CHRISTOLOGY AFTER CHALCEDON

Severus of Antioch and Sergius the Monophysite

CHRISTOLOGY AFTER CHALCEDON

Severus of Antioch and Sergius the Monophysite

IAIN R. TORRANCE

THE CANTERBURY PRESS NORWICH

The Canterbury Press Norwich, St Mary's Works,
St Mary's Plain, Norwich, Norfolk NR3 3BH
The Canterbury Press Norwich is a publishing imprint
of Hymns Ancient & Modern Limited

The Syriac script was generated on an IBM PC XT
using the package *Multi-Lingual Scholar* from
Gamma Productions, Inc.,
710 Wilshire Blvd., Suite 609
Santa Monica, CA 90401

and a Syriac font supplied by
George A. Kiraz
Alaph Beth Computer Systems
5030 Maplewood Ave. #203
Los Angeles, CA 90004

ISBN 0-907547-97-4

First published 1988

The design on the front cover shows part of Folio 17a of the manuscript Add. 17154 and it is reproduced by permission of The British Library. The design was prepared by Richard Morgan.

Filmset by Eta Services (Typesetters) Ltd, Beccles, Suffolk
Printed and bound in Great Britain by Cambridge University Press

To
Morag

Contents

Part Two

The Letters between Severus of Antioch and Sergius the Grammarian

Preface

This study began life as a thesis submitted to the University of Oxford. My research was supervised by Dr Sebastian Brock, and his kindness and thoroughness were an example which I hope will never leave me. The thesis was examined by The Revd Dr Lionel Wickham and Bishop Kallistos of Diokleia. Their graciousness and careful attention to detail taught me a great deal. Archbishop Methodios of Thyateira and Great Britain encouraged me at every stage, and did me the honour of publishing an earlier draft of my translation of the *Letters* in *Abba Salama* 9 (1978), and of the theological introduction to them in *Ekklesia kai Theologia* 2 (1981); 3 (1982); 4 (1983) and 5 (1984).

The Very Revd Dr Henry Chadwick took an interest in this study from the beginning, and that it is now being published is due entirely to his prompting and sound advice. I would also like to thank Mr Gordon Knights of The Canterbury Press Norwich, who has helped me through all the hurdles of preparing a typescript for publication.

I would express my gratitude to The British Academy for its support in the provision of an award towards the publication of this book.

My parents, Thomas F. Torrance and Margaret E. Torrance, have been a constant support to me, morally, financially and spiritually. I owe them more than I could ever say.

My wife, Morag, has helped me at every stage, and this study is a part of both our lives. In gratitude and love I dedicate it to her.

Canty Bay, East Lothian, Scotland.
August 1987 Iain R. Torrance

Abbreviations

SEVERUS OF ANTIOCH

EM	*Eiusdem ac Sergii Grammatici: Epistulae Mutuae*, ed. and transl. J. Lebon, *Corpus Scriptorum Christianorum Orientalium*, 119, 120 (Syr. 64, 65) (Louvain, 1949).
Select Letters	*The Sixth Book of the Select Letters of Severus, Patriarch of Antioch, in the Syriac Version of Athanasius of Nisibis*, ed. and transl. E. W. Brooks, 4 vols. (London, 1902–4).
Collected Letters	"A Collection of Letters from Numerous Syriac Manuscripts", ed. and transl. E. W. Brooks, *Patrologia Orientalis*, 12, 14 (Paris, 1919–20), 163–342; 1–310.
Philalethes	*Le Philalèthe*, ed. and transl. R. Hespel, *Corpus Scriptorum Christianorum Orientalium*, 133, 134 (Syr. 68, 69) (Louvain, 1952).

CYRIL OF ALEXANDRIA

Adv. Nest.	*Adversus Nestorii Blasphemias Contradictionum Libri Quinque.*
Apol. contra Theod.	*Apologeticus contra Theodoretum pro XII Capitibus.*
Apol. pro XII Cap. contra Orient.	*Apologeticus pro XII Capitibus contra Orientales.*
Contra Diod. Tars. Episc.	*Fragmenta contra Diodorum Tarsensem Episcopum.*
Contra Syn.	*Fragmenta contra Synousiastas*
De Recta Fide ad Theod.	*De Recta Fide ad Theodosium Imperatorem*
Ep. I, II ad Succ.	*Epistola I, II ad Succensum*
QUSC	*Quod unus sit Christus*
Pusey edn.	Cyril of Alexandria, *Opera*. Text ed. P. E. Pusey, 7 vols. (Oxford, 1868–77), repr. 1965.

JOSEPH LEBON

Le Monophysisme	*Le Monophysisme sévérien* (Louvain, 1909).
Chalkedon	"La Christologie du monophysisme syrien", in *Das Konzil von Chalkedon: Geschichte und Gegenwart*, ed. A. Grillmeier and H. Bacht (Würzburg, 1951), I, 425–580.
ACO	*Acta Conciliorum Oecumenicorum* (Berlin and Leipzig).
CSCO	*Corpus Scriptorum Christianorum Orientalium* (Louvain).
PG	*Patrologia Graeca*
PL	*Patrologia Latina*
PO	*Patrologia Orientalis*
JSS	*Journal of Semitic Studies*
JTS	*Journal of Theological Studies*
HTR	*Harvard Theological Review*
RHE	*Revue d'histoire ecclésiastique*
The Syriac Chronicle	*The Syriac Chronicle Known as that of Zachariah of Mitylene*, trans. F. J. Hamilton and E. W. Brooks (London, 1899).
H. syr. 22	Harvard (Houghton Library) syr. 22.

Part One

A THEOLOGICAL INTRODUCTION TO THE LETTERS BETWEEN SEVERUS OF ANTIOCH AND SERGIUS THE GRAMMARIAN

I Introduction

A. Severus, Antoninus and Sergius

The correspondence between Sergius and Severus comprises three letters from Sergius, three replies by Severus and an apology by Sergius. The first letter from Sergius was addressed originally not to Severus, but to Antoninus, the Bishop of Aleppo, who seems to have asked Severus to reply.

The outline of Severus' life is relatively well known.[1] Apart from his own very numerous letters,[2] and hints which he gives in his theological writings, there are three ancient "Lives of Severus".[3] Though we may doubt their historical value, these lives even attempt to give something of a description of Severus. Thus, Athanasius says that Severus was a man "delicate in body and fine in person".[4] When he did the work of his brethren in the monastery, the blood used to run from his hands. Athanasius again stresses that Severus was a compassionate man,[5] and, as we will see, this is an important quality in understanding him. All the early biographers emphasise Severus' asceticism, and Severus himself, writing to Justinian, says that his life was habitually frugal.[6]

Severus was born in Sozopolis in Pisidia about 465. His family was well-to-do, and as a young man, not yet baptised, he was sent to Alexandria to study *γραμματική* and *ῥητορική*. From Alexandria he went to Beirut, to study Roman law. At Beirut Severus came under the influence of a group of Christian students, and began to study Basil and Gregory Nazianzen. At this stage he was baptised, at the shrine of Leontius at Tripoli.[7]

We are told that after his baptism Severus became increasingly ascetic, spending much of his time in church. He qualified as an advocate, and visited Jerusalem, where he decided to follow the monastic life. From Jerusalem, looking for a still more ascetic life, he went into the desert of Eleutheropolis. Here he eventually became ill, and was persuaded to enter the convent of Romanus. At this time he shared out with his brothers the property he inherited from his parents, and after giving most of his share to the poor, bought a convent near Maiuma.

Severus was already actively involved in opposing the Council of Chalcedon. Maiuma had been the episcopal seat of Peter the Iberian, one of the two(?) bishops who consecrated Timothy Aelurus;[8] and Severus was to follow in this tradition. He already belonged to the more extreme Monophysite party, which rejected the Henoticon of Zeno.[9] Liberatus, the archdeacon of Carthage, wrote of Severus that "dum sederet prius in monasterio Iberi, non suscipiebat Zenonis edictum, nec Petrum Mongon ... exinde missus est permanere Constantinopolim ..."[10] Severus was indeed sent to Constantinople. A Chalcedonian monk, Nephalius, stirred up the bishops in Palestine against the anti-Chalcedonian monks, who began to be harassed. John of Beth Aphthonia tells us that Nephalius even wrote an *Apologia* for Chalcedon, which Severus destroyed as if it had been a cobweb, with his two *Orationes*.[11] This was the first important anti-Chalcedonian work of Severus that we have, and it was written around 508.[12] Cobweb or not, Evagrius tells us that Severus was expelled from his own monastery by Nephalius and his party, and thence proceeded to the imperial city, to plead the case of himself and those expelled with him.[13]

Severus spent the years 508–11 in Constantinople. He seems quite quickly to have gained the sympathy of Anastasius, who was already not over-fond of the Patriarch Macedonius, who had definite leanings towards Chalcedon. The Chalcedonians in the capital made a collection of edited excerpts from Cyril, in an attempt to show that Cyril himself supported the Chalcedonian account of the two natures. This work was apparently given to Macedonius, who gave it to the emperor. Severus, in turn, wrote his *Philalethes*, giving the true context of the quotations from Cyril.[14] Relations between Severus and Macedonius steadily deteriorated. Macedonius' position was not strong. He had already undermined his support with the extreme Chalcedonians by promising to uphold the Henoticon.[15] In addition, Anastasius had a personal grudge against him. Euphemius, the previous Patriarch, had withheld his approval from the elevation of Anastasius, unless he wrote an agreement to maintain the faith of Chalcedon inviolate. This document had passed into the hands of Macedonius, and according to Evagrius, Anastasius' objection to the document was largely the cause of Macedonius' expulsion.[16] In 511 he was replaced by Timothy.

The removal of Macedonius was only part of a concerted effort by the Monophysites. While Severus had been in the capital, Philoxenus had been busy in Palestine, undermining the position of Flavian of Antioch. At Anastasius' order, a Synod was assembled at Sidon

in 512. Flavian was presented with a list of seventy-seven anathemas, as well as the request openly to anathematise Chalcedon. Flavian refused, being unwilling to "arouse the sleeping dragon, and corrupt many with his poison".[17] This was not to satisfy Philoxenus: his monks informed Anastasius that Flavian was a heretic, and they received an order for his ejection. In November 512, Severus was consecrated Patriarch of Antioch in his place.

In his enthronement address,[18] Severus affirmed Nicea, Constantinople and Ephesus. He affirmed the Henoticon of Zeno as "an orthodox confession of the faith", but explicitly anathematised Chalcedon and the Tome of Leo, as well as Nestorius and Eutyches, and Diodore and Theodore, "the masters of Nestorius". Added to the list are Ibas of Edessa, Barsumas of Nisibis, and Cyrus and John of Aigai.[19] In a Synod held at Tyre around 514,[20] the assembled bishops openly anathematised Chalcedon and the Tome, and Severus joined with Philoxenus in expounding the Henoticon as annulling Chalcedon.[21] Evagrius also tells us that Severus ceased not daily to anathematise Chalcedon.[22]

In Antioch he must have made his presence felt. John of Beth Aphthonia tells us that on becoming bishop, he sent away the cooks from the episcopal palace, and demolished the baths he found there.[23] In his Cathedral Homilies, he warned his people against resorting to the races[24] and the theatre,[25] and his letters show his energy, and the trouble he had in financial matters. But his time as Patriarch was not to be long.

Anastasius died in July 518, and Evagrius tells us that, many contentions having arisen in the church, Justin, in the first year of his reign, ordered him to be arrested and punished.[26] Severus, with a number of the Monophysite bishops, managed to escape to Egypt. Philoxenus was sent into exile at Gangra. In Egypt, Severus lived a harried existence,[27] but wrote some of his most important works. As we will see shortly, he completed his correspondence with Sergius from his exile. Lebon dates his great anti-Chalcedonian work, the *Liber contra impium Grammaticum*, to around 519.[28] Rather sadly, the exiled Monophysites began to quarrel amongst each other, and Severus' works against Julian of Halicarnassus also belong to this period.[29]

Around 530 Justinian relaxed persecution of the Monophysites, and in 532 he summoned the leading Monophysites to a "*collatio*" with the Chalcedonians in Constantinople. Though invited, and promised immunity by Justinian, Severus did not attend this conference.[30] He came instead, again at the summons of Justinian, in the

winter of 534/5. At about the same time Anthimus of Trebizond, whom Zacharias tells us would not receive the Synod of Chalcedon into the faith,[31] succeeded Epiphanius as Patriarch of Constantinople, and Theodosius, a friend of Severus, became bishop of Alexandria.

This unity in the Monophysite camp so alarmed the orthodox Ephraim of Antioch that he sent a special envoy to Agapetus in Rome.[32] Justinian was engaged in an operation to regain Rome, and the Goths sent Agapetus to Constantinople to treat with Justinian on their behalf. Agapetus arrived in Constantinople in 536. Zacharias tells us that he perverted the love of the king to Severus and Anthimus. Justinian's interest clearly lay in the West, and Anthimus was replaced by Menas as Patriarch of Constantinople. Though Agapetus died in April 536, the position of Severus and the Monophysites was lost.

Severus, and his friends, were condemned[33] at a *σύνοδος ἐνδημοῦσα* in Constantinople lasting from May to June 536. The synod was confirmed by an edict of Justinian on the 6th of August 536. According to the edict, Severus was guilty of both Nestorianism and Eutychianism,[34] his books were to be banned,[35] and he was to be banished.[36]

According to Athanasius, Severus left Constantinople with the help of the Empress Theodora.[37] He returned to Egypt, and there, about 538, "the Lord visited him with a light disorder, and .... he fell asleep".[38]

Antoninus was Bishop of Aleppo (ܚܠܒ). His predecessor was Peter, one of the bishops who assisted at the consecration of Severus in 512.[39] While he was Patriarch, Severus wrote to him several times.[40] Antoninus was expelled in 519, taking refuge in Alexandria. The Chronicle to the year 846 records that having suffered persecution in various places, Antoninus died in Constantinople.[41]

Of Sergius, Lebon notes, "nous ne connaissons ni sa patrie, ni les événements de son histoire, en dehors de la polémique dont nous avons parlé".[42] We can see from his letters that he was a monophysite of an exaggerated sort. He seems to have remained in the East,[43] after Justin became emperor, so it is not unreasonable to assume that though he had a certain prominence, he was not a bishop.

We do not know all the background of the origin of the correspondence between Sergius and Severus, but we can surmise some of it. In the unnamed town where Sergius was living, a severe attitude was taken to converted Dyophysites. Sergius had a brief statement or *κεφάλαιον*, which seems to have been used as a doctrinal test[44] to

the converted Dyophysites. This was, "We do not speak of two natures or (two) proprieties after the inexpressible union".[45] Sergius' κεφάλαιον had been submitted to an assembly, of which Antoninus of Aleppo was a member. The opinion of the assembly corrected Sergius, stating, "We do not speak of divided proprieties".[46] Sergius claims to find this judgement difficult to understand, and it is a question of prime importance for the commentator to ask if ܕܝ̈ܠܝܬܐ is meant in the same way, in both Sergius' κεφάλαιον, and the answer of the assembly. Sergius characterises the judgement as a concession,[47] rehearses several of his objections to it, and begs the assembled Fathers to help him. The request is passed to Severus and the correspondence begins.

The question of the exact date of the correspondence is not easy. Sergius was clearly addressing an assembly of bishops when he wrote, "O Good Fathers...."[48] Lebon asks, "Etait-ce un synode?"[49] We cannot say. Was Antoninus at its head? Possibly, as Sergius writes to him, but Severus himself was not available at the time, being, as he says, "Far off".[50] If it was a synod, can we deduce more about it? Lebon suggests it was the Synod of Tyre in 514,[51] which would allow a date of perhaps 515[52] for Sergius' *First Letter*.

There is easier internal evidence for dating the end of the correspondence, for both Sergius' and Severus' *Third Letters* point to a date after 518. To take these points in turn: in Sergius' *Third Letter*, he speaks of the spark of his feeble tongue being used, "because of the remoteness of bishops in the east",[53] which very probably refers to the expulsion of the Monophysites after the death of Anastasius in 518. Later in the same letter,[54] Sergius, having prayed that Severus be given long life, says he looks forward to when he will say to the Lord God, "Thou hast turned away the captivity of Jacob...".[55]

Severus, in his *Third Letter*, clearly demonstrates a post-518 date, when he challenges Sergius, "Therefore show (me) when, in the six years I spoke in the Church of the Antiochenes, and wrote many letters, at any time I once said Emmanuel is one ousia, and of one signification and of one particularity".[56] Later in the same letter, Severus describes himself as put to flight by enemies in his tracks,[57] and at the end of the letter, Severus refers to Dioscorus II of Alexandria, who died on 14th October, 517[58] as if he were already dead.

B. An outline of the events following Chalcedon, as a background to the life of Severus

The ninety to a hundred years following Chalcedon were a highly

involved period of history. Nevertheless, it is possible to derive a little clarification from pointing to certain broad factors which were at work. Wigram,[59] for example, points to the policy of the emperors, who soon after Chalcedon lost Rome, and in the 6th century tried to recover it; the growing national feeling of certain parts of the empire; and the jealousy of the great sees: Canon 28 of Chalcedon gave patriarchal jurisdiction rather than just an honorary precedence in the East to Constantinople, and Rome unwaveringly held to Chalcedon, which approved the Tome of Leo.

The account which follows in no way attempts to provide a history of the period.[60] It is intended, rather, to set Severus' life against the background of his times, and to show him as the consistent, though conservative, follower of his predecessors.

After Chalcedon in 451, Dioscorus of Alexandria was exiled to Gangra in Paphlagonia, and Proterius, a Chalcedonian, was appointed in his place. The Alexandrians greeted him with a riot. In Jerusalem, the anti-Chalcedonian monks rejected Juvenal, their Chalcedonian bishop, and in his place appointed Theodosius. Before Marcian, the emperor, was able to replace Juvenal, Theodosius was able to consecrate a number of bishops, among whom were Peter the Iberian, who became bishop of Maiuma near Gaza, and Theodotus, the bishop of Joppa.[61]

On the death of Marcian in 457, the people of Alexandria renewed their feud against Proterius. Those who had been expelled by Marcian returned, and though Proterius was still alive and discharging the functions of his office, the people elected a Monophysite, Timothy Aelurus, as their bishop.[62] Peter the Iberian was one of those who took part in his consecration.[63] There was another riot, and Proterius was murdered in the baptistry. The emperor Leo then sent circular letters throughout the empire, asking the bishops to declare their opinion regarding the ordination of Timothy Aelurus, and the Synod of Chalcedon. The bishops expressed their adherence to Chalcedon, and unanimously condemned the ordination of Timothy Aelurus, who was sentenced to banishment at Gangra.[64] In his place, the Alexandrians elected another Timothy, a moderate Chalcedonian, nicknamed Basilicus or Salophaciolus.

Zeno became emperor in February 474, but, as a result of a palace conspiracy in which his mother-in-law, the Augusta Verina, took a leading role, he was ousted in 475 by Basiliscus, who reigned for 20 months. Basiliscus recalled Timothy Aelurus from his exile to Constantinople, where he was joined by Peter the Fuller, the exiled Monophysite bishop of Antioch. Timothy, according to Evagrius

and Zacharias, persuaded Basiliscus to send a circular letter to the bishops of the empire, explicitly anathematising Chalcedon and the Tome of Leo. His letter even commanded that such doctrine should be burned.[65] Zacharias tells us that Acacius, the bishop of Constantinople, was impressed with Timothy's doctrinal arguments, but that he hesitated to sign the Encyclical which anathematised Chalcedon, and so diminished the jurisdiction of his see.[66] However, Peter the Fuller of Antioch signed, as did Paul of Ephesus, Anastasius of Jerusalem, and five hundred other bishops.[67]

Timothy then went to Ephesus, where he convened a synod, and restored to that see the dignity of the Patriarchate, of which it had been deprived by Chalcedon.[68] From there he proceeded to Alexandria. Historically, we may notice two points in this: first, Timothy was making it the standard of his party explicitly to anathematise Chalcedon. Secondly, and equally explicitly, the anathematisation of Chalcedon was against the interests of Constantinople, and brought into play the jealousy of that see.

On his return to Alexandria, Timothy showed himself to be a truly remarkable man. Although a Monophysite, he insisted on the doctrine of the double consubstantiality, and from his exile he had written not only against the Chalcedonians, but also against the Eutychians. But even this he did with toleration and restraint: he waited four years before exposing by name the Eutychians Isaiah of Hermopolis and Theophilus of Alexandria.[69] Again, from exile, he had urged that converted Dyophysites (members of Proterius' party) should be treated with pastoral moderation. He referred explicitly to the regulation of Cyril and Dioscorus, that when a bishop, a presbyter or a deacon is converted, he should have one year of repentance, and after that be re-established in his former rank.[70] In Alexandria all he required of members of the Proterian party was that they should anathematise the Synod and the Tome.[71] This moderation earned him enemies: Theodotus of Joppa apparently wanted a much more severe attitude to be taken to the converted Proterians, and even practised re-anointing.[72] He left Timothy's party to form an extreme separatist group. Zacharias, rather interestingly, tells us that Peter the Iberian did not at all agree with this faction, but was warmly attached to Timothy.

Historically and theologically, we can see in Timothy Aelurus and Peter the Iberian a Monophysite position which is clearly Cyrillian, rather than Eutychian.[73] Pastorally, it practised moderation. We have already seen that Severus expressed his admiration for Peter the Iberian, and from his letters, we can see that he made a particular

point of following the pastoral practice of Timothy Aelurus. In the case of converted followers of Theodotus,[74] Severus wrote that they should only be subject to the periods of penance which Timothy recommended,[75] and in the case of converted Chalcedonians, he wrote that he again followed the example of Timothy, who, when he reached Alexandria, received those who came from the heresy of the Dyophysites, upon their anathematising the heresy in writing, and accepting such a period of separation for penitence as he judged to be good.[76] He explicitly repudiated re-anointing.[77] Thus, we can see a consistent line of practice from Cyril, through Timothy, to Severus. We can also see the emergence of a more extreme Monophysite group, marked by its Eutychian leanings and its pastoral severity. It is tempting to see here the theological and pastoral ancestry of Sergius, whom we will study shortly.

While Timothy Aelurus was in Alexandria, Acacius in Constantinople intrigued to bring back Zeno. Basiliscus, now too late, repudiated his Encyclical and restored the rights of the see of Constantinople. Zeno returned in August 476, and Basiliscus was sent to Cappadocia and beheaded. Zeno expelled Peter the Fuller from Antioch,[78] and but for Timothy's age would have expelled him from Alexandria. He soon died, and in his place the Alexandrian bishops elected, on their own authority, Peter Mongus.[79] Zeno, in exasperation, expelled Peter and in his place recalled Timothy Salophaciolus, the now aged Chalcedonian successor of Proterius.

The Alexandrians then sent a presbyter, John, to Constantinople, to obtain permission for them to elect as their bishop a person of their own choice, on the death of Timothy Salophaciolus.[80] However, in Constantinople, John was apparently caught canvassing his own nomination, and only returned under an oath that he would never accept the see. Zeno issued a precept that, on the death of Timothy, that person should be bishop whom the clergy and people might elect. Timothy very soon died, and John broke his oath, and by means of a bribe, procured his own nomination as bishop.[81]

When Zeno heard this, he ordered that John should be ejected from the see as a liar, and that Peter Mongus should be restored, on condition that he subscribe to a document which Zeno addressed to the Alexandrians, and admit into communion the party of Proterius. This document was the Henoticon of July 482.[82] It was a masterpiece of diplomacy and clear-thinking.

In 476 Odoacer had deposed the last Roman emperor, Romulus Augustulus, and proclaimed himself king. With the loss of Rome and the West, there was lost that section of the empire which was

most deeply committed to the theology of Chalcedon. As we saw at the time of Basiliscus, Acacius of Constantinople was impressed by Timothy Aelurus' doctrinal arguments, but hesitated to sign an Encyclical anathematising Chalcedon. His concern was with Canon 28 and the precedence of his see: if this could be safeguarded, he was quite prepared to have monophysite leanings. The time was ripe for an attempt to conciliate the monophysites doctrinally, yet without formally anathematising Chalcedon. This is what the Henoticon set out to do.

It declared the three Councils of Nicea, Constantinople and Ephesus to be standards of the faith, received the Twelve Chapters (Anathemas) of Cyril, and anathematised Nestorius and Eutyches. Doctrinally, the Henoticon avoided the contentious technical phrase (ἐν δύο φύσεσιν), and indeed taught a positive doctrine which both sides could accept. Thus, it affirmed the double consubstantiality, stated that Christ is "one and not two", and said that both the miracles and the sufferings are those of a single person.[83] Finally, it anathematised any one who held any other opinion, "whether at Chalcedon or in any synod whatever".[84] This was not an explicit condemnation of Chalcedon, but amounted to a downgrading of it, so that its main importance lay in its condemnation of Nestorius and Eutyches.

Clearly, the *prima facie* purpose of the Henoticon was to create peace in Egypt between the Monophysites and the Proterians, and to provide a reconciliation between Constantinople and Alexandria. However, after some hesitation as it contained no explicit anathema on Chalcedon and the Tome, Peter Mongus subscribed to it,[85] as did Peter the Fuller of Antioch (who was replaced in his see after the expulsion of Calendio, the Chalcedonian bishop of Antioch who refused to sign and complained to Zeno), and the bishops of Ephesus and Jerusalem.[86] The Henoticon thus quickly became not just a test for Peter Mongus, but something of a government creed.

Peter Mongus' hesitation in signing was justified: in Egypt the Henoticon soon ran into stormy water. In Alexandria, a sizeable number of Monophysites,[87] under the leadership of Theodore of Antinoe, seceded from the communion of Peter Mongus, on the grounds that the Henoticon contained no clear and decided anathema on Chalcedon and the Tome. To pacify this faction, Peter explicitly anathematised both Chalcedon and the Tome, which provoked the wrath of Constantinople and Rome, but because he entered into communion with those who had uttered no anathema, the extremists withdrew from him into their monasteries, but with-

out appointing a bishop instead of Peter. They thus became known as the "Akephalists" (ἀκέφαλοι) or the Separatists (ἀποσχίσται).

We should notice several points in this. Evagrius, with justification, called Peter "a double dealer, a waverer, and a time-server".[88] Zacharias tells us that he tried to show to the Separatists that the Henoticon nullified Chalcedon, by accepting the twelve Chapters of Cyril and anathematising Nestorius and Eutyches.[89] This interpretation, that the Henoticon by itself annulled Chalcedon, was, as we shall see, one which was to become increasingly popular. Secondly, the Separatists were not all extremists in the Eutychian sense, though without doubt they were intransigently conservative. They were supported, it would seem, in their demand for an anathema on Chalcedon, by Peter the Iberian,[90] who, as we saw at the time of Timothy Aelurus, was not of the pastorally extreme party. We can argue that some were simply following the Alexandrian tradition which Timothy Aelurus laid down, that converted Proterians would be accepted if they explicitly anathematised the Synod and the Tome. As we have already seen, Severus aligned himself with this group, rejecting both Peter Mongus, and the idea that the Henoticon, by itself and without explicit anathema on Chalcedon, was sufficient to heal disunity in the Church.

Peter Mongus died in 490 and the emperor Zeno in 491. Zeno was succeeded by Anastasius, who continued the policy of trying to unite the eastern empire on the basis of the Henoticon. Evagrius tells us that he was averse to the introduction of change, and that therefore, "during these times, the Council of Chalcedon was neither openly proclaimed, nor yet repudiated by all; but the bishops acted each according to his own opinion".[91] Euphemius, a Chalcedonian, was bishop of Constantinople, but was deposed in 496 and replaced by Macedonius. In 498 Flavian became bishop of Antioch. It was at this stage that Severus began to play a significant role in the history of his time. With the removal of Macedonius and Flavian through the efforts of Severus and Philoxenus, and with the consent of Anastasius, the balance of the Henoticon was lost, and for a short time the Monophysites were supreme.

We have already covered some of this ground, but now see the background against which Severus can be understood. Severus went up to the capital in 508 and gained the sympathy of Anastasius. Though Macedonius signed the Henoticon at the beginning of his episcopacy, Zacharias leaves us in no doubt as to his Chalcedonian leanings. He even tells us that Macedonius used to celebrate the memory of Nestorius every year.[92] Athanasius of Antioch tells us

that Macedonius was a self-confessed Chalcedonian.[93] In addition, he had a personal quarrel with Anastasius. Clearly, the removal of such an extremist could hardly signal the overthrow of the Henoticist cause, which depended on the maintenance of a moderate position by all parties.

The removal of Flavian of Antioch was more significant. As we have already seen, Flavian refused at Sidon in 512 explicitly to anathematise Chalcedon for Philoxenus, though he was prepared to anathematise Nestorius and the school of Diodore.[94] Evagrius tells us that Flavian admitted the Synod only as far as regards the deposition of Nestorius and Eutyches, and not as a definition of the faith.[95] Severus himself, in a letter to the monks in the East, after his expulsion from Constantinople in 536, seems to endorse this assessment of Flavian.[96] Flavian, then, unlike Macedonius, was a true Henoticist. But this did not satisfy Philoxenus, who insisted on an explicit anathema on Chalcedon, and Flavian was expelled in 512. Severus became Patriarch, and as we have seen, both explicitly condemned Chalcedon, and, at Tyre in 514, expounded the Henoticon in an anti-Chalcedonian way.[97] The Henoticist compromise was now dead.

We have already seen that the monophysite supremacy was to be short-lived. Anastasius died in 518, and the new emperor, Justin, was committed to healing the breach with Rome. Pope Hormisdas was able to make peace with Constantinople on his own terms, and in March 519 John of Cappadocia, Patriarch of Constantinople, duly anathematised his predecessor, Acacius, who had been the author of the schism.[98] Severus, as we know, fled to Egypt, but the tide had now turned against the Monophysites. We have already seen in outline the rest of Severus' life, including his final condemnation in 536. Let us, in conclusion, draw together the points which have emerged from his historical background.

We have seen that quite apart from his theological "fathers", Cyril and Gregory Nazianzen, Severus refers to and acknowledges the influence on him of Timothy Aelurus and Peter the Iberian. Both of these men condemned Eutychianism as explicitly as they condemned Nestorianism. Their monophysitism was thus Cyrillian, and as will become clear in the examination of his letters to Sergius, Severus follows them in this.

Timothy Aelurus before the Henoticon, and Peter the Iberian, during the time of Peter Mongus, explicitly anathematised Chalcedon. Yet, we suggest that this condemnation was not fanatical: neither of them was a pastoral extremist, for they were both opposed

to the re-anointing of converted Proterians practised by Theodotus of Joppa. Similarly, Severus insisted on an explicit anathema against Chalcedon, refusing the compromise of the Henoticon, but again, we suggest that his condemnation was that of the conservative, not the fanatic, and this is borne out by his pastoral moderation. The extreme group was that which practised re-anointing, and there is no doubt but that Severus condemned this.

We suggest, then, that Severus was very consciously a member of a particular tradition. He was a conservative, but as we will try to show, the tradition to which he belonged was one of great theological depth, and to it he brought his own subtlety.

C. Earlier studies of Severus, and the orientation of this introduction

Beyond question, the greatest work that has been produced on the Monophysites is that by Lebon: *Le Monophysisme sévérien*. This was published in Louvain in 1909, and Lebon brought it up to date[99] with his long article, "La Christologie du monophysisme syrien", which was published in 1951. Much of the material of the earlier book is covered by this superb 160-page article, and it is to this that we will mainly refer.

Lebon sets out to give an over-all view of Monophysite theology, and so considers Timothy Aelurus and Philoxenus as well as Severus. His study falls into two parts: the first, entitled "La doctrine monophysite de l'incarnation" is short and descriptive;[100] the second, entitled "La dogmatique monophysite de l'incarnation"[101] is far longer and more analytical.

In his first section, Lebon sketches where the Monophysites may be placed in terms of the widely accepted distinction between Alexandrian and Antiochene Christologies. He immediately introduces the Christology of Cyril of Alexandria, showing that this becomes central to the Monophysites.[102] He then gives us an outline description of Monophysite doctrine, picking out particular key concepts. Thus, he stresses the Monophysite exclusion of any type of change from the incarnation.[103] God the Word was made flesh, but remained who he was. Similarly, the Monophysites go to great pains to deny that the union to one nature involved any mixture or confusion.[104] He shows the Monophysite use of the union of body and soul as a model, with the insistence that this union does not produce an identity of ousia, of such a kind as would be destructive of the difference of the things which have been united.[105]

Commenting on this, Lebon writes that, however frequently the Monophysites denied it, they were always suspected of introducing a mixture or confusion into the union. He, however, sees them as terminological traditionalists,[106] who borrowed the vocabulary of the Cappadocians and Cyril, who used "mixture" words to express a very intimate union, but without ever wanting to imply any idea of confusion.

From this we can already see the style of Lebon's study. As a good historian of dogma, he notes for us the Monophysite denials of confusion in the union, and the terminological parallels with earlier writers. In concentrating on just one text, and making use of Lebon's categories, we will try to answer the different question of why any idea of confusion, in Severus, is out of place. This is an attempt to move, in a small way, from questions which are basically historical to questions which are basically theological.

Lebon begins his second section by taking two questions around which the Monophysite quarrel raged:

(1) The question of whether there are one or two natures in Christ. This is the question raised by the Chalcedonian ἐν δύο φύσεσιν.
(2) The question of whether the ἰδιότης of the natures in the union is preserved or not. This is the question raised by the Chalcedonian σωζομένης δὲ μᾶλλον τῆς ἰδιότητος ἑκατέρας φύσεως.

He divides the section into two parts: one to examine each question. To answer question (1), he leads us through a careful and detailed study of the vocabulary of the Monophysites, to show how their terms and usages differed from those of the Chalcedonians.

This study falls into three sub-sections. In the first, "Les éléments de l'incarnation",[107] Lebon shows that the Monophysites use φύσις, ὑπόστασις and πρόσωπον as perfectly synonymous.[108] Thus φύσις, like ὑπόστασις and πρόσωπον, refers to what is concrete and individual. According to Lebon, then, the Monophysites ultimately confused the Chalcedonians with the Nestorians, and reduced all Dyophysitism to the confession of two really distinct beings.

In the second sub-section, "L'acte de l'incarnation", Lebon stresses that to the Monophysites, the incarnation is an *act*, a ἕνωσις. The Monophysites never formally define the term, and Lebon tries to illustrate it by considering the conditions required for "un groupement de choses" to merit the name "ἕνωσις".[109] ἕνωσις, for example, has no more radical enemy than number: if the constituent elements in a ἕνωσις could be numbered, it would follow, within the

Monophysite presuppositions, that they were independently existing and ununited entities. Similarly, to illustrate the concept of ἕνωσις, Lebon contrasts it with συνάφεια and παράθεσις,[110] and shows that to note the act of the incarnation the Monophysites use other terms: συνδρομή, σύνοδος, σύμβασις, and in Severus, σύνθεσις.[111]

In the third sub-section, "Le terme de l'incarnation", Lebon turns to the major formula of the Monophysites: μία φύσις τοῦ Θεοῦ Λόγου σεσαρκωμένη. He explains that the nature of which the formula affirms the unity is that of God the Word, who is the subject in the incarnation. The formula is thus distinctively Cyrillian and anti-Nestorian.[112] Illustrating his main point, as before, through comparisons, he briefly discusses the phrases μία φύσις σύνθετος, and μία φύσις διττή,[113] and then turns to consider apparently Dyophysite expressions permitted by the Monophysites. We have already seen the Monophysite condemnation of Chalcedon and Nestorianism, and understanding that ἐν δύο φύσεσιν implied two natures in independent existence. Lebon now shows that to defend himself against the accusation of teaching a confusion, Severus allowed that one could speak of δύο φύσεις, but only ἐν θεωρίᾳ.[114] Similarly to defend himself against the charge of confusion, Severus taught that the Word incarnate is (μία φύσις) ἐκ δύο.[115] For both these expressions, Lebon shows Severus' dependence on Cyril.[116]

In the second part to his second section, Lebon turns to the second question he outlined at the beginning: the "conservation ou destruction de la propriété des natures après l'union".[117] He first shows the problem. On the one hand Severus was presented with the Tome teaching, "Agit enim utraque forma cum alterius communione *quod proprium est*", and Chalcedon stating that "σωζομένης δὲ μᾶλλον τῆς ἰδιότητος ἑκατέρας φύσεως", which appeared to argue for the preservation of the ἰδιότης of the natures which came to union, but in such a way that the independent existence of each nature seemed also to be implied. On the other hand, Severus was presented with the extreme Monophysitism of a writer like Sergius, who wanted to exaggerate the nature of the unity to such an extent that he preached unification of ἰδιότης as well as of φύσις in the union.

In an excellent terminological examination, Lebon shows that in the face of this dilemma Severus hammered out his own concept of ἰδιότης. Qualifying ἰδιότης as "φυσική"; "ἡ κατὰ φύσιν"; "ὡς ἐν ποιότητι φυσικῇ",[118] he consciously followed Cyril, saying that ποιότης φυσική expresses ὁ λόγος τοῦ πῶς εἶναι of a thing.[119] According to Lebon, ποιότης φυσική expresses "l'essence spécifique",[120] and it is the continuing difference between the natures in this that Sever-

us insists on. This definition enabled Severus to steer between the apparent Nestorianism of recognising two independent natures in the union, and the apparent Eutychianism of allowing that one or both of the natures in the union lost its integrity of identity.

But here again, while the foundations have been laid, Lebon makes what is largely a terminological point. The *theological* point is that Severus, in making this distinction, was doing something totally different from either Nestorianism or Eutychianism, quite apart from steering a terminological path between the two extremes. This is the area our introduction will try to explore.

We have described Lebon's paper at some length, because he has produced a quarry of detailed references, terminology and historical background from which all who study the Monophysites must borrow. Our own debt to him will be seen in the frequent references made to his works. However, as we have tried to show, though his contribution is enormous, his work is essentially map-making over new and difficult terrain. In showing us so helpfully what terms are used, and how and when, he has somehow managed to remain external to the concepts he describes.

Working within the framework Lebon has given us, there is room for a supplementary study. The ἕνωσις of which Severus tells us, and which Lebon describes for us, was not simply a union, but a union, an act of God the Word, *for a purpose*. We will want to suggest that this purpose, far from being exterior to the union, is part of what makes the union what it is. To see the goal of the union as a determinative part of the nature of the union is to inject a new dimension into the study of Severus. This soteriological dimension does not appear when one is map-making. As we will try to show, it is to see the terms in a dynamic as well as a static descriptive way. By confining ourselves to one short but dense text of Severus, and bearing in mind his purpose as much as his terminology, we will hope, in a small way, to ask new and fruitful questions.

As we have said, Lebon's paper was published in 1951. Since then there has been a growing interest in the Monophysites. A recent work is that by Roberta Chesnut.[121] Chesnut's interest is to study the relationship between Christ and our knowledge of God in the three very different theological systems of Severus, Philoxenus and Jacob of Serug. We have already shown that the aim of our study of the letters between Severus and Sergius is to try to show Severus' Christology and terminology in its soteriological dimension. Though Chesnut gives a detailed description of some of Severus' major terms and concepts, she is concerned neither with soteriology,

nor with Severus' relation to Cyril, and so her work is able to contribute relatively little to our study. Another modern work, though of necessity a very general one, is that by John Meyendorff. In his *Christ in Eastern Christian Thought*,[122] he provides a perceptive account of the debates after Chalcedon, showing Severus' important role in the formation of the theology of the separating Monophysite churches.

It is within the Monophysite churches that some of the most stimulating modern work on Severus is being done. Since 1964 there have been unofficial theological conferences between theologians of the Eastern and Oriental Orthodox Churches.[123] The Panorthodox Conference at Chambésy in 1968 decided that a Theological Dialogue should start between the Eastern and Oriental Orthodox Churches. Consequently, the Orthodox Churches set up a Commission for the Theological Dialogue with the Ancient Oriental Churches.[124] This Commission first met in Addis Ababa in 1971, and then with the Non-Chalcedonian Commission in Athens in 1973 and in Addis Ababa in 1975. This introduction is written with the kind of questions raised by these Theological Commissions in mind.

We will refer, in the broadest terms, to some points raised by Professor V. C. Samuel of the Syrian Orthodox Church, and Professor N. A. Zambolotsky of the Russian Orthodox Church. Samuel tells us his aim very frankly. It is to question the view that because Severus criticised Chalcedon and the Tome, he could not have taught the faith of the Church in its purity.[125] The question is whether the rejection of Chalcedon by Severus was the result of a Christology which explained away the human reality of Christ.[126] To show that Severus did not dissolve the human nature of Christ, Samuel points to the heresies he rejected: Manichaeism, Apollinarianism and Eutychianism.[127] He also considers the accusations made against Severus in 536.[128] On the basis both of this, and of Severus' positive teachings, Samuel argues "that Severus was not a Monophysite".[129] This is a provocative line to take, but Samuel justifies it in a very interesting statement: "Severus never objected to the dynamic continuance of the two natures in the one Christ, and the ascription of the term 'monophysite' to his theological position is nothing but the legacy of the polemics of a bygone age".[130] As a consequence of this, Samuel argues that in the dispute between Severus and John the Grammarian, the issue was not whether or not the manhood of Christ was real, but how the manhood was to be understood and interpreted.[131] Throughout all of this argument, Samuel shows beyond doubt the Cyrillian foundation on which Severus stood.

If Severus was not a Monophysite, what was he? Samuel tells us that Severus did not object to the *dynamic continuance* of the two natures: our introduction will attempt to study in detail the status and role of the human nature in the incarnation, and what implications this has for our understanding of the union.

From the Chalcedonian side, Zambolotsky shows himself to be in considerable agreement with Samuel.[132] He approaches Severus through Lebon, and sees him as rooted in the theology of Cyril. We will take just two points which illustrate Zambolotsky's approach. First, Zambolotsky takes up Samuel's contention, which we have already seen, that as regards the Monophysite formula *μία φύσις τοῦ Θεοῦ Λόγου σεσαρκωμένη*, "Severus' position cannot agree with such interpretation of '*μία*' as simply 'one'".[133] The point is that Severus is not a Monophysite in the bad sense, which would involve dissolving the human nature in the union. Zambolotsky examines this contention carefully,[134] and concludes that the reality of Christ's humanity is indeed strongly confirmed by Severus. Our concern is then to ask how it is confirmed, what is its status and what is the nature of the union. Zambolotsky hints at an answer to this, and this is the second point we will draw from his paper. We showed above how Samuel spoke of the "dynamic continuance" of the two natures in Severus' Christology. Zambolotsky tells us that "Severus' human nature is not 'hypostatic' but like the human nature of Leontius of Byzantium and John of Damascus 'hypostatised', received to the unity of the hypostasis of the Logos".[135] This is an approach we will try to explain and develop in our theological introduction.

D. Manuscript and Translation

The letters between Severus and Sergius were, of course, written in Greek. In the preface to his edition of the Syriac text, Lebon refers to A. Baumstark, who judged that the Syriac translation was made by Paul of Kallinike.[136] M. Brière agrees with this.[137] Paul was banished from his see around 519. He later went to Edessa, where he translated many of Severus' works. He died in exile.[138]

The manuscript translated is that edited by Lebon in 1949.[139] It is BL Add MS 17154. Wright describes the manuscript as being of vellum, about $7\frac{7}{8}$ inches by $6\frac{5}{8}$, and consisting of 52 leaves, some of which are slightly stained, especially at the beginning. Each page is divided into two columns, of from 31–42 lines, and he tells us that the volume is written in a good, regular Estrangela hand of the 7th

century.[140] Lebon tells us that Wright has forgotten to note that there is a gap in the manuscript between the present folios 6 and 7; photography seems to reveal that 3 folios have been cut out.[141]

Lebon believed Add 17154 to be the only manuscript of the letters.[142] In an article published in 1975 Dr Sebastian Brock has shown that fragments of the letters survive in an 8th or 9th century manuscript, Harvard (Houghton Library) syr. 22.[143] In this preliminary report, Brock describes the manuscript as containing 80 folios, the vast majority of which are loose, and many of which are badly damaged.[144] The folios are out of order and many have been lost. Keeping to the order of the modern foliation Dr Brock has been kind enough to give me a list of what fragments of the letters the manuscript preserves. This goes slightly beyond the list he gives in his report.[145] The reference is to the pagination of Lebon's edition.

H. syr. 22
f.12^{b} = Lebon p. 70.3–25
⟨7 ff lost⟩
50 = 90.29– 94.16
39 = 94.16– 98.11
37 = 98.12–101.25
23 = 101.25–105.10
47 = 105.10–108.19
59 = 108.19–112.1
⟨1 f lost⟩
45 = 115.15–118.20
⟨3 ff lost⟩
26 = 129.23–133.17
25 = 133.17–136.26
36 = 136.26–140.6
33 = 140.6 –143.16
24 = 143.16–146.25
⟨4 ff lost⟩
44 = 160.24–[164.3]
72 = 164.3–167.18
⟨1 f lost⟩
34 = 171.1 –174.18
35 = 174.18–177.28
62 = 177.28–181.12
⟨end lost⟩

Brock tells us that the Harvard manuscript provides the same translation as that found in Add 17154.[146] It has not yet been published, but in the translation of Lebon's edition I refer in several instances to the Harvard reading, which Dr Brock most generously made available to me.

The translation is fairly literal. As the letters were written in

Greek, it is a version, not an original that is translated here, and inevitably certain obscurities and difficulties remain. One, in particular, is the translation of ܒܪ ܟܝܢܐ.[147] In the letters, ὁμοούσιος in Greek quotations is rendered by both ܒܪ ܟܝܢܐ[148] and ܫܘܝܘܬ ܟܝܢܐ.[149] Very interestingly, in both of the cases where ὁμοούσιος can be seen to be rendered by ܫܘܝܘܬ ܟܝܢܐ in Add 17154, H. syr. 22 happens to be preserved, and reads ܒܪ ܟܝܢܐ.[150] In the English version, ܒܪ ܟܝܢܐ is rendered consistently by "consubstantial". ܫܘܝܘܬ ܟܝܢܐ is rendered by "consubstantial" in the two cases where it can be seen to render ὁμοούσιος but otherwise it is rendered more literally by "equality of nature". This is because out of four occasions where ܫܘܝܘܬ ܟܝܢܐ cannot be anchored to ὁμοούσιος, it occurs three times (EM p. 125.25; p. 126.4; p. 127.4) in the context of a discussion of the word συμφυΐα, and once (EM p. 129.17) at the conclusion to the discussion of the word συμφυΐα. It is therefore translated "equality of nature", in case on those occasions it might be a rendering of συμφυής. The translation of ܕܝܠܝܬܐ is more complex as it brings in the different theological views of Sergius and Severus. We examine this at length in the theological introduction.

Words supplied for the sense, but absent in the Syriac, are placed in round brackets ( ). The page references to Lebon's edition are given in *italics* within round brackets. Where a suggested emendation, or a variant in Harvard syr. 22, is translated instead of Add 17154, the word or phrase is placed in square brackets [ ]. Diamond brackets ⟨ ⟩ are used to show a lacuna in the manuscript.

Footnotes in the translation have been kept to a minimum: the aim has been to write a theological introduction, not a footnote-commentary.

Notes

1. A number of modern histories of doctrine give the basic facts: cf. e.g. J. Lebon, *Chalkedon*, p. 426, n. 4; W. H. C. Frend, *The Rise of the Monophysite Movement* (Cambridge 1972), esp. pp. 201–8; W. A. Wigram, *The Separation of the Monophysites* (London 1923), esp. pp. 57–60; R. C. Chesnut, *Three Monophysite Christologies* (Oxford 1976), pp. 4–5.

2. See *Abbreviations* and *Bibliography*.

3. By Athanasius of Antioch, John of Beth Aphthonia and Zacharias Rhetor (See *Bibliography*). A fourth ancient life has recently been discovered by A. Vööbus: cf. "Découverte d'un memra de Giwargi évêque des arabes, sur Sévère d'Antioche", *Le Muséon* 84 (1971), pp. 433–436, and "Discovery of New Important *memre* of Giwargi, the Bishop of the Arabs", JSS 18 (1973), pp. 235–237. This ms. has not yet been published, but Vööbus says that Giwargi made use of the biographies of Severus

by John of Beth Aphthonia and Zacharias Rhetor, as well as some other sources of unknown provenance.

4. Athanasius of Antioch, *The Conflict of Severus*, PO 4, p. 602.

5. *Ibid.*, p. 613.

6. *The Syriac Chronicle*, Bk. 9, ch. 16, p. 257 (See *Abbreviations*).

7. Athanasius, John of Beth Aphthonia and Zacharias Rhetor concur in telling us that Severus received baptism at the shrine of Leontius. What is more interesting is that there is evidence in Coptic, though not in Syriac, that until the time of his studies in Beirut, Severus was a pagan, and came from a pagan family. This evidence is presented by G. Garitte, from a Coptic homily which has parallels to the Syriac Homily 27. The Coptic homily (ch. 4, sections 2–6), contains a passage in which Severus, at the shrine of Leontius, prayed that he might be saved from pagan worship and the customs of his family. Garitte argues that the Coptic represents the original Greek of Severus' sermon, and that this detail has been suppressed in the Syriac version. See G. Garitte, "Textes hagiographiques orientaux relatifs à saint Léonce de Tripoli. II L'Homélie copte de Sévère d'Antioche", *Le Muséon* 79 (1966), pp. 335–386.

8. On Peter the Iberian, cf. John of Beth Aphthonia, *Vie de Sévère*, PO 2, pp. 219–223; D. M. Lang, "Peter the Iberian and his biographers", JEH 2 (1951), pp. 158–168. In his letters, Severus acknowledges the influence of Peter on him (cf. *Select Letters*, Section 5, Letter 11).

9. We will explain the background to this in the next section.

10. *Breviarium causae Nestorianorum et Eutychianorum*, *XVIIII*, ACO 2.5, p. 133.13–16. For Severus' own condemnation of Peter Mongus, cf. *Select Letters*, Section 4, Letter 2.

11. cf. John of Beth Aphthonia, *op. cit.*, p. 232.

12. For the dating, cf. Lebon, *Le Monophysisme*, pp. 120–121.

13. cf. Evagrius, *The Ecclesiastical History*, ed. J. Bidez and L. Parmentier (London 1898), Bk. 3, ch. 33.

14. Between 509–511. cf. Lebon, *Le Monophysisme*, pp. 124–125.

15. cf. Zacharias Rhetor, *Vie de Sévère*, PO 2, p. 113.

16. Evagrius, *op. cit.*, Bk. 3, ch. 32.

17. *The Syriac Chronicle*, Bk. 7, ch. 10, p. 179 (Hamilton and Brooks' translation).

18. PO 2, pp. 322–325.

19. It is interesting to note that in his *Letter of Apology*, Sergius also condemns "Persia" (presumably Barsumas of Nisibis) and Cyrus and John (cf. EM p. 186.24).

20. See Honigmann, *Évêques et Évêchés Monophysites* (CSCO 127, Sub. 2, Louvain, 1951), pp. 16–17, for the difficulties in dating the Synod.

21. *The Syriac Chronicle*, Bk. 7, ch. 10. For Severus' attitude to the Henoticon, see his *Collected Letters* (ed. Brooks), PO 12, Letters 46 (p. 320) and 49 (p. 324). He held that though it contained an orthodox confession of faith, by itself (without an explicit anathema on Chalcedon) it was unable to bring the healing that was needed.

22. Evagrius, *op. cit.*, Bk. 4, ch. 4.

23. John of Beth Aphthonia, *op. cit.*, p. 243.

24. Homily 26. See *Bibliography*.

25. Homily 54.

26. Evagrius, *op. cit.*, Bk. 4, ch. 4.

27. He mentions this twice in his *Third Letter* to Sergius: EM p. 158.6–7; p. 176.14–17.

28. cf. Lebon, *Le Monophysisme*, p. 153.

29. Lebon dates them to between 518 and 528: cf. *Le Monophysisme*, p. 174. *The Syriac Chronicle*, Bk. 9, chs. 9–13, shows the reluctant way in which Severus entered this quarrel. On Julian, see R. Draguet, *Julian d'Halicarnasse et sa controverse avec Sévère d'Antioche sur l'incorruptibilité du corps du Christ* (Louvain, 1924), and the useful review of Draguet's work by R. P. Casey, "Julian of Halicarnassus", HTR 19 (1926), pp. 206–213.

30. *The Syriac Chronicle*, Bk. 9, ch. 16, gives Severus' letter to Justinian, refusing to come to the royal city.

31. *Ibid.*, Bk. 9, ch. 19.

32. *Ibid.*, Bk. 9, ch. 19.

33. Among other things, Severus was accused of being an "Akephalist" (ACO 3, p. 137.8–10); a Eutychian and Manichaean (ACO 3, p. 147.35–36); of conducting uncanonical baptism (ACO 3, p. 112.35–36); and of holding illegal meetings (ACO 3, p. 113.14–16). The old slur about his pagan background was also brought up (ACO 3, p. 40.16–24).

34. cf. ACO 3, p. 121.5–9.

35. *Ibid.*, lines 22–27.

36. *Ibid.*, lines 30–34.

37. Athanasius, *op. cit.*, pp. 709–710.

38. *Ibid.*, p. 716.

39. cf. *Chronicon anonymum ad AD 846 pertinens*, ed. E. W. Brooks (CSCO 3, Syr. 3, 1904), p. 221, line 12.

40. cf. *Select Letters*, Section 1, Letters 14, 15 and 16 (pp. 63–70 in Brooks' text). Also *Collected Letters*, Letter 29, PO 12, p. 260.

41. *Chron. a. 846*, *op. cit.*, p. 226, lines 7–11. Also cf. Honigmann, *op. cit.*, pp. 25–26.

42. *Le Monophysisme*, p. 170.

43. EM p. 156.4–7.

44. At EM p. 95.22, Severus, answering Sergius' *First Letter*, urges him instead to make the Nicene Creed his test.

45. EM p. 71.1–3. ܠܘ ܗܘܐ ܒܟܝ̈ܢܐ ܐܘܣܝܐ ܚܕ ... ܘܠܐ ܕܬܠܝܬܐ

46. EM p. 71.4–5 ܠܘ ܕܬܠܝܬܐ ܡܬܦܠܓܢܝܬܐ ܐܘܣܝܐܝܬ

47. EM p. 70.23.

48. EM p. 72.27.

49. *Le Monophysisme*, p. 166.

50. EM p. 158.22.

51. *Le Monophysisme*, p. 168.

52. Lebon is followed by Honigmann, *op. cit.*, p. 26 n. 6, on this date.

53. EM p. 156.6.

54. *Ibid.*, p. 157.6–7.

55. Ps. LXXXIV.2. All OT references are to LXX.

56. EM p. 172.19–23.

57. *Ibid.*, p. 176.14–15.

58. Honigmann, *op. cit.*, p. 144. (Cf. Schwartz, ACO 2.5, p. 134 note 7).

59. Wigram, *op. cit.*, p. 9 ff.

60. For an historical account of the period, see Wigram, *op. cit.*; Frend, *op. cit.*, R. V. Sellers, *The Council of Chalcedon* (London, 1961); J. B. Bury, *History of the Later Roman Empire* (London, 1923). Wigram's work contains useful tables, giving the dates of the emperors and principal bishops.

61. An outline of these events is given in Evagrius, *op. cit.*, Bk. 2, ch. 5.

62. cf. *ibid.*, Bk. 2, ch. 8.

63. Severus, *Select Letters*, Section 2, Letter 3 (p. 252 in Brooks' text).

64. cf. Evagrius, *op. cit.*, Bk. 2, chs. 9–11.

65. cf. *The Syriac Chronicle*, Bk. 5, ch. 2; Evagrius, *op. cit.*, Bk. 3, ch. 4. See the text of Basiliscus' encyclical and counter-encyclical edited by E. Schwartz, "Codex Vaticanus graecus 1431, eine antichalkedonische Sammlung aus der Zeit Kaiser Zenos" (*Abh. der Bayer. Akad. der Wiss.*, Phil.-philol. u. hist. Kl. 32.6, 1927), No. 73, p. 49 and no. 74, p. 52.

66. *The Syriac Chronicle*, Bk. 5, ch. 1.

67. cf. Evagrius, *op. cit.*, Bk. 3, ch. 5. Zacharias puts the number of bishops at seven hundred.

68. *Ibid.*, Bk. 3, ch. 6.

69. cf. *The Syriac Chronicle*, Bk. 4, ch. 12. Peter the Iberian was equally anti-Eutychian, and anathematised John the Rhetorician of Alexandria, who wrote works under Peter's name: cf. *ibid.*, Bk. 3, ch. 10.

70. *Ibid.*, Bk. 4, ch. 12.

71. cf. *ibid.*, Bk. 5, ch. 4, and Evagrius, *op. cit.*, Bk. 3, ch. 6.

72. *Ibid.*, *The Syriac Chronicle*, Bk. 5, ch. 4; Evagrius, Bk. 3, ch. 6.

73. On Timothy Aelurus, see his *Fragments*, ed. F. Nau, PO 13, pp. 202–236; R. Y. Ebied and L. R. Wickham, "A Collection of Unpublished Syriac Letters of Timothy Aelurus", JTS 21 (1970), pp. 321–369; and J. Lebon, "La Christologie de Timothée Aelure", RHE 9 (1908), pp. 677–702.

74. Severus tells us that Theodotus adhered to the fatuities of John the Rhetorician of Alexandria: *Select Letters*, Section 5, Letter 6 (pp. 356–357 in Brooks' text). In Severus' eyes, then, Theodotus was a Eutychian.

75. Severus, *Collected Letters*, Letter 34, PO 12, p. 277.

76. Severus, *Select Letters*, Section 1, Letter 60 (pp. 201–202 in Brooks' text).

77. cf. *Select Letters*, Section 5, Letter 6; *Collected Letters*, PO 12, p. 277.

78. Evagrius, *op. cit.*, Bk. 3, ch. 8.

79. *Ibid.*, Bk. 3, ch. 11.

80. This is the version in Evagrius, *op. cit.*, Bk. 3, ch. 12. According to *The Syriac Chronicle*, Bk. 5, ch. 6, John was sent as the representative of the Chalcedonian party, to ask that the Alexandrians should not receive Peter Mongus as their next bishop.

81. cf. Evagrius, *op. cit.*, Bk. 3, ch. 12; *The Syriac Chronicle*, Bk. 5, ch. 7.

82. See Evagrius, *op. cit.*, Bk. 3, ch. 14. There is an English translation of the text in Evagrius in Frend, *op. cit.*, pp. 360–362.

83. cf. Evagrius, *op. cit.*, Bk. 3, ch. 14, p. 113.8–10.

84. *Ibid.*, p. 113.22–24.

85. cf. *The Syriac Chronicle*, Bk. 5, ch. 7.

86. *Ibid.*, Bk. 6, ch. 1.

87. Zacharias speaks of thirty thousand monks, with ten bishops: *ibid.*, Bk. 6, ch. 2.

88. Evagrius, *op. cit.*, Bk. 3, ch. 17.

89. *The Syriac Chronicle*, Bk. 6, ch. 2.

90. cf. *ibid.*, Bk. 6, ch. 1.

91. Evagrius, *op. cit.*, Bk. 3, ch. 30, p. 126.5–8.

92. *The Syriac Chronicle*, Bk. 7, ch. 7.

93. Athanasius of Antioch, *op. cit.*, pp. 646, 664.

94. *The Syriac Chronicle*, Bk. 7, ch. 10.

95. Evagrius, *op. cit.*, Bk. 3, ch. 31.

96. *The Syriac Chronicle*, Bk. 9, ch. 20.

97. cf. *ibid.*, Bk. 7, 10 and 12.

98. cf. The *Libellus Ioannis Episcopi Constantinopolitani*, PL 63.443–445.

99. Lebon, *Chalcedon*, p. 453.

100. *Ibid.*, pp. 425–450.

101. *Ibid.*, pp. 451–580.

102. *Ibid.*, p. 431.

103. *Ibid.*, p. 440.

104. *Ibid.*, p. 442 ff.

105. *Ibid.*, pp. 447–449.

106. *Ibid.*, p. 444 and cf. pp. 578–579.

107. *Ibid.*, p. 454 ff.

108. *Ibid.*, p. 461 ff.; pp. 464–465.

109. *Ibid.*, p. 467.

110. *Ibid.*, p. 468.

111. *Ibid.*, p. 472.

112. *Ibid.*, p. 483.

113. *Ibid.*, pp. 486–490.

114. *Ibid.*, pp. 489–504.

115. *Ibid.*, pp. 510–516.
116. *Ibid.*, p. 505 and p. 514 f.
117. *Ibid.*, pp. 534–576.
118. *Ibid.*, pp. 537–538.
119. *Ibid.*, cf. pp. 538–539.
120. *Ibid.*, p. 539.
121. *Three Monophysite Christologies* (Oxford, 1976).
122. Washington and Cleveland, 1969.
123. At Aarhus in 1964; Bristol in 1967; Geneva in 1970 and Addis Ababa in 1971. The papers from these conferences may be seen in *The Greek Orthodox Theological Review*, 10 pt. 2 (1964–5) (Aarhus); 13 pt. 2 (1968) (Bristol); 16 pts. 1 and 2 (1971) (Geneva and Addis Ababa).
124. cf. Methodios Fouyas, *The Person of Jesus Christ in the Decisions of the Ecumenical Councils* (Addis Ababa, 1976), p. 223 ff.
125. "The Christology of Severus of Antioch", *Abba Salama* (Athens), 4 (1973), p. 126.
126. cf. "Further Studies in the Christology of Severus of Antioch", *Ekklesiastikos Pharos* (Athens), 58 pts. 3–4 (1976), p. 284.
127. *Ibid.*, pp. 286–296 and cf. *Abba Salama*, pp. 145–151.
128. *Ibid.*, pp. 283–286.
129. *Abba Salama*, p. 145 and cf. pp. 160–161.
130. *Ibid.*, pp. 161–162.
131. cf. *Ekklesiastikos Pharos*, p. 277, and *Abba Salama*, p. 173.
132. "The Christology of Severus of Antioch", *Ekklesiastikos Pharos*, 58 pts. 3–4 (1976), pp. 357–386.
133. Zambolotsky, *ibid.*, p. 367; cf. Samuel, *Abba Salama*, p. 145 and 160–161 and "One Incarnate Nature of God the Word", *Greek Orthodox Theological Review*, 10 pt. 2 (1964), p. 48.
134. Zambolotsky, *ibid.*, pp. 367–373.
135. *Ibid.*, p. 377.
136. EM p.v.
137. "Introduction Générale à toutes les Homélies", PO 29, p. 17.
138. Honigmann, *op. cit.*, p. 54.
139. CSCO 119 (Syr. 64).
140. W. Wright, *Catalogue of the Syriac Manuscripts in the British Museum* (London, 1872), pt. 2, pp. 557–558.
141. Lebon, *Le Monophysisme*, p. 163, n. 2.
142. cf. EM p. iv.
143. "Some New Letters of the Patriarch Severos", *Studia Patristica* 12 (*Texte und Untersuchungen zur Geschichte der altchristlichen Literatur*, Band 115), Berlin 1975, pp. 17–24.
144. *Ibid.*, p. 18.
145. *Ibid.*, pp. 19–20.
146. *Ibid.*, p. 19.
147. For notes on this, see A. de Halleux, "La Philoxénienne du Symbole", *Symposium Syriacum 1976* (*Orientalia Christiana Analecta* 205, Rome, 1978), pp. 301–302; R. Y. Ebied and L. R. Wickham, "A Collection of Unpublished Syriac Letters of Timothy Aelurus", JTS 21 (1970), p. 325; L. Abramowski and A. Goodman, *A Nestorian Collection of Christological Texts* (Cambridge, 1972), Vol. 2 (Introduction, Translation and Indexes), p. li.
148. 13 times: cf. EM p. 87.17; p. 128.24; p. 129.1; p. 129.5; p. 129.6; p. 129.7; p. 131.22; p. 131.24; p. 131.25; p. 131.26; p. 131.27; p. 131.28; p. 132.1.
149. Twice: EM p. 107.22; p. 167.9.
150. At EM p. 107.22, H. syr. 22 reads ܒܬܪ ܒܬܪܟܐ; at p. 167.9 it reads ܒܐܬܐ ܒܡܡܟܐ.

II The Misunderstanding between Sergius and Severus

We have already seen in the introduction that Sergius found the answer of the episcopal assembly hard to understand. The *κεφάλαιον* of Sergius was, "We do not speak of two natures or (two) proprieties after the inexpressible union".[1] The opinion of the assembly corrected Sergius saying, "We do not speak of divided proprieties".[2] We need to ask, "Is there a misunderstnding here?" "Is ܕܝܠܝܬܐ being used in the same sense by both speakers?" This is a question which must be carefully examined before there can be any attempt at giving a summary of Sergius' Christological position.

In *Appendix A*, after the translation, there is given a list of every occurrence of the words ܕܝܠܝܬܐ, ܕܝܠܝܘܬܐ, ܡܫܘܕܥܢܘܬܐ, ܡܫܘܕܥܢܝܘܬܐ and ܦܘܪܫܢܐ, in the Severus-Sergius Letters, together with the underlying Greek word, where there has been a quotation of Greek. There are 176 occurrences of the word ܕܝܠܝܬܐ (in singular and plural forms), and 13 occurrences of the word ܕܝܠܝܘܬܐ (in singular and plural). ܕܝܠܝܬܐ (in singular and plural) translates the Greek words *ἡ ἰδιότης*; *τὸ ἴδιον*; *τὰ ἴδια*; *τὰ ἰδιώματα* and the Latin word, *proprietas*. The translation pattern, where it can be checked against quotations from Greek, may be set out in a table, as follows:

ἡ ἰδιότης	is rendered by	ܕܝܠܝܬܐ	×2
τὰ ἴδια	are rendered by	ܕܝܠܝ̈ܬܐ	×8
τὸ ἴδιον	is rendered by	ܕܝܠܝܬܐ	×1
τὰ ἰδιώματα	are rendered by	ܕܝܠܝ̈ܬܐ	×4
proprietas	is rendered by	ܕܝܠܝܘܬܐ	×1
proprietas	is rendered by	ܕܝܠܝܬܐ	×2

There is too little information here to allow us to see a pattern in the Greek to Syriac translation, which would allow us to distinguish between different occurrences of ܕܝܠܝܬܐ. Any such distinguishing will have to emerge from an argument based first on context, and then on theological meaning and sense.

In the Syriac translation of these letters, both Severus and Sergius use the word ܕܝܠܝܬܐ. Is it possible to find, in their various uses of the word, certain paradigm instances of uses—uses which are such that

they can point both to distinctions within the usage of each writer, and to differences between the uses by the writers?

The usage which it is perhaps easiest initially to isolate and recognise, is when in Severus, ܕܝܠܝܬܐ is used in the plural, to mean "properties", in the context of a discussion of the *communicatio idiomatum*. We can give two examples of this. In his *First Letter*, Severus quotes Cyril, saying, "Therefore the properties (ἴδια/ܕܝ̈ܠܝܬܐ) of the Word became (properties) of manhood, and the properties (ἴδια/ܕܝ̈ܠܝܬܐ) of manhood, (properties) of the Word. For thus one Christ and Son and Lord is understood."[3] In the second example, although it is out of the context of the *communicatio idiomatum*, Severus makes it clear that it is of "properties" that he is speaking. He rebukes Sergius, saying, "But apart from this, how is it not absurd to speak of *two* properties (ܕܝ̈ܠܝܬܐ) or two activities? For there are many properties (ܕܝ̈ܠܝܬܐ) and not just two of every nature."[4]

Secondly, ܕܝܠܝܬܐ is used with what might be called a "definitional" sense in Severus, and has been translated "propriety". Severus, for example, writes, "Who does not know that the faculty of laughter is the propriety (ܕܝܠܝܬܐ) of 'man', and neighing of 'horse'?"[5] Giving what is virtually a definition of the concept, and so is certainly a paradigm of the use, he writes, "Because a propriety (ܕܝܠܝܬܐ), expressed precisely, is that thing which belongs to something alone, and without sharing with another".[6] He uses the word in the same strict sense at the beginning of his *Second Letter*: "Is the soul of a man *changed*, that it should become flesh? .... For this is the peculiarity (ܕܝܠܝܬܐ) of mixture".[7]

These are two distinct usages and meanings of ܕܝܠܝܬܐ in Severus, but there is a third, which Severus developed from Cyril, and which became one of his most powerful and subtle theological distinctions. In the translation of the *Letters*, I have rendered this usage as "particularity". The concept will be fully examined later: for the meantime, let us suggest that "particularity" refers to the integrity of being of a particular thing. Flesh is flesh, and is not stone, simply for the reason that it is flesh. It might be blackened, crushed or cooked, but while it remains *flesh*, while it retains that identity, it is not something else. It is to this possession of identity that "particularity" refers, and two examples will illustrate it clearly. In his *First Letter*, Severus writes, "And we call this a particularity (ܕܝܠܝܬܐ) and name it: (that is,) that which (lies) in difference of natural quality, which (definition) I will not cease repeating many times, and not that (which lies) in (independent) parts, and natures in independent existence are implied".[8] In a second example of this usage, Severus

quotes Cyril, but from a passage only extant in Syriac: "Because we say too that, with respect to particularity (ܕܝܠܝܘܬܐ), flesh is completely of another nature from the Word which sprang from God and the Father".[9]

We have distinguished three distinct usages of ܕܝܠܝܬܐ in Severus. Are there the same three usages in Sergius, or are there not, and is this part of their misunderstanding? We shall suggest that Sergius knows the first and second usages (that of "property" and "propriety"), but not the third ("particularity"), and furthermore, that he quite radically develops and sharpens the second usage.

We can give first an example of our first type of usage, that meaning "property". In his *Third Letter*, Sergius writes, "But I, from (my) first words, was of the same mind, and in every respect have believed that the invisible and intangible God the Word, along with the flesh also accepted the properties (ܕܝ̈ܠܝܬܐ) of the flesh, and became visible and tangible on our behalf".[10] The word ܕܝܠܝܬܐ is here used in the plural, and the context points beyond any doubts to the meaning "properties". We can also find contexts demanding the definitional sense, which we have translated "propriety", in Sergius. For example, in his *First Letter*, he writes, "For just as laughter is the propriety (ܕܝܠܝܬܐ) to 'man', and none of the other animals is like him in this, so also there is one propriety (ܕܝܠܝܬܐ) of Christ, in which no-one from those who are invisible or visible shares".[11] Sergius here emphasises the singularity of the ܕܝܠܝܬܐ, and this, together with the definitional connotations of the references to laughter, force the conclusion that there is something here quite different from what was meant in the previous example. We will return to this.

ܕܝܠܝܬܐ is not the only word over which Sergius and Severus clash, or misunderstand each other. Another word is ܫܘܕܥܐ,[12] which we shall suggest shortly is used, on occasion, by Sergius, in contexts very similar to those which we have called "definitional uses" of ܕܝܠܝܬܐ. But before asking for the meaning of ܕܝܠܝܬܐ and ܫܘܕܥܐ, let us illustrate the clash between the usages of Severus and Sergius. All the occurrences of ܫܘܕܥܐ, ܡܫܘܕܥܢܘܬܐ and ܡܫܘܕܥܢܝܬܐ[13] in the Letters are listed in *Appendix B*, after the translation. Certain conclusions can be drawn from that table.

Both Severus and Sergius use ܫܘܕܥܐ with the sense of "meaning"; "signification"; "mark". Thus, there are Severus' uses at p. 94.22; p. 134.2 and 12 (Where Cyril is quoted, and the underlying Greek is δήλωσις); p. 161.27; p. 165.20; p. 166.30. Sergius uses ܫܘܕܥܐ in a similar way at p. 99.31, and ܡܫܘܕܥܢܝܬܐ at p. 100.4. However, in three places, Sergius shows a more extended use of

ܫܘܘܕܥܐ, and, going to what is important for our purpose, Severus both repudiates Sergius' extended usage, and even, though of course we only see the Syriac translation, rephrases Sergius, when he quotes him. Our concern is not with differences of just words, but with pointing out where there is a real clash of concepts, ideas and intentions. We shall list the verbal details of this clash between Sergius and Severus, but then ask what lies behind it.

Sergius uses ܫܘܘܕܥܐ in a more extended sense at p. 102.2; p. 150.26 and p. 155.4, 7, 9. Summarising his arguments, the instances are as follows. At p. 102.2, he suggests that blackness is a sign (ܫܘܕܥܐ) of that which is laid down. At p. 150.26, he says that as ousiai can be simple or composite, so too, the signs (ܫܘܘܕ̈ܥܐ) of ousiai are simple or composite. At p. 155.4, 7, 9 he argues that as we could not recognise ousiai without (identifying) signs (ܫܘܘܕ̈ܥܐ), therefore when we combine two ousiai, we also combine the signs (ܫܘܘܕ̈ܥܐ) [= the means of identifying the new compound].

Severus objects, at p. 164.11 saying that none of the orthodox Fathers called the Word one ousia or sign (ܫܘܘܕܥܐ) when it was composed (to be one) with flesh, and at p. 172.22 he asks when did he ever, during his six years in Antioch, say that Emmanuel is one ousia, and of one signification (ܫܘܘܕܥܐ), and of one particularity. ܫܘܕܥܐ as used by Sergius on p. 102.2, appears as ܡܫܘܕܥܢܘܬܐ where it is quoted by Severus at p. 136.4. Similarly, Sergius uses ܡܫܘܕܥܢܘܬܐ at p. 152.3, but when Severus quotes him, ܡܫܘܕܥܘܬܐ appears instead at p. 162.26, and ܡܫܘܕܥܢܘܬܐ at p. 168.15.

Having gone some way towards illustrating the Sergius to Severus clash at a verbal level, let us ask what lies behind it. It has already been shown very briefly that Severus has a usage of ܕܝܠܝܘܬܐ which we translated "particularity", saying it referred to the integrity of being of a particular object. How does Sergius misunderstand this: what does he mean by ܕܝܠܝܘܬܐ in his *First Letter*? We shall proceed in the same way as before, looking for a "paradigm" or "base" statement, where the meaning seems clearer, and argue outwards from there.

We find such a "base" statement at p. 71.28–72.1: "But every propriety belongs to an underlying nature, and if we speak of two proprieties, we are obliged also to speak of two natures".[14] Here Sergius shows his hand. To him, there is a one-to-one relationship between proprieties and natures. If you speak of two proprieties, you will be implying two natures. A consequence is that for any nature, there will be just one propriety. We can now look back to Sergius' clash with the episcopal assembly. The κεφάλαιον of Sergius was, "We do

not speak of two natures or (two) proprieties after the union".[15] The answer of the assembly, "We do not speak of divided ܕܝ̈ܠܝܬܐ",[16] could, as we can now understand, certainly puzzle Sergius. The assembly had in mind the "particularity" concept of Severus, which we will examine later, but Sergius, looking at the plural word, understood it as an affirmation of undivided proprieties, which to him would imply a plurality of natures. It is no wonder he viewed this answer as a concession![17]

Arguing on the basis of what we take to be one of his fundamental presuppositions, namely that a propriety implies a nature, Sergius fights back. The very Biblical facts[18] will contradict the suggestion that there are two proprieties in Christ, that is, the propriety of God and the propriety of flesh. The propriety[19] of God is that he is not seen or touched, but Christ came visibly. The propriety[20] of flesh is that it is brought forth from two parents, but no man was the father of Christ. Thus, Sergius argues, the person of Christ contradicts the two proprieties idea: neither of the two proprieties will fit. Now, we can draw two points from the argument so far, the first to do with the meaning of "propriety", and the second to do with Sergius' presuppositions.

First, it is important to notice that Sergius uses "ܕܝܠܝܬܐ" in the singular. It is the propriety of God that he is not seen or touched,[21] it is the propriety of flesh that it should be brought forth of two parents, and later be corrupted.[22] The concept underlying the singular ܕܝܠܝܬܐ seems to be something like "peculiarity"; "defining characteristic". It is this, we suggest, that Sergius means by ܕܝܠܝܬܐ in this context: a propriety is a "unique identifier". It is worth noting that on this point Joseph Lebon is not completely clear. Summarising some of Sergius' views in a very illuminating footnote, he writes, "En effet, alors que ce sont des propriétés de Dieu d'être invisible et intangible. . . . Pour la chair, à son tour, ce sont des propriétés d'être engendrée de deux parents et d'être corruptibles . . .".[23] The text in both places uses ܕܝܠܝܬܐ in the singular, and we suggest it is this which gives a clue to the meaning. We suggest that Sergius is saying, "It is the *peculiarity* of God that he is a and b; it is the *peculiarity* of flesh to be x and y, and these peculiarities do not fit in the case of Christ". Our second point is one we can note now, but will explore later. Sergius seems to think that he can specify what a propriety is. He seems to think that he can say whether one does or does not apply. This implies that if proprieties are "indicators", they are very fixed and rigid ones. But if the indicators which specify the peculiarities of objects are fixed and rigid, this will be because the objects themselves

are fixed and rigid. Using words we will return to later, in Sergius' thought-world, objects are "static" rather than "dynamic".

To continue with Sergius' argument, he gives up as useless the idea of two proprieties, suggesting that, "just as we believe Christ is one from two natures, so also we accept one propriety from two of God incarnate".[24] He then draws some consequences: there is to be seen no propriety either of God or of flesh in Christ,[25] but "the entire manner of the economy points towards one propriety: that which is with God incarnate".[26] Sergius concludes that as laughter is the propriety of "man", none of the other animals sharing it, so too there is just one propriety of Christ, which no-one, either visible or invisible, shares in.[27] We can see Sergius' argument: an object which is distinct, or independently recognisable, possesses a propriety, a peculiarity, which somehow marks it out as being itself. Christ is someone different, or new: he is unlike anyone visible or invisible, and he has his own propriety. It is this concept of identity, or mode of marking the identity of Christ, that we shall suggest Sergius opposes to Severus' concept of one nature in which it is possible to discern differences in natural quality.

We can give one further point, which may clarify Sergius' concept. We saw above that Sergius suggested that just as we believe Christ is one from two natures, so also we should accept one propriety from two. We have seen as well that he suggested this because he believed that a propriety characterised in a peculiar way, and so "indicated", one object. Later on in the *Letters*, Sergius complains that he is called to judgement, on the grounds that he set aside ousiai, and interwove composition from signs (ܫܘܕ̈ܥܐ).[28] He defends himself: "I do not acknowledge that I suffered (from) this ignorance. For a quality does not exist without an ousia, nor should we recognise ousiai without (identifying) signs (ܫܘܕ̈ܥܐ). Therefore when I said that two ousiai were composed, along with them I was also uniting the signs (ܫܘܕ̈ܥܐ)".[29] We may understand this as an illustration of the "from two proprieties, one propriety" of Sergius' *First Letter*. The argument is the same: from the presupposition of there being a tight connection between a propriety and the object to which it applies, it follows that when you compose two ousiai, you also unite their identifying signs, thus obtaining one sign of the (new) compound. We can see that we must examine the concept of composition which Sergius presupposes here, but we will come to that later. For the meantime, this use of ܫܘܕܥܐ, with its parallels to the *First Letter*, is an additional argument that ܕܝܠܝܬܐ is there meant in a denoting or ostensive sense, as a defining characteristic.

Finally, if now the different concepts are clearer, we will offer an example of how the Sergius–Severus misunderstanding is acted out. The argument between them on particular points frequently spans several letters. In this case, Severus quotes Cyril to Sergius in his *First Letter*. He says of Christ that ". . . . he is composed so as to be one in the middle from human properties (ܕܝ̈ܠܝܬܐ) and from those which are above man".[30] Sergius, in his *Second Letter*, then quotes the passage from Cyril, but obviously interpreting it out of context and in accordance with his own presuppositions, adds, "The Father seems to say that the incarnate Word was one in every respect, I mean both nature and propriety (ܕܝܠܝܬܐ), when he mingled the natures along with the proprieties (ܕܝ̈ܠܝܬܐ)".[31] Sergius' interpretation of Cyril, that the Word incarnate was one nature and propriety, is of course very reminiscent of his suggestion in his *First Letter*, that Christ is one from two natures, and that we should accept one propriety from two.[32] His second point that the Word mingled the natures along with the proprieties, is reminiscent of the passage we have just examined from Sergius' *Third Letter*, where he argued that when two ousiai were composed, along with them, the signs should also be united.[33] We have already tried to show that Sergius' emphasis upon the "one propriety" is his way of expressing that Christ, as presented by the Biblical facts, does not fit any previous propriety, but is utterly new, different and unique. "There is one propriety of Christ, in which no-one from those who are invisible or visible shares."[34] To understand Sergius, we must give due weight to his attempt to express this radical newness and difference of the figure of Christ.

But how does Severus react? In his *Second Letter*, he quotes again the same passage from Cyril, complaining to Sergius, ". . . . you say, 'The Father seems to say that the Word incarnate made to cleave natures along with properties, and is one in every respect, I mean both nature and particularity (ܕܝܠܝܬܐ)'".[35] Severus finds this astonishing, "For, while (Cyril) (uses) a plural word, and discriminates (between properties) by difference, and says, 'Of human properties and of those which are above man,' you mingle everything to one particularity, as you have expressed it above, (namely) that at one time there took place one ousia or quality".[36] Severus' reference to "one quality" shows that he takes Sergius to be speaking of one particularity, not understanding Sergius' "one propriety" doctrine. It is, as we shall see, one of Severus' own most emphasised points that in the union, the particularity of the natures in Christ remained without confusion, and particularity implies difference in natural quality.

Were there just one quality in Christ, the difference in the quality of the natures would have been lost, and the flesh, for example, might no longer be flesh. Severus' fear is that Sergius' doctrine is Eutychian or Synousiast. Thus, while Sergius understood the answer of the episcopal assembly ("We do not speak of divided particularities"), as affirming two proprieties, thereby implying two natures, and being virtually Nestorian, Severus understood Sergius' "one propriety" as "one particularity", and so as virtually an affirmation that the flesh had become consubstantial with the Word, through losing its intrinsic difference.

This, we suggest, is the scale of the misunderstanding! We will now turn to consider, in summary form, the theological argument of Sergius' *Letters*.

Notes

1. EM p. 71.1–3. ܠܐ ܬܪܝܢ ܟܝ̈ܢܝܢ ܐܡܪܝܢ ܚܢܢ ... ܘܠܐ ܕܝ̈ܠܝܬܐ
2. This, I suggest, is how Sergius understood the answer. EM p. 71.4–5. ܠܐ ܕܝ̈ܠܝܬܐ ܦ̈ܠܝܓܬܐ ܐܡܪܝܢ
3. EM p. 80.6–8 and PG 76.137C (=*Adv. Nest. Lib. III.* Pusey edn. Vol. 6, p. 153.30–154.3).
4. EM p. 86.18–20.
5. EM p. 136.15–16.
6. EM p. 138.29–139.2.
7. EM p. 105.17–20.
8. EM p. 80.23–81.1.
9. EM p. 75.6–9.
10. EM p. 153.8–12.
11. EM 72.20–24.
12. cf. R. Payne Smith, *Thesaurus Syriacus* (Oxford, 1879–1901), Col. 1562. Among the Latin translations which the *Thesaurus* gives, are: *signum; indicium; symbolum; signum characteristicum*. An occurrence is listed where the word is used, "*de notis quibus res aliqua describitur ut agnosci possit*".
13. cf. *Thesaurus. op. cit.*, Col. 1561. Translations include *significatio, indicatio*.
14. ܟܠ ܕܝܢ ܕܝܠܝܬܐ ܕܒܟܝܢܐ ܕܗܘܝܐ ܐܝܬܘܬܗ̇. ܘܐܦ
ܗܠܝܢ ܐܡܪܝܢ ܚܢܢ ܕܝ̈ܠܝܬܐ: ܗܠܝܢ ܘܒܟܝ̈ܢܐ ܡܬܐܡܪܝܢ ܕܐܝܬܝܗ̇.
15. cf. EM p. 71.1–3.
16. cf. EM p. 71.4–5.
17. cf. EM p. 70.23.
18. cf. EM p. 71.18 ff.
19. ܕܝܠܝܬܐ EM p. 71.17. It is important to note that this is singular.
20. ܕܝܠܝܬܐ EM p. 71.22. Note that this is singular.
21. cf. EM p. 71.16–18.
22. cf. EM p. 71.22–24.
23. J. Lebon, *Chalkedon*, p. 548, n. 43. One might note that "propriété" in French can mean both "property" and "peculiar property", so the exact point is obscured.
24. EM p. 72.9–11.
25. cf. EM p. 72.17–18.

26. EM p. 72.19–20.
27. cf. EM p. 72.20–24.
28. EM p. 155.3.
29. EM p. 155.5–9.
30. EM p. 92.28–30. The reference to Cyril is PG 76.1193B. (= *De Recta Fide ad Theod.* Pusey edn. Vol. 7, p. 134.13–14).
31. EM p. 102.10–12.
32. cf. EM p. 72.9–11.
33. cf. EM p. 155.8–9.
34. EM p. 72.23–24.
35. EM p. 121.5–8.
36. EM p. 121.8–13.

III The Theological Argument of Sergius' Letters

Introduction

We attempt in this section to give a summary account of the main argument of Sergius' *Letters*. Not every detail of Sergius' counter arguments against Severus can be considered here: to attempt to do so would be to lose sight of the wood for the trees. Where possible, footnotes in the translation will attempt to clarify points not covered here.

The translation of the various "mixture" terms presents a problem. English is not precise enough to provide an easy one-to-one correspondence with the distinctions involved in the Greek *σύγχυσις*, *κρᾶσις* and *μίξις*. In the translation of the *Letters*, I have made use of the English distinction between "confusion" and "mixture", translating the Greek *σύγχυσις* as "confusion" and *κρᾶσις* as "mixture". The Greek word *μίξις* might seem to imply the translation "mixture", in English, but to enable the reader to see immediately that a different verb is being used, I have translated the Syriac "ܚܠܛ" consistently as "mingle" or "mingling", even though such an inflexible translation can appear strained. Where they can be checked against quotations of Greek, the Syriac roots ܒܠܒܠ and ܫܓܫ would seem to translate *σύγχυσις* or a related word, ܡܙܓ would seem to translate *κρᾶσις*, and ܚܠܛ *μίξις*. *Appendix C*, at the end of the translation, lists every occurrence of the words in the *Letters*, giving the Greek which the Syriac has translated, where this is available. The meaning of the distinction between the words will be examined later.

Letter I

As has been said, Sergius' *First Letter*, is addressed to Antoninus of Aleppo. He asks an episcopal gathering what expression of belief he may impose on converted Dyophysites. His own expression is summed up as "We do not speak of two natures or (two) proprieties

after the inexpressible union".[1] The assembly appeared to Sergius to make a serious and unintelligible concession: it corrected his κεφάλαιον to "We do not speak of divided particularities",[2] which, as we have seen, Sergius took to mean that the assembly would affirm that there were two undivided proprieties after the union.

He asks what the advantage of affirming two proprieties would be. Could it be to thwart the Changers of Ousiai:[3] if the two proprieties are retained, the flesh remains flesh, and the divinity is not confused?[4] But Sergius objects that as a line of defence, this goes too far. He states what we have suggested is one of his basic presuppositions: "Every propriety belongs to an underlying nature, and if we speak of two proprieties, we are obliged also to speak of two natures".[5] Thus, this defence against the Changers of Ousiai will supply one with two natures, not just two proprieties.

But there is a second objection to it. The affirmation that the proprieties of God and of flesh persist after the union is contradicted by the Biblical facts. It is the propriety of God that he is not seen or touched,[6] and the propriety of flesh that it is brought forth from two parents, and later is corrupted.[7] Christ does not fit these proprieties: God came visibly and had dealings with men, and no man was his father. So much for saying that the proprieties persist! Sergius adds, "because he was not born in accordance with the propriety of the flesh, neither did his flesh see corruption".[8]

But Sergius has yet another argument against the opinion of the assembly: to proclaim "two undivided proprieties", when it is understood that every propriety belongs to a particular nature, is no different from the Dyophysite confession itself, which proclaims two undivided natures.[9] There is no safeguard in saying "undivided", so how may the Dyophysites be outflanked? Sergius canvasses his own solution: just as we believe Christ is one from two natures, so let us accept "one propriety from two of God incarnate".[10] "He who out of kindness undertakes to be seen" (i.e. moves out of the divine propriety), at the same time "transcended the human propriety".[11] As a result, Christ could do what was foreign both to God and man: he could walk, which God does not do, but could do this on water, which man does not do. Closed doors could not prevent his entering.

As a result, Sergius concludes, no propriety either of God[12] or of flesh[13] may be recognised in Christ, but "the entire manner of the economy points towards one propriety, that which is with God incarnate".[14] This propriety belongs only to Christ, with no-one, visible or invisible, sharing it with him.[15] Sergius then appeals to the assembly: may the good Fathers enquire into and correct his con-

temptible thoughts; may they not reject his youth. He concludes his letter.

We may draw three main theological presuppositions from this letter, all of which will guide us later in understanding Sergius' position. First, in his reference at the beginning of the letter to the Changers of Ousiai, Sergius implicitly denied a change or confusion of the elements from which Christ was formed. Though Severus several times accused him of introducing change and confusion, Sergius claims he avoids this error. We must take his denial seriously. Even when it looks as if he is introducing confusion, we must consider whether he may not be doing something else. Secondly, one can see the presupposition that a propriety implies a nature, and that two proprieties, even if undivided, imply two natures, in the Dyophysite sense of two natures with their own activities. Thirdly, one can see the presupposition that the scope of a propriety is quite narrow and rigid. The Biblical Christ just does not fit the predetermined proprieties of God and of flesh. In consequence, our previous presupposition—that a propriety implies a nature—applies in reverse: a distinct nature demonstrates its distinctness by implying its own propriety, even if the propriety can only be defined in a notional way, as when Sergius in his *Second Letter* says, "all the propriety of the inhomination of the Word is a mystery".[16]

Letter II

Sergius begins his *Second Letter* by recounting a visionary experience, thanking Severus for his letter and its teaching, and telling how his ignorance has been removed.[17] He says that he acted as a mediator between the Chalcedonians, who published two proprieties, and some who held his own former opinion, and condemned a plurality of proprieties.[18] After that we come to the meat in the *Letter*.

Sergius confesses that he still finds Cyril as quoted by Severus, unintelligible, and, besieged once again by his former doubts, he explains his difficulties to Severus. Severus, in his *First Letter*, had quoted Cyril, saying, "Not confusing with each other and mixing the natures".[19] Sergius allows that there is no confusion[20] in the union, but argues that the natures in the union must be thought of as mixed, "in a divine and inexpressible mingling and in an hypostasis".[21] He produces two arguments to back up this contention. First, how could one affirm one incarnate nature of the Word, and how could one rebuke the Dyophysites, unless one were to admit this

mixing and mingling in an hypostasis?[22] Secondly, he asks "Is Cyril at odds with Gregory Nazianzen?" How could he, Sergius, ever find fault with Gregory the Theologian who says that the natures are mixed in a composition which is beyond description,[23] which he calls *συμφυΐα*, through which Sergius understands that the natures are not merely placed beside each other, but are utterly mingled, to become one image and one hypostasis,[24] so that, with the composition being so understood, the ousia of the Trinity, which is only concerned with three persons, is not increased.[25]

In consequence, Sergius claims that he gives a more orthodox explanation of the formula, "One nature of God the Word incarnate", than "The Opposition" (the Dyophysites). Though they claim to speak of one nature of the Word, in the word "incarnate" they see a mark (ܪܘܫܡܐ) of the other nature, standing independently in its own right,[26] and thus they affirm an accidental union.[27] Sergius then returns to the quotation from Cyril, allowing that some may object and claim that the Son can be understood as one in this way, that is, without mixture of the natures. He rebuts the objection by saying that Nestorius too claimed this.

Sergius then draws his conclusions. He argues that unless the natures were inconfusedly mixed, one cannot say that those things which have remained unmixed are hypostatically united.[28] There is no necessity to consider a union of natures which are not mixed.[29] In a rather obscure statement, but in one which more nearly approaches a formula, he says that "the combination of two or more simples into one belongs to the principle of composition, in which what is complete is also a (constituent) part, and (yet) afterwards the (constituent) parts are not from then on adjudged according to the principle of duality, since once and for all one ousia and quality has come into being".[30] Obscure though this is, it is neither as new nor as definitional as it appears, because it in fact incorporates bits from Sergius' previous argument. Thus before, in the argument against the quotation from Cyril, Sergius argued that the elements of the union are mixed in "*a composition* which is beyond description",[31] which he says Gregory calls *συμφυΐα* and he claims that this involves not a "mere placing beside each other"[32] of the natures, but an "utter mingling"[33] to become "one image and one hypostasis".[34] Here, for the moment, Sergius rests his case. This is what he understands, and nothing else makes sense. He is under pressure from the Chalcedonians, and begs for Severus' advice.

As with the *First Letter* we must now ask whether we can see any more clearly what Sergius' theological presuppositions are. First, as

we saw before, though Sergius repudiates confusion (*σύγχυσις*), he allows *κρᾶσις* and *μίξις*. Secondly, juxtaposition is seen by Sergius as the primary enemy of union. How is this seen? Sergius denies that union is thought of when the natures are unmixed; he understands that in union the natures are not merely placed beside each other; he claimed that the Nestorians understood the word "incarnate" as being a mark of a nature standing in its own right. If juxtaposition is the state to be avoided, it is avoided by having recourse to *κρᾶσις* and *μίξις*. This is what the mixture concepts are required for.

Another way of making this point is to say that Sergius clearly sees no alternative between Nestorianism and a union based on mixture. Thus, when it was objected that the Son could be understood as one on the Cyrillian model (i.e. without mixture or confusion), Sergius said this was Nestorius' idea. So he gives the alternative of either juxtaposition, with no mixture (Nestorianism), or his theory. This is important in itself, as it shows why Sergius finds Cyril paradoxical,[35] for Cyril both denies mixture and condemns Nestorius, but it is even more important to ask what are the blinkers, which permit Sergius only to see this alternative. Surely his ultimate presupposition is that all natures are free-standing, independent natures. Where this is understood, it brings Sergius' fear of juxtaposition into perspective. If each item in the external world exists in independent existence, and two items are to be combined in a union closer than juxtaposition, then some sort of mixture will have to be appealed to. To Sergius, "unmixed" equals "juxtaposed". The presupposition that all natures are independent natures is also in accord with Sergius' previous statement that "every propriety belongs to an underlying nature, and if we speak of two proprieties, we are obliged also to speak of two natures".[36]

A third presupposition which we must draw from this *Letter* is Sergius' emphasis that the unification of the natures is to something unitary. Referring to Gregory, he says that the natures are "utterly mingled to (become) one image[37] and one hypostasis".[38] Describing his own account of composition, he says that the (constituent) parts are not afterwards adjudged according to the principle of duality,[39] one ousia and quality having come into being.[40] Although a unitary result of a union may seem too obvious to be worth mentioning, we shall examine its implications later.

The remainder of Sergius' *Second Letter* contains a few loose ends. Sergius refers to Severus' answer to his *First Letter*, and tries to defend himself against a criticism. Sergius had suggested that as we believe Christ is one from two natures, so also we should accept one

propriety from two. Severus had objected that it was foolish[41] to say Emmanuel was composed from two properties, which was certainly a misunderstanding of Sergius, saying that no-one would say a man was composed from "thinking" and "blackness". Sergius accepts the criticism, but objects that "being rational" and "blackness", where applied to a man, are not of equal status: "being rational" is part of the definition of man, and if "being rational" is removed from an object, that object is not a man. "Blackness", however, is a purely contingent property.[42]

As an explanatory additional point on the same topic, Sergius produces another of Severus' quotations from Cyril, and tentatively trying to interpret him along his own lines, says, as we have seen, "The Father seems to say that the incarnate Word was one in every respect, I mean both nature and propriety, when he mingled the natures along with the proprieties".[43] In conclusion, Sergius asks where else he fails. He denies that he suddenly and rashly began to discuss theology, and promises to accept Severus' bridle in what he says.

Letter III

Sergius begins his *Third Letter* by apologising for his foolish arguments.[44] He recognises that his reasoning is as fragile as an earthenware pot.[45] He admits that he will be accused of the teaching of the changers of ousiai, and says that he will explain his understanding of them, showing how foolish he considers them.[46] Sergius' *Third Letter* is a mixture of what is mercifully concrete, and of what is very obscure. His main aim in the letter is to defend himself against the charge of confusing the natures from which Christ is composed. His defence offers some further illumination as to how he, himself, understands the product of the union.

First, then, distinguishing his own views from those of the "changers of ousiai", he claims that they ignore the unique nature of the divine birth. If the flesh had been dissolved, then it was no great thing that Mary's virginity was preserved.[47] In turn, he asks how he could be accused of doing away with the flesh, when, like the orthodox Fathers, he confesses that a composition took place. But what is composition? Here Sergius gives us an example. If a man took pure gold and impure gold, and refined the impure, uniting it to the pure gold, this would be an "addition" of ousia, not a composition.[48] He denies that he understands the union in terms of an addition. We will return to this.

To protect himself still further against this accusation, he offers a number of declarations. First, just as the Word was embodied, and has not endangered the ousia of divinity, so too, Sergius declares, he has preserved his own true flesh.[49] Thus, he continues, the prophets did not lie about the advent, saying God comes visibly. Using another concrete example, Sergius explains that were we to say that the body of the Lord, by the mingling[50] with divinity, was dissipated like morning mist in the sun, then God was not seen, did not die and was not examined by St Thomas.[51] Secondly, unlike the Eutychians, Sergius declares that he does not vitiate the incarnation in any way.[52] He accepts the reality of the body and of the soul of Christ. He affirms that God was truly incarnate, even so that he could die, and that he rose in a fleshly way from the dead. He affirms that the Word still keeps at the Second Advent the marks (ܠܘ̈ܫܡܐ) of the crucifixion. He claims that he acknowledges Christ, "wholly perfect God, who was perfectly made man".[53]

After this denial of change or dissolution of the human nature, and we must remember that this was his persistent plea, Sergius offers some conclusions. Through whatever term it is said that it came about, whether *κρᾶσις*, *μίξις* or *σύνθεσις*,[54] he recognises one fact: the supreme union of God to flesh endowed with a soul, without there being a confusion.[55] Again we see that he explicitly denies a confusion or a change: "even if iron is said by us to be hot, it is not thought that it was changed into fire itself".[56] Then, in another suggestive example which we will return to shortly, Sergius says, "For if the fire that we know rejects the ousia of matter, it is destroyed, since it does not naturally persist in another way than by being mingled (ܬܬܚܠܛ) with some ousia of matter".[57]

Sergius then begins to make a defence of some of his earlier statements which have been criticised by Severus. He says that first he will give a definition of composition, and he gives us the definition he gave before: "the principle of composition is like this: (namely) the coming together from two or more simples, which have come to some one thing, in which also what is complete (in itself) is a part, (and) afterwards the (constituent) parts are not investigated with regard to the principle of duality, since once and for all there has come into being one ousia or quality".[58] Sergius next gives us the argument that we have looked at earlier, that just as some ousiai are simple, and some are composed, so too there are some simple and some composed signs of ousiai.[59]

Sergius is now ready to defend the point which provokes Severus most: his statement that the Word incarnate, the product of the

union, is one ousia. He begs Severus' indulgence: he does not contradict him, but merely wishes to avoid a false opinion,[60] and he produces his first argument, which is one from equivalence. He says that to him, *φύσις* and *οὐσία* mean the same, and he justifies this by quoting a passage where Severus had used the two words as equivalent.[61] He then argues: if they are equivalent, and we say, "From two natures, one nature of the Word incarnate", why may we not also say, "From two ousiai, one ousia of the Word incarnate"?[62,63] Sergius adds that he leaves out the "incarnate", but says that he does not dissolve the composition because of this.

After arguing from equivalence, Sergius appeals to Aristotle, quoting from *The Categories*, "To give a rough idea, examples of substance are man, horse".[64] He adds, "But it is not the case that he does not acknowledge the composition of the living creature because of this",[65] and then asks, "How therefore do I defraud the truth, when I call the incarnate Word '(one) ousia', and understand this (ousia) (to be) incarnate?"[66] We must ask what the point of this argument is. What does Sergius think it achieves? Why is it important to him to call the Word incarnate "one ousia", and at the same time say that this is not to do away with the composition?

As a first part of an explanation, we must recognise that Sergius is trying to defend himself against Severus. He realises that Severus disapproves of the Son being called "one ousia". In his *Second Letter*, Severus accused Sergius, in his "one ousia and one quality" doctrine, of producing a "real confusion of ousia".[67] Later in the same letter, Severus expounded his own theory, that it was wrong to "confuse the difference in ousia of those things which have run together inexpressibly to union".[68] Severus, then, attacks Sergius for teaching, as he understands it, a confusion of the elements. But Sergius has little or no understanding of Severus' elaborate terminological and theological precautions against confusion,[69] and thinks he needs only to appeal to obvious points of current usage,[70] and to re-explain his concept of unity in the light of several concrete examples which he has chosen to exclude the idea of confusion.

Does Sergius manage to clarify his concept of unity in his *Third Letter*? We suggest that he does, to a certain extent. We have seen that Sergius' basic concern is to avoid justaposition. Following from this, we have also seen his insistence that if the natures are to be united, they must be mixed and utterly mingled. Indeed, we have seen that in this *Third Letter* Sergius speaks of *κρᾶσις*, *μίξις* and *σύνθεσις* as if they were almost equivalent.[71] We have seen that the union leads to something unitary: once united the parts are not

adjudged according to the principle of duality. At the same time, this letter tells us that such unity was not achieved at the expense of one of the elements. The body was not dissipated by the mingling with divinity, like morning mist in the sun. We can look back to Sergius' intriguing remark that if fire rejects the ousia of matter, it is destroyed, as fire only continues when it is mingled with something to burn.[72] Surely his image here is to show us that though the elements unite, there remains a kind of tension: though there is "a one", there is not a destruction of either element; there is no dissolving of the composition.[73]

Sergius' denial that one of the elements is done away with is further illustrated by the distinction he draws between his concept of composition and "addition", in the example of the gold.[74] How is composition different from addition? If you add purified gold to pure gold, you still have just gold. Therefore, the previously defined and previously possessed propriety of gold will still apply to the product. In Sergius' *First Letter*, we saw that the proprieties of God and of flesh did not fit the fact of the Biblical Christ. Because of this, a new propriety was called for. This was because, as Sergius saw it, an utter mingling, a *σύνθεσις*, a *συμφυΐα* had taken place. Thus we can see that "composition" is unlike "addition", because even though the elements become one, and even though Sergius claims they are not changed in themselves, the end result is different from both constituent parts, and comes under a different propriety of its own. This contrast, then, of addition and composition, is to emphasise the newness and difference of the product of the union, and yet its unconfused nature.

Going back now to Sergius' appeal to the usage of Aristotle, and to the equivalence in some instances of *φύσις* and *οὐσία*, we can see that whatever his terminological preference, behind it lies the deeper distinction between a unit from addition and a unit from mixture. We have seen that he does not consider a "union" of unmixed, which is to him, juxtaposed, natures to be a unit at all.[75] We shall have to ask later whether Sergius' concept of a union from mixture is adequate for a Christology: for the meantime we can allow that he recognises that a man or a horse are "mixtures" rather than "additions", and sees no harm in appealing to the usage of Aristotle, and calling the living creature "one ousia".

Sergius produces a second argument along basically similar lines, but before coming to that, in a particularly obscure passage, he says that he should explain matters concerning quality, and that "the quality of the ousia of the Word who shared with me in flesh and

blood, also shared in the corporeal signification (ܡܫܘܕܥܢܘܬܐ)".[76] We will return to this passage very shortly. Severus refers to it in his *Third Letter*,[77] taking it as Sergius' explanation for his statement that the composition of the natures results in (one ousia and) one quality. The affirmation of one quality in Christ is, as again we shall see, in flat contradiction to the argument of Severus, who wants to preserve difference in natural quality for the elements from which Christ is composed.

Sergius then gives us his second argument in defence of his statement that the Word (incarnate) is one ousia. This argument is in syllogistic form.[78] A "living creature" is an ousia endowed with a soul and sensation. A man, a horse, a bull are each ousiai endowed with souls and sensation. Therefore, a man, a horse, a bull are "living creatures", as the generic name of the ousia is applied to the hypostases which are the particular ousiai. Similarly, Sergius suggests, if we call the simple Son one hypostasis, even though we know he is endowed with a body and composite, "why may we not also take the name of the highest genus, and call the Son 'ousia', while defining that this was incarnate?"[79]

What is Sergius trying to do in this argument? On the one hand, certainly, he is showing that calling the Son incarnate an "ousia" is no more to be feared as "dissolving the composition" than calling a man a "living creature" is to be avoided for the same reason. But if this usage is not to be feared, what does it contribute? Is it informative to say the Son is an "ousia", where "ousia" is "the name of the highest genus"?[80] Let us ask, "Is it informative to say a man is a "living creature"? To call a man a living creature is to bring him under the umbrella of a class which also holds bulls and horses. As such, it is not very informative. But it can also be seen as a way of saying that a man is a one *something*, until he has been marked off by his propriety (perhaps as being two-legged and rational, rather than horse- or bull-like). So, it could be a way of affirming the individuality of an as yet undefined particular: "it falls under the umbrella of the class, but we haven't yet found a slot for it".

Perhaps it is just this that Sergius is trying to do, when he says that the Son (incarnate) is an "ousia". We can suggest that once again he is affirming the unitary nature of the product of the composition: it is a "one", even if an undefined "one". Sergius ends the argument by quoting Cyril, whom, seemingly, he can always interpret in his own way, saying that "one" is applied not only to simples, but also to composites, like man.[81]

Sergius produces three more arguments in defence of criticisms

from Severus. First, he says that it is thought that he denied to the Word incarnate the properties of the flesh. He now assures us that the intangible Word, along with the flesh also accepted the properties of the flesh, becoming visible and tangible on our behalf.[82] These, he tells us, are not properties of simple divinity, but of (divinity) embodied.

How convincing is this as an answer? We may first ask why it should be thought that Sergius denied to the Word incarnate the human properties. If we turn back to his *First Letter*, it will be remembered that he said of the Word, "because he was not born in accordance with the propriety of the flesh, neither did his flesh see corruption",[83] and, "there is one propriety of Christ, in which no-one from those who are invisible or visible shares. For only God who was incarnate is born from the Virgin, and performed everything and suffered on our behalf...".[84] We have just seen that Sergius argues that the end result of a "composition", if "composition" is to be distinguished from "addition", is different from the constituent elements, and has its own propriety. We have also seen, behind Sergius' fear of juxtaposition, his presupposition that all natures are independent, free-standing natures. It is not a large step then to see that on Sergius' system, the product of a composition will also be a different, independent nature. If this is so, we would not expect it to have the properties of either of the constituting natures, but its *own* properties, which would be a product of the properties of the natures from which it came.

Sergius makes himself clearer in his second argument. He says it was believed that he understood that the lower was changed into the higher.[85] True to the distinction which we have seen that he makes between addition and composition, Sergius denies the charge. A change from the lower into the higher is renounced by those who confess composition. The composition in Christ is not like heating water, "to change the wet ousia to air".[86] This example of the dissolution of one element is just an extreme case of the "addition" model: the water is changed to air, and so there is more air. Instead, and in a very suggestive argument,[87] Sergius describes for us how the product of composition is not like this. Neither body nor flesh are possessed of soul. However, the flesh which is common to all things which breathe, both to us, and the other living creatures, is mixed from four elements. Thus, on the one hand the rational and the irrational share the same flesh, while on the other hand, the presence of soul introduces an important change, though without changing the nature of human flesh. Similarly, he argues, both we and the

Word incarnate share ensouled flesh, yet, in so far as this flesh was composed to be one with God, it had special properties in comparison with our flesh. Thus, it was not obliged to hunger, and thirst and sleep.

This argument, together with what we have seen before, that the product of the union will be different from the constituent parts, and that it will be an independent nature with its own propriety, strongly suggests that it is an implication of Sergius' ideas that Christ too will be an independent nature, with his own, special, "Christly" properties.

Can this really be what Sergius is saying? We suggest that his whole argument leads in this direction. In both his *Second* and *Third Letters*, Sergius gave what was virtually a definition of composition. It will be remembered that it was an important part of that definition that once composition was achieved, "the (constituent) parts are not afterwards investigated with regard to the principle of duality, since once and for all there has come into being one ousia or quality".[88] What does this imply? It was a commonplace in Patristic theology to have some means of saying that in Christ, the divine element shared in the properties of humanity, and the human element shared in the properties of divinity. This was a way of expressing the unity of Christ, and was called the "*communicatio idiomatum*". We will examine the concept more fully when we come to Severus. The point here is that if the "parts" are truly not to be considered from the point of view of duality, in any respect, then one cannot speak of a *communicatio idiomatum*. If there is no duality, there cannot be any interchange. This will imply the situation which has just been suggested: Sergius' Christ, instead of being one person in two natures, with two sets of properties, will be a new compound with his own emergent properties. When Sergius is interpreted in this light, more sense can perhaps even be made of his statement that the product of the composition is "one quality"[89] as well as "one ousia", and his saying that the "quality of the ousia of the Word shared in the corporeal signification".[90] If the new compound is indeed to be thought of as an independent nature with a range of its own distinctive properties, it would seem reasonable to speak of it as having one quality as well. To speak of "two qualities" or "difference in quality" would be either meaningless in the context, or would be, as Sergius would see it, to refer back illegally to independent, and so juxtaposed, parts, thereby destroying the unity.

Sergius' last argument is one that we have met already. He says he is accused of having set aside ousiai, and of interweaving composi-

tion from signs (ܫܘ̈ܘܕܥܐ). He answers, as we know, that just as a quality (ܡܫܘܕܥܢܘܬܐ) does not exist without an ousia, so we should not recognise ousiai without signs. Thus when two ousiai were composed, along with them were also united the signs.[91] Sergius adds a little more. Accurately speaking, he suggests, we should speak of God as being above ousia. However, taught by the "ὁ ὢν ἀπέσταλκέν με" of Exodus, he suggests we may call God "ousia", and "above ousia",[92] "for God is, and is above those things which are".[93] He then looks for the propriety of God, suggesting that Severus[94] has defined this to be "goodness", from the verse, "Why do you call me good? No-one is good, except one, God", and on the principle that a propriety is that thing which belongs to someone and to him alone.[95] Having suggested this, he admits it is inappropriate: "God is in truth above ousia and propriety".[96]

Sergius ends his letter with a plea that Severus should make a ruling that those who have read his (Severus') *Second Letter*, should also read Sergius' defence: he has been left as something of a spokesman in the East,[97] and does not wish the churches he influences to come under a rebuke which was really caused by a misunderstanding.

In introducing the content of Sergius' *Third Letter*, we have already to some extent drawn out its implications, and can summarise these very briefly. The concern of the *Third Letter* is to characterise the product of the union in the most orthodox terms of which Sergius is capable. We have seen that in his account of the union, neither element is dissipated or dissolved. There is neither a confusion nor a change.[98] These denials are summed up in Sergius' example of the gold: he understands the union not as an addition, but as a composition. We have seen what follows from this: the product of the composition will be different, being independently definable[99] from either of its constituents; it will be unitary; and, as we have argued, will have properties of its own, and of one type. If this uncovers Sergius' understanding of the union, it remains for us to place it against some kind of backcloth, and assess its Christological adequacy.

The Apology of Sergius

The *Apology* of Sergius is quite short, but like his other *Letters*, it is regrettably obscure. We will describe its contents, and then examine the structure of its argument. In it, Sergius presents a very different

and quite exciting approach. We will see that he has now not just come to terms with the earlier misunderstanding between himself and Severus, but that he has tried to come to grips with what lay behind it, seeing that quite different doctrines were masked by the same form of words.

After his opening apologies, Sergius says that two sorts of opponents are rising up against him, as some people misrepresent the words of Severus, while others, from his own party, have been misled by the ambiguity of the term "propriety" (ܕܝܠܝܘܬܐ).[100,101] To illustrate further the idea of doctrinal and verbal ambiguity, Sergius gives three examples of cases where, though a basic formula seems to be accepted, verbal agreement hides very different theologies. Thus, the wise pagans, the Jews and the Christian orthodox all agree that "God is cause".[102] The Manichaeans, Sabellians and Arius, in their own way, all agree with the orthodox in confessing the Trinity.[103] Mani, Apollinaris, Eutyches and the orthodox all confess "one nature of God the Word after the birth from the Virgin".[104] But there agreement ends. Mani supposed the inhomination to be imaginary; Apollinaris stumbled to an imperfect opinion, while Eutyches introduced a complete change.[105] These were their accounts of the one nature. What was Sergius'? As his account, which is obviously intended to be more adequate than those of the just-mentioned heretics, and to offer a solution to their problems, Sergius gives the following statement, but without a supporting argument: "It is clear that the flesh did not exist before (the union), but comes (into existence for the purpose of) that mystical union".[106] We will return to this shortly.

Continuing his theme on ambiguity, Sergius says that even Nestorius professes properties (ܕܝ̈ܠܝܬܐ), but not properties of the incarnate Word, but only of the two natures which he understands in Christ.[107] Sergius quite clearly understands the "Nestorian" approach to Christology as affirming that Christ is a dual being, or a being with two parallel and independently operating natures. He quotes short passages from Nestorius, Theodoret, Leo and the Chalcedonian Definition in an attempt to substantiate this.[108]

He then turns to Severus: "Did he, like those who were quoted before, set up two natures, understanding these in Christ after the union, and attributing (an individuating) particularity[109] to each one of them?"[110] "Not at all", Sergius answers. Severus attributes the properties of the flesh to the Word incarnate.[111] Thus, while the Nestorians, speaking as they do of the properties of the natures, say that the Temple of the Word was seen, suffered and rose, Severus

proclaims that Emmanuel, the Word, was born and touched, thirsted, died and rose.[112] Severus, that is, sees the Word himself as active and an agent.

Sergius then asks, "How did this happen to the Word—that he should be seen, touched and suffer?"[113] The answer is because he was incarnate.[114] "(Even) as he remained the Word, thus preserving to himself the properties of divinity, yet preserving the integrity of the flesh, ... he receives these (properties) of our flesh."[115] In consequence of this, the same Word was visible and invisible, passible and impassible, yet, "we do not say that the natures exist, and each one (of) them is seen out of its own properties and activities, but we hold that the Word himself became flesh, and displayed these (properties) of the flesh".[116]

Sergius then tries to defend this account. Just as when a man is wounded, he does not receive cutting in one nature, and in another show perception, but there appear both cutting of the body and perception of the soul in the one and the same composite nature,[117] so too in the case of the composite nature of Christ, one cannot attribute certain actions purely to the divine nature or purely to the human nature, as if they were working independently of each other. Sergius argues, "Let them show me what was done after the incarnation (which) was merely human. And I will not say a tear, for that came divinely, for he was immediately summoning Lazarus.... They speak of sweat and perplexity in relation to the Passion? But these things also (happened) divinely, and surpass our reasonings, so that by means of human passions he might lead men to impassibility."[118]

Sergius concludes the *Apology* with a catena of quotations from Severus' letters, in support of the points he has made,[119] and final apologies and praise for Severus.

Let us now consider the extent to which Sergius has changed his position in the *Apology*. When he was discussing the different interpretations of the formula, "One nature of God the Word after the birth from the Virgin",[120] after showing that Mani, Apollinaris and Eutyches all reached heretical conclusions, Sergius offered as his solution, "the flesh did not exist before (the union), but comes (into existence for the purpose of) that mystical union".[121] This statement is neither argued for, nor explained.[122] However, by relating it to the rest of the *Apology*, it may be possible to see its implications, and so some of its importance.

After giving, in something of a caricature, the opinions of the heretics, Sergius asked, "How do we (judge) concerning the one nature which was composed from divinity and *perfect* man-

hood?"[123] The listed opinions of the heretics in some way or other made the manhood less than perfect (i.e. imaginary, incomplete, changed), and Sergius' solution would seem to claim implicitly that it keeps the manhood perfect. But how can this be? Is not to keep the manhood perfect to fall into the trap of the Dyophysites, and to assert two parallel natures, yoked by an external connection?

We saw that Sergius then gives us a short account of how he understands the Nestorian position. Nestorius does not attribute the properties to the Word, but to the natures. Thus, the Temple of the Word is seen. In other words, according to Sergius, Nestorius does not affirm a union in Christ. Though the natures are yoked by some connection, they are not united. This is the juxtaposition which Sergius so feared in his *Second Letter*. But, if Nestorius does not teach a union, Severus does. He attributes the properties to the Word, and thus the Word hungered and thirsted. Sergius, at this stage, has adopted Severus' position as his own, so we may take it that Sergius implies by his reference to Severus that his solution both keeps the manhood perfect, *and* affirms a true union.

But we have seen that Sergius both asserted that the manhood was perfect and claimed a union before. We remember his account of composition: "In which *what is complete* is also a (constituent) part, and (yet) afterwards the (constituent) parts are not from then on adjudged according to the principle of duality...".[124] There, mixture[125] and "utter mingling"[126] were the means of unification. Is this what Sergius is still asserting? Does he still see *κρᾶσις* and *μίξις* as the answer to *παράθεσις*? We can see that he has changed his ground. Before,[127] Sergius called Severus a Nestorian, unless he would agree to a mixture. Now, he refers to Severus as affirming a union, opposing him to Nestorius, and, indeed, in the whole of the *Apology*, none of the mixture words are mentioned.[128]

So Sergius now accepts that one can have a union, and preserve the humanity undiminished, without resorting to mixture. But how? "Whence do these things (come) to the Word, that he should be seen and touched ...?"[129] Sergius' answer is, "because he was incarnate".[130] But how does Sergius understand this? We saw above that Sergius denied that one could attribute certain actions purely to the divine nature, or purely to the human nature, as if they were working independently of each other. Instead, if one speaks of the sweat and perplexity, one must see that these also came divinely, that he might lead men to impassibility.[131] What does this mean? Surely it implies that Sergius now understands the union of God and man in the incarnation not as the result of an operation (i.e. mixture) performed

on two static and preexistent natures, which in turn produce a new compound with its own fixed properties, but as the active soteriological initiative of the Word, who became man for a specific purpose, and then adapted what he did to that point. If a compound produced by mixture has a property Y, it always has the property Y. Sergius has come to see that though Christ is God become man, he is not obliged, as if he were a compound, always to display divine properties. At the Passion, he was perplexed, but was not compelled to this because of the composition, but chose to endure it for the sake of the salvation of men. The human and divine properties were displayed, each as was appropriate to his purpose, and in proportion to each other. For Sergius to see this is for him to see that the incarnation is quite different from a mixture. At the beginning of his debate with Severus, Sergius looked at the Biblical Christ as if he were a compound which did not fit existing definitions. He tried to map his uniqueness and individuality. Now he sees that the Word is an active subject, adapting his activities to his purpose, and cannot be, as it were, frozen in a photographic "still", and brought under definition.

Even though Sergius' argument is not explicit, we can see the extent to which he has changed his ground. Following from his acceptance of the idea that the flesh did not pre-exist the union, Sergius is able to understand that Severus can both deny mixture and profess union. But this is a union of quite a different sort. It is not static, like a chemical composition, but a "becoming": the becoming man of the Word. To say this is also already to imply the preservation of the difference of the natures, upon which Severus insists. What we see here in a rather unargued way, we will see much more explicitly and within an inter-related system, when we examine Severus' letters. But before coming to that, we must illustrate and try to evaluate some of Sergius' concepts from his letters before the *Apology*.

Notes

1. EM p. 71.1–3.
2. EM p. 71.4–5.
3. EM p. 71.10 ܗܘܠܐ ܐܘܣܝܐ.
4. EM p. 71.11.
5. EM p. 71.28–72.1.
6. EM p. 71.16–18.
7. EM p. 71.22–24.
8. EM 71.27–28.

9. cf. EM p. 72.1–6.
10. EM p. 72.10–11.
11. EM p. 72.11–12.
12. EM p. 72.17–18.
13. EM p. 72.18.
14. EM p. 72.19–20.
15. cf. EM p. 72.22–24.
16. EM p. 101.22–23.
17. EM pp. 96–98.
18. EM p. 98.15–28.
19. EM p. 77.26 (PG 76.85B = *Adv. Nest. Lib. II.* Pusey edn. Vol. 6, p. 113.14); EM p. 99.12–13.
20. EM p. 99.14–15.
21. EM p. 99.15–16.
22. EM p. 99.17–19.
23. EM p. 99.21.
24. EM p. 99.22–24.
25. EM p. 99.25–27.
26. ܟܝܢܐ ܕܡܠܬܗ ܘܠܗ ܒܣܪ (EM p. 100.4).
27. cf. EM p. 99.27–100.6. The Syriac for "an accidental union" is ܚܘܝܕܐ ܕܠܘܬ ܦܪܨܘܦܐ. The underlying Greek is possibly ἕνωσις κατὰ θέσιν: it refers to the "relational", "non-essential" union affirmed by the Nestorians.
28. EM p. 100.16–19.
29. EM p. 100.20–22.
30. EM p. 100.11–16. cf. also the same formula, at p. 150.19–24.
31. EM p. 99.21.
32. EM p. 99.22–23.
33. EM p. 99.23–24.
34. EM p. 99.24.
35. EM p. 99.12.
36. EM p. 71.28–72.1.
37. ܨܘܪܬܐ = εἰκών.
38. EM p. 99.23–24.
39. cf. EM p. 100.14–15.
40. cf. EM p. 100.15–16.
41. cf. EM p. 86.7–9.
42. For Sergius' argument, cf. EM p. 101.21–102.4.
43. EM p. 102.10–12. It is worth noticing how Sergius slips in his "mixture term" (ܚܠܛ), "mingled", in his paraphrase of Cyril.
44. EM p. 145.3–25.
45. EM p. 145.29.
46. EM p. 146.9–13.
47. EM p. 146.14–17.
48. EM p. 146.26–27: ܬܫܡܫܬܐ ܗܘ ܕܐܢܫܘܬܐ ܗܝܢܐ ܕܐܬܚܙܝ ܗܘܐ ܘܠܐ ܪܘܡܐ
49. EM p. 147.6–8.
50. ܚܘܠܛܢܐ ܕܐܠܗܘܬܐ It will be remembered that the root ܚܠܛ translates μίξις.
51. EM p. 147.12–21.
52. EM p. 148.2–3.
53. EM p. 149.1–2.
54. EM p. 149.12–13. The Syriac is ܡܕܝܢ ܐܠܐ ܚܘܠܛܢܐ ܘܡܘܙܓܐ
55. EM p. 149.12–18.
56. EM p. 149.21–22.
57. EM p. 149.23–26.
58. EM p. 150.19–24. (cf. EM p. 100.11–16).
59. EM p. 150.24–28.
60. EM p. 151.2–6.

61. EM p. 151.7–12.

62. EM p. 151.12–18.

63. J. Lebon, *Chalkedon*, pp. 519–521, while writing of the Monophysite use of the formula *ἐκ δύο φύσεων*, refers to John the Grammarian, the opponent of Severus, who claimed that he must see the two *φύσεις* as *οὐσίαι*, to avoid confessing that Christ is *ἐκ δύο προσώπων*. (cf. *Contra impium Grammaticum*, *CSCO* 3 (Syr. 58), p. 179.11–21. cf. Severus' reply: p. 179.29–180.6). Against this, Severus asserted that the *φύσεις ἐξ ὧν* Christ is formed are fully concrete and particular, namely the hypostasis of the Word, and the flesh endowed with a reasonable soul. Lebon then writes, "A l'extrême opposé, le grammarien Sergius, à peine revenue de ses erreurs eutychianistes, ne voyait dans les natures, dont le Christ est formé, que des essences spécifiques et des formes". We suggest that this interpretation of Sergius is not consistent with the fear of juxtaposition which we have seen him to have. (For this, cf. p. 99.22–23: in his own account of composition, Sergius says that the natures are not merely placed beside each other, but are utterly mingled; and p. 100.10–11, where Sergius equates Cyril's account of an unmixed union with that of Nestorius.) It is precisely because he fears juxtaposition, and sees it as the only other alternative, that Sergius insists upon and requires *κρᾶσις* and *μίξις* to bring the elements to unity. (For this, cf. p. 100.16–19: "unless the natures, from which Christ is, were mixed (ܐܬܚܠܛ ܗܘܘ) inconfusedly, how shall I say that those things which thus remained unmixed with each other were hypostatically united?" and p. 100.20–22: "there is no necessity that I should consider a union of (natures) that are not mixed with each other, as those men say. . . .") We find a wide variety of meanings for "*οὐσία*/ܐܘܣܝܐ" in Sergius, but it is quite evident that in one of its senses, *οὐσία* refers to the particular concrete individual. (cf. for example, p. 152.17, which mentions "hypostases which are particular ousiai"; cf. also p. 100.15: "once and for all one ousia has come into being", and p. 99.23–24, which speaks of an utter mingling to "one image and one hypostasis".) At, for example, p. 146.26 and p. 154.2, "ousia" has the meaning "stuff" or "material": addition is an increase of "stuff", and, heating water changes the wet "stuff" into air; at p. 155.10, "ousia" means "being": God is above "being". At p. 152.16, "ousia" means "species": the generic name of the "species". For a modern account of the range of the meanings of *οὐσία*, cf. C. Stead, "The Concept of Divine Substance", *Vigiliae Christianae*, 29 (1975), especially pp. 10–13.

However, the comparison to John the Grammarian is useful. If, for the sake of illustration, we may use the grossest caricature, we suggest that here we have that interesting case, where both the Dyophysite and the (extreme) Monophysite share the same, ultimately dualist, presuppositions. If it is an absolute presupposition that all natures are particular and independent, then how are any two of them to be united? The Dyophysite (and this is a caricature) tries to yoke the two by some external union, or under one person; the Monophysite grasps the nettle, and forces unity by absorbing the humanity into the deity. Both answers are in fact evasions of the problem. We will later examine Severus' solution.

64. *Categories*, 4.1b.27: *ἔστι δὲ οὐσία μὲν ὡς τύπῳ εἰπεῖν οἷον ἄνθρωπος, ἵππος*. Professor J. L. Ackrill's translation above: cf. *Aristotle's Categories and De Interpretatione* (Oxford, 1963), p. 5.

65. EM p. 151.26.

66. EM p. 151.28–152.1.

67. EM p. 106.27–29.

68. EM p. 129.25–27.

69. I.e. that part of affirming an unconfused union is not denying difference and particularity with respect to natural quality of the natures from which Christ is formed (cf. e.g. p. 93.24–28).

70. I.e. equivalence and Aristotle.

71. cf. EM p. 149.12–14.

72. cf. EM p. 149.23–26.

73. cf. EM p. 151.17–18 and 26.

74. cf. EM p. 146.24–27.
75. cf. EM p. 100.20–23.
76. EM p. 152.1–4.
77. EM p. 168.
78. cf. EM p. 152.11–18.
79. EM p. 152.21–23.
80. EM p. 152.21.
81. EM p. 152.26–28, and PG 77.241B (= *Ep. ii ad Succ.* ACO I, 1, 6a, p. 160.2–4).
82. EM p. 153.9–12.
83. EM p. 71.27–28.
84. EM p. 72.22–26.
85. EM p. 153.27–28.
86. EM p. 154.2–3.
87. EM p. 154.4–20.
88. EM p. 150.21–24.
89. cf. e.g. p. 150.23–24; p. 100.15–16.
90. cf. EM p. 152.1–4.
91. cf. EM p. 155.4–9.
92. EM p. 155.15–16.
93. EM p. 155.14–15.
94. cf. EM pp. 137–139.
95. cf. EM p. 138.29–139.2.
96. EM p. 155.23–24.
97. As has been noted, this points to a date after the banishment of the Monophysite bishops in 518–519.
98. Sergius seems to see "confusion" and "change" as being inter-related: cf. p. 149.15–18: "For I understand the supreme union of God to flesh endowed with a soul, and without confusion maiming the meaning, for (the flesh) has not changed to that which is eternal".
99. I.e. having a different propriety.
100. I.e. Thinking of "propriety" (ܕܝܠܝܘܬܐ) in its single, definitional sense, they opposed and could not understand how or why Severus could speak of two "particularities" (ܕܝ̈ܠܝܘܬܐ) in Christ after the union. Severus' "particularity" refers to the integrity of the identity of a nature, and affirming two particularities in Christ is a corollary of asserting that the natures are not confused.
101. cf. EM p. 178.22–179.6.
102. EM p. 179.7 (cf. p. 179.7–13).
103. EM p. 179.13–23.
104. EM p. 179.23–24.
105. cf. EM p. 179.25–28.
106. EM p. 179.30–31.
107. cf. EM p. 180.3–6.
108. cf. EM pp. 180.7–181.4.
109. ܘܠܟܠ ܚܕ ܡܢܗܘܢ ܝܗܒ ܕܝܠܝܘܬܐ. Sergius seems here to refer to a concept of "particularity as to independent existence" which Severus specifically rejected, and from which he distinguished his own concept of particularity, which referred to the integrity of the identity of an object *without* thereby implying its independent existence. (Here, cf. p. 78.22–23; p. 80.26–81.1; p. 158.26–27). We have already seen in Sergius' first three letters that the idea that "the definition of the identity of x" (= the "propriety" of x) implied the independent existence of x, formed part of his presupposition, and created the misunderstanding between him and Severus. Now, it would seem that Sergius understands that one can mention the preservation of the identity of x (= Severus' "particularity") without thereby necessarily implying that x exists independently.
110. EM p. 181.6–8.
111. cf. EM p. 181.10.

112. cf. EM p. 181.8–17.
113. cf. EM p. 181.18–19.
114. EM p. 181.19–20.
115. EM p. 181.22–25. Though he does not use the actual terms, we can see here that Sergius has grasped what lay behind Severus' insistence that one recognises the particularities of the natures from which Emmanuel is. (Here, cf. Severus, p. 80.19–81.4.)
116. EM p. 182.7–10.
117. cf. EM p. 182.16–23.
118. EM p. 183.8–15.
119. cf. EM p. 183.25–185.23.
120. EM p. 179.23–24.
121. EM p. 179.30–31.
122. However, we suggest it is of key importance in the *Apology*. cf. also in *The Apology*, p. 180.5–6;p. 181.6; p. 182.7–10; p. 182.11–12; p. 184.19–20; p. 186.5–8 for references where an attack is made on the idea of two parallel and independent natures in Christ.
123. EM p. 179.28–30.
124. EM p. 100.13–15, and cf. p. 150.21–23.
125. cf. e.g. EM p. 99.21.
126. EM p. 99.23–24.
127. cf. EM p. 100.10–11, 16–23.
128. cf. *Appendix C*.
129. EM p. 181.18–19.
130. EM p. 181.19–20.
131. cf. EM p. 183.13–15.

IV Concepts and Comparisons

Sergius' argument is brief and obscure. Having given a somewhat descriptive analysis of it, we will now place certain of his basic concepts in contrast with those of several other Patristic authors. Our aim here is not to show literary dependence,[1] or even direct theological influence. By seeing Sergius in certain contrasts, our aim is simply to see more sharply the movement of his thought.

The question of mixture

In his first three letters, Sergius both uses himself, and advocates the use of, certain concepts of mixture. Analysing Sergius descriptively, we suggested that his use of mixture concepts led him to portray the Word incarnate as a *tertium quid*, a new compound with his own peculiar properties. We will now place Sergius and his expressions in contrast to the Aristotelian and Stoic accounts of mixture. This is not done in a regulative way, to prove Sergius an Aristotelian or a Stoic, but to provide a foil, which may let us better appreciate Sergius' language.

Aristotle's account of mixture is largely in his *De Generatione et Corruptione*.[2,3] Aristotle begins by considering whether there is such a thing as mixture: *πότερον ἔστι μίξις ἢ τοῦτο ψεῦδος*.[4] He sets out three prerequisites: in mixture, the ingredients cannot remain unaltered, staying just as they are;[5] the ingredients are not mixed, if one ingredient is destroyed,[6] and again, there is no mixture if both ingredients are destroyed when they come together.[7] Following from these prerequisites, Aristotle is able to distinguish *σύνθεσις* (composition) from *μίξις* or *κρᾶσις* (mixture).[8] In a *σύνθεσις*, the ingredients form an aggregate, or as Joachim puts it, "the smallest parts of the whole are different in character from the whole",[9] while in a mixture, the resultant is uniform throughout.[10]

But how does the uniform resultant, or *ὁμοιομερές*, occur? Aristotle argues that the ingredients act on each other, when they are brought together, in virtue of their contrariety.[11] However, the ingredients must not merely act on each other, but must be more or

less balanced.[12] If one ingredient swamps the other, this does not produce a mixture, but an increase of the predominant ingredient,[13] or in Aristotelian terms, a *φθορά* of the passive ingredients, and a *γένεσις* of the dominant one. More concretely, the interacting ingredients, if they produce a *μιχθέν*, reach a *μέσον*, which is not a single point, but a balance over a certain range between the conflicting powers.[14]

But what is the reciprocal interaction and alteration of the ingredients to become a *ὁμοιομερές*? We have seen that Aristotle has denied that the ingredients are destroyed: this would be the *φθορά* of the ingredients and the *γένεσις* of the *ὁμοιομερές*. So the ingredients are retained, but in what sense? Aristotle writes: *ἐπεὶ δ' ἐστὶ τὰ μὲν δυνάμει τὰ δ' ἐνεργείᾳ τῶν ὄντων, ἐνδέχεται τὰ μιχθέντα εἶναί πως καὶ μὴ εἶναι, ἐνεργείᾳ μὲν ἑτέρου ὄντος τοῦ γεγονότος ἐξ αὐτῶν, δυνάμει δ' ἔτι ἑκατέρου ἅπερ ἦσαν πρὶν μιχθῆναι, καὶ οὐκ ἀπολωλότα.*[15] Thus, we see that Aristotelian mixture involves a sort of tension of identity: the ingredients have truly united to something uniform and different, but in a sense they have been preserved.[16]

Summing up from Aristotle, we can see three points which are important to us: (1) an Aristotelian *μιχθέν* is *ὁμοιομερές*; (2) there is in *μίξις* what we have called a tension of identity: the ingredients are preserved, but they are altered and unified; (3) there is the idea that the *μιχθέν* is itself a balance, or a *μέσον*.

Let us turn now to the Stoic account of mixture, as it is presented and criticised by Alexander of Aphrodisias. According to Alexander, Chrysippus distinguished between *παράθεσις* (for example of beans and wheat-grains), *σύγχυσις*, and *κρᾶσις*.[17] Chrysippus' *παράθεσις* corresponds to Aristotle's *σύνθεσις*, and is an external juxtaposition of objects. We need not examine it further here.

But how are *σύγχυσις* and *κρᾶσις* distinguished? Alexander writes, *τούτῳ γὰρ ἡ κρᾶσις αὐτοῖς τῆς συγχύσεως διαφέρει, ὅτι ἐπὶ μὲν τῆς συγχύσεως ἕν τι τὸ ἐκ τῶν συγχεομένων γίνεται, μηδενὸς τῶν ἐν τῇ συγχύσει μήτε κατὰ τὴν οὐσίαν σωζομένου, μήτε κατὰ τὰς ποιότητας, ἐπὶ δὲ τῆς κράσεως ἑκάτερον τῶν ἐν τῷ κεκραμένῳ σωμάτων ἔτι σώζεται καὶ κατὰ τὸ ὑποκείμενον καὶ κατὰ τὰς ποιότητας, καίτοι δι' ὅλων ἀλλήλοις κεκραμένων τῶν σωμάτων.*[18] We see that Stoic *σύγχυσις* is a *φθορά* of the ingredients, and the *γένεσις* of an *ὁμοιομερές*. Stoic *κρᾶσις*, on the other hand, involves the preservation both of the ingredients, and of their *ποιότητες*.

But if the ingredients and their *ποιότητες* are preserved, how is the resultant a *κραθέν*? How is *κρᾶσις* to be distinguished from *παράθεσις*? Alexander says that Chrysippus explains *κρᾶσις* in terms

of the mutual co-extension of two or more bodies in their entirety. He writes, τὴν γὰρ δύο ἢ καὶ πλειόνων τινῶν σωμάτων ὅλων δι' ὅλων ἀντιπαρέκτασιν ἀλλήλοις οὕτως, ὡς σώζειν ἕκαστον αὐτῶν ἐν τῇ μίξει τῇ τοιαύτῃ τήν τε οἰκείαν οὐσίαν καὶ τὰς ἐν αὐτῇ ποιότητας, λέγει κρᾶσιν εἶναι μόνην τῶν μίξεων.[19] This account sharply distinguishes Stoic κρᾶσις from σύγχυσις, but, as we will learn from Alexander, does not adequately distinguish it from παράθεσις. Stoic κρᾶσις has been a popular explanatory model with the patristic commentators. Commenting on the passage just quoted, R. A. Norris calls κρᾶσις "a mutual and total interpenetration of two material substances, in which each retained all of its characteristic properties unaltered, so that even in their intimate union, the two substances remain distinct".[20] Our concern is simply to note that Stoic κρᾶσις preserves the ποιότητες of the ingredients.

As we have suggested, Alexander finds the Stoic account of κρᾶσις paradoxical, or even incoherent.[21] He argues that in the Stoic terms, there is no alternative between παράθεσις and σύγχυσις: either the constituents are preserved as they are (παράθεσις),[22] or the compound becomes uniform, as the ingredients are destroyed (σύγχυσις).[23] As a solution, he turns back to Aristotle, re-explaining Aristotle's account in his own words.

After discussing the nature of the constituents of μίξις and κρᾶσις, Alexander, to distinguish κρᾶσις from φθορά and γένεσις, writes, ἴδιον δὲ κράσεως πρὸς τὴν γένεσίν τε καὶ φθορὰν τὸ ἐπὶ μὲν τούτων τέλεον θάτερον εἰς θάτερον μεθίστασθαι καὶ μεταλαμβάνειν τὰς ἐναντιώσεις, καθ' ἃς παθὸν ἀπέβαλε τέλεον, ἃς εἶχε πρὸ τούτου, ἐπὶ δὲ τῶν κιρναμένων οὐ τοῦτον ἔτι γίνεται τὸν τρόπον.[24] The τρόπος or process of κρᾶσις is that when bodies with the capacity for mutual interaction act on each other, and are to some extent balanced in their powers,[25] they lose the sharpness of their competing contrarieties, producing one quality (μία ποιότης), as their underlying matter is unified and becomes one thing.[26] What can we see in this? First, there is the denial of a total change of the constituents, where "total change" is interpreted as φθορά. This is to assert that there is a continuity between the constituents and the κραθέν. We saw the same idea in Aristotle, where we called it a "tension of identity", between "being preserved" and "being altered". Secondly, we see the idea that the κραθέν is the result of a "balance" between the competing powers. Aristotle spoke of the μιχθέν as a μέσον. Thirdly, the κραθέν is unified so that it has μίαν ποιότητα. Similarly, we saw that Aristotle spoke of the μιχθέν being ὁμοιομερές.

From our analysis of Sergius' first three letters, we suggested that

he understood the Word incarnate as a *tertium quid*: not as the Word become man, but that the Word and a human nature had become some sort of inbetween thing, with peculiar properties of its own. Is this interpretation of Sergius' account of the union in Christ substantiated and clarified, or refuted, by considering Sergius' account of mixture in the light of that of Aristotle and Alexander? We suggest that the interpretation is both clarified and substantiated, and will now try to show the similarity of Sergius' account of mixture to that which we have seen in Aristotle and Alexander, and what the implications of this are for his Christology.

We have seen Sergius' insistence upon mixture, as being the mode of the union, in opposition to any sort of mere juxtaposition. For example, in his *Second Letter*, he writes, "Therefore unless the natures from which Christ is, were mixed unconfusedly, how shall I say that those things which thus remained unmixed with each other were hypostatically united?"[27] We have seen how Sergius defends his account of mixture, distinguishing it from confusion, and furthermore, that he clarifies what he understands by confusion. Thus, in his *Second Letter*, he says that when the divine union is being thought of, ideas of confusion are set aside,[28] and in his *Third Letter*, he writes that he "understands the supreme union of God to flesh endowed with a soul, and without confusion maiming the meaning, for (the flesh) has not changed to that which is eternal".[29] The flesh has not *changed into* something else: Sergius repeats elsewhere his rejection of confusion, interpreted in this way. Thus, the flesh has not been dissolved into[30] the divinity; it is not dissipated[31] by the μίξις, like a cloud by the rays of the sun; it is not turned into the dominant constituent.[32] This, as we can see, is very much in agreement with the Aristotelian account: κρᾶσις or μίξις is neither a mere σύνθεσις (in the Aristotelian sense, where it means a juxtaposition), nor merely the φθορά of the more passive constituent, and the αὔξησις of the more dominant.

Instead, according to Sergius, the constituents form one ousia and one quality.[33] If we interpret Sergius along Aristotelian lines, his assertion that the union forms one quality (which was certainly misunderstood by Severus[34]) indicates his final rejection of a union by juxtaposition. We remember that to Aristotle, the distinguishing characteristic of μίξις, as contrasted with σύνθεσις, was that its resultant was ὁμοιομερές,[35] and with Alexander, κρᾶσις yields a κραθέν which has μίαν ποιότητα.[36] At another point, Sergius hints that he understands the coming together to one οὐσία and ποιότης as "a coming to the middle".[37]

We can allow that there is a considerable similarity between Sergius and Aristotle (and Alexander). But what illumination may we draw from this? According to Aristotle and Alexander, the product of μίξις is a μιχθέν (or a κραθέν from κρᾶσις). As we have seen, it is ὁμοιομερές; of one ποιότης; its constituents are not destroyed, but no longer exist independently. We can see all of this in Sergius, and may suggest that he understood Christ to be a μιχθέν in these terms. Interpreting Sergius in this way allows one to see how he could affirm that the resultant, the μιχθέν, was *one*, and still claim that this unity was such that it did not dissolve the composition.[38] We can also see that in his own terms, Sergius was offering a viable alternative to confusion/destruction (which was the view of the heretics: the Synousiasts, the Eutychians, the Apollinarians), and juxtaposition (which he sees as the view of the Nestorians).

But what Christological price does Sergius have to pay for arguing like this? What implications does this structure have for his Christology? On the credit side, to view Christ as a μιχθέν is to take seriously his unity. It is also to recognise and stress his novelty. But on the debit side, to understand Christ as a μιχθέν and so as ὁμοιομερές, is to do away with the *communicatio idiomatum*. Is this a loss? What is the point of the *communicatio idiomatum*? Without pretending to give a full account of it, part of its point is certainly explanatory: one being both hungers and feeds the hungry. Another part of its point is to recognise a soteriological fact: as God become man, Christ fulfils the law, ministering to God the things of man, while at the same time he redeems man, ministering to him the things of God. But to say this presupposes the preservation of the identity of the divinity and the humanity.

If Christ is a μιχθέν, a fixed, identifiable and static entity, operating within the range of the μέσον between two contrary ousiai, this dynamic soteriological interplay is absent. What becomes of the constituents of a μιχθέν? They do not remain as they were, but merge to one quality in the μέσον. To what extent is their identity unchanged? Aristotle would say that they were present potentially but not actually.[39] But is the potential presence of God the Word in Christ sufficient for the redemption of man? We can conclude that Sergius was more interested in unity than soteriology.

A further objection is this. In understanding Christ as a μιχθέν, that is, as an entity recognisably different from its constituents,[40] and from the other entities, one is compelled to bring him under a class. If the μιχθέν is a unit different from its constituents, it is a one "something". If it can be identified, this can only be on the basis of

some general concept, or class, embracing it. The μιχθέν is an x, having the properties of Class X. This is a logical implication of calling Christ a μιχθέν, but does it make theological sense to say Christ has "Christly" properties? Would not such properties be static, fixed, and as removed from any soteriological purpose as the unity itself?

We can see that Sergius' "solution" is not without its drawbacks. But why is it a solution at all? What problem does it answer? Sergius' insistence on μίξις is his way of avoiding juxtaposition, and it is not until his *Apology* that he sees that Severus' account of the union is different from juxtaposition. Sergius' "solution" is not in fact an avoidance of juxtaposition, but an acceptance of it (i.e. that there were two independent, pre-existing natures), and a later attempt to annul it. Need one accept the basic presupposition, that the divine and the human natures both pre-existed independently? Is Sergius' "solution" an inadequate answer to a false problem? In relation to the same presupposition,we will consider very briefly the answers of Apollinaris, and Eutyches. When we turn to Severus, we will see how he attacked the presupposition.

Thus, again for the sake of making a contrast with Sergius, and so of bringing out the logic of his argument, let us briefly consider the position of Apollinaris. As a great and recognised heretic, Apollinaris posed questions which none of his successors could afford to ignore. We have already seen that Sergius refers to Apollinaris in his *Apology*,[41] indicating that his was a position which he avoided. We will assess shortly what the implications of this avoidance were for the structure of Sergius' Christology.

What was the problem of Apollinaris, and what were his solutions? As a first step, we must understand that Apollinaris had a basic objection to the soteriological inadequacy of the Antiochene position, which he interpreted as being unable to account for the union in Christ. In the *Anacephalaeosis* to his book against Diodore, we find him saying,"Ἄνθρωπος θεῷ παραζευχθεὶς ἕτερος παρὰ τὸν θεόν ἐστι ταῖς ζωτικαῖς κινήσεσι λογιστικαῖς τε καὶ παθητικαῖς.[42] Similarly, in *Fragment 95*, he says, ἀνθρώπου θάνατος οὐ καταργεῖ τὸν θάνατον.[43] What lies behind this inadequacy in the account of union given by the Antiochenes? Here Apollinaris writes, καὶ εἰ ἀνθρώπῳ (φησὶ) συνήφθη ὁ θεός, τέλειος τελείῳ, δύο ἂν ἦσαν, εἷς μὲν φύσει υἱὸς θεοῦ εἷς δὲ θετός.[44] We find elsewhere in Apollinaris similar denials that the union can be a juxtaposition of two "perfects", but most interesting is the principle in Pseudo-Athanasius, δύο τέλεια ἓν γενέσθαι οὐ δύναται.[45]

If to affirm δύο τέλεια was to pose a juxtaposition, and so to undo

the work of salvation which only the incarnate Word could complete, what was Apollinaris' solution? This, of course, is famous: it was to deny the presence of a human mind in Christ.[46] But what did this mean: what was the nature of the unity which followed from this? According to Apollinaris, in man, the spiritual and material constituents are complementary. Neither of them is independent of the other, or perfect, and they come together to form a vital, or organic unity. Thus, in a passage giving an analogy to the constitution of Christ, Apollinaris writes, *ὅπερ ⟨καὶ⟩ ἐπὶ τοῦ κοινοῦ ἀνθρώπου ἐκ δύο μερῶν ἀτελῶν γίνεται, φύσιν μίαν πληρούντων....*[47] These "imperfect" constituents come together to a *ἑνότης ζωτική*:[48] a unity which is a unity because the constituents share the same life.[49] This unity is not simple (*τὸ ἁπλοῦν*[50]), but a composite: Apollinaris writes against Diodore, *οὐκ ἄρα ἄλλη καὶ ἄλλη οὐσία θεὸς καὶ ἄνθρωπος, ἀλλὰ μία κατὰ σύνθεσιν θεοῦ πρὸς σῶμα ἀνθρώπινον.*[51] Using the constitution of man as an analogy for the union in Christ, Apollinaris describes this union as a *κρᾶσις*,[52] and a *μίξις*[53] and calls the nature of Christ *σύγκρατος*.[54] But this is not to say that he understood the constituents as being confused in their union: he writes, *τῶν συγκιρναμένων αἱ ποιότητες κεράννυνται καὶ οὐκ ἀπόλλυνται, ὥστε τινὰ καὶ διΐσταται ἀπὸ τῶν συγκερασθέντων καθάπερ οἶνος ἀπὸ ὕδατος.*[55] R. A. Norris interprets him as accepting the Stoic account of *κρᾶσις*,[56] which, we remember, we met before, when we considered Alexander of Aphrodisias' criticism of Chrysippus.[57] Stoic *κρᾶσις*, it will be remembered, involved the complete mutual co-existence of the constituents, with the original substances and their qualities being preserved. We can see that such a background accords with Apollinaris' idea of a unity in a *σύνθεσις*, and of complementary parts coming to a *ἑνότης ζωτική*.

But if this is to describe the nature of the union, how did Apollinaris understand it theologically? What does it mean to say that God the Word has entered into a *ἑνότης ζωτική* with human flesh? In another famous phrase, Apollinaris says *σάρκωσις κένωσις*: the incarnation is to be understood as a self-limitation: *σάρκωσις κένωσις· ἡ δὲ κένωσις οὐκ ἄνθρωπον, ἀλλα υἱὸν ἀνθρώπου τὸν κενώσαντα ἑαυτὸν ἀπέφηνε κατὰ τὴν περιβολήν, οὐ κατὰ μεταβολήν.*[58] But what is the importance of this? Christ was not a figure who stood still. He was not "static". He was born a child, and grew physically to manhood. As a man, he was active. In patristic theology one approach at expressing the unity of Christ was to attribute certain things (like growth, suffering, eating) to his human nature, and others (like forgiving sins, healing the sick) to his divine nature. But this way of expressing the

unity of Christ is inherently unsatisfactory. A divine nature and a human nature, especially when the point of their partnership is not explained, do not make easy partners, and the unity tends towards dualism. Apollinaris' σάρκωσις κένωσις is an attempt to answer this problem. By saying that incarnation is a κένωσις, a self-limitation of the Logos, Apollinaris makes the Logos the unique subject[59] of all his activity. Again, as the subject, the "owner" of all that he does, a *communicatio idiomatum* occurs: εἰ δὲ ἓν πρὸς τὸν κύριον γέγονε τὸ σῶμα τοῦ κυρίου, τὰ ἴδια τοῦ σώματος ἴδια αὐτοῦ κατέστη δὶα τὸ σῶμα.[60] What previously and properly belonged to either nature, now, κατὰ τὴν μίαν ζωήν, belongs to the Word incarnate.

But what follows from this? These concepts, "The Logos incarnate is subject, is owner, of all that he does", are not *static* ways of expressing the unity in Christ. Despite its obvious shortcomings, the strength of Apollinaris' account of Christ's unity is that by referring everything to the Logos, it is intrinsically flexible enough to allow us to make sense of what we might call the "inconsistencies" in the actions of Christ. Christ exercised divine power to heal the sick, but not to turn stones into bread. He raised the dead, but did not come down from the cross. Why? Because the Logos was the subject of all his actions, and his actions were voluntary, and performed for a purpose.[61] To include an understanding that the actions are voluntary, is to be able to unite even discontinuous actions under one will. This is totally different from viewing the actions of the Incarnate as if they were the involuntary concommitants of a new divine-human amalgam.

When it is understood that the life of Christ in its dynamic activity and variety must be allowed for, it will be recognised that Christ, and the unity in Christ, cannot be defined or encapsulated in static terms. We have seen that the system of Apollinaris is flexible enough to recognise the dynamic aspect of Christ. We have seen, too, that his system holds together with an internal logic: there is a recognition that the Logos is the same person before and after the incarnation; the σάρκωσις κένωσις concept; the *communicatio idiomatum*. Inter-related with these concepts we found his actual description of the unity: the denial that a union could result from two "perfects", and the concept of ἑνότης ζωτική.

We noted earlier that in his *Apology*, Sergius referred to Apollinaris,[62] indicating that his was a position which he avoided: Sergius' account was of a single nature composed from divinity and *perfect* manhood.[63] Apollinaris could see a union of divine and human elements in Christ, when the manhood was stripped of a human mind.

Sergius, unlike Apollinaris, tried to describe a real union of two "perfects". But how could this be achieved? Would it not lead straight to juxtaposition and Nestorianism? We have already seen that this was Sergius' fear, and suggested how he answered the problem. The two perfect constituents united to become an Aristotelian μιχθέν or κραθέν. But what did this cost Sergius? We can now answer this clearly. Apollinaris' Christology, defective though it was, remained flexible by seeing the Logos as the same person both before and after the incarnation, and as the subject of all that was done in his incarnate life. Can the same be said for Sergius, or is his Christology intrinsically inflexible? When we examined Sergius' account of mixture, we saw that according to him, the composition of the Logos and the humanity yielded one ousia and one quality.[64] Now, if the Logos has come to form a being of one quality,[65] can he still sometimes do A, and sometimes do B? Could he on one occasion turn water into wine, and on another not turn stones into bread? We suggest that Sergius, by understanding the incarnate Logos to be a being of one quality, has robbed him of his soteriological self-determination. He would be obliged to act as a being of one quality, namely, consistently.

Why is Sergius' description of Christ so limited? We suggest that this is so because, at least in the three letters which we have, he viewed the incarnation merely as a puzzle of union: an operation to be satisfactorily performed on two static and pre-existent natures. He does not seem to have viewed the incarnation (again, in these letters) as a theological action creatively undertaken by the Logos. This tendency of Sergius' can be seen in his *First Letter*. It will be remembered that there, rather than beginning with the Logos and considering the purpose of the action of the Logos, he began with the biblical picture of Christ,[66] showing that he was unlike both God and man. Sergius' question then was, "How was this unity achieved?" "What sort of union produces that sort of result?" Against Sergius, we would suggest that in the incarnation that nature of the unity is determined by the purpose of the unity, and that the question as to the nature of the unity cannot be asked in the abstract. The issue in Christology is a theological and soteriological one, concerning the action of the Word, not a technical one, about the advantages of κρᾶσις over παράθεσις for producing a union.

We can see this criticism implicit in Severus' criticism of Sergius. In his *Second Letter*, Sergius quoted back to Severus Severus' own quotation of Cyril: "Not confusing with each other and mixing the natures".[67] Sergius found this unintelligible: he asked himself the

(unanswerable) technical question, "How can there be a union when there is not mixture?" Severus, in his *Second Letter*, commenting on Sergius' difficulty, shows that the question as to the union is not to be asked at a merely technical level, but is to be understood within the sphere of the *activity* of the Word: "For why, when the Doctor did not present his doctrine (only) this far, (namely), "not confusing or mixing the natures amongst each other", but wisely added, "But with the Word of God *becoming a partaker* in flesh and blood, one Son is understood and named in this way as well", do you not learn from (this) addition the inexpressible nature of the union?"[68]

Is this criticism of Sergius fair? Are we right so to stress the implications of the "of one quality", and thus the conclusion that Sergius' Christ was a static divine-human amalgam, a μέσον between two opposite natures? Can we not find passages which imply a soteriological preservation of the flesh, rather than a mixing of it to some new μέσον?

As we have already noted, in his *Third Letter*, Sergius tries to defend himself against the charge of introducing confusion into the union. Thus, with the aim of defending himself from that charge he writes, "But just as he was embodied, and has not endangered the ousia of divinity .... so too he has preserved his own true flesh".[69] He says that if the body of the Lord had been dissipated like a cloud going up into the air, then he "undertook none of those things which are ours".[70] Again, and in the passage which appears most promising, he says as follows, "But that which is beyond all speech (is this): he sits in heaven God incarnate at the right hand of majesty. For he established us along with him, and made us sit along with him with his Father".[71] But the apparent soteriological import of these passages is never developed, or at least, not until Sergius' *Apology*.[72] Sergius' concern in his *Third Letter* is not to develop a theological account of the flesh, but to deny its confusion.[73] Again, we have already seen how, in the same letter, he interpreted the confusion of the flesh: "I understand the supreme union of God to flesh endowed with a soul, and without confusion maiming the meaning, for (the flesh) has not changed to that which is eternal".[74] Thus, what Sergius denies is that there is a φθορά of the flesh, *not* that the divinity and the humanity have come to form a new ὁμοιομερές, a μέσον different from both of them.

To form some understanding of the rationale of Sergius' Christology, we have approached him negatively. Being unable to say what positions or Fathers he would support, we can to some extent understand him through examining the positions he rejects. Thus, avoid-

ing what he understands as Nestorianism, with its consequent union based on an external connection, we have suggested that Sergius turns to a model of unity which yields a being of one quality. We have also suggested that Sergius avoided Apollinarianism, with its implication that the manhood be less than perfect, but have argued that in his answer, concentrating as he does on the technical problem of unity, Sergius has all but lost sight of the purpose of the union, and thus runs the risk of seeing it in static, inadequate terms.

Let us now turn to Sergius' third heretic, Eutyches. In his *Third Letter*, facing the criticism of Severus, Sergius says, "I shall be accused of the teaching of the changers of ousiai. Therefore I shall make a defence about what my opinion is concerning them .... (to show that) those men are reckoned foolish by me, and followers of the madness of Eutyches".[75] He continues, "For, when the flesh has been *dissolved into* divinity...."[76] In his *Apology*, after mentioning Mani and Apollinaris, Sergius says, ".... but mad Eutyches introduces not only a shadow, but a complete change, outside the mystery".[77] We can understand, then, that Sergius recognises that union is not to be achieved through dissolving one element in the juxtaposition, and consequently we will expect a preservation of the flesh to be a part of his Christology. But what is the nature of this "preservation", and what role does it play? Let us look at Eutyches: was he in fact dissolving one of the constituents of the union? Let us see just how different the logic of his position is from that of Sergius', and thus just how deeply Sergius' own Christological position is affected by the concept of unity which he has adopted.

Eutyches is chiefly notorious for his unwillingness to say that Christ was ἐκ δύο φύσεων[78] and for his denial that Christ was ὁμοούσιος ἡμῖν.[79] On both counts he was accused of docetism, and charged with teaching that the Lord brought his body from heaven. But let us examine each of his denials more carefully. We will take first the question of ἐκ δύο φύσεων. Does Eutyches deny this because he is a docetist? He tells us that he does not accept it as it is neither scriptural nor credal. He himself holds to the teachings of Nicea, Ephesus and St. Cyril, and furthermore he refuses to try to explain God in materialistic terms: .... μὴ γένοιτο ἐμὲ .... φυσιολογεῖν τὸν θεόν μου.[80] More concretely, along with his denial that Christ is ἐκ δύο φύσεων, Eutyches affirms that Christ was born of the Virgin,[81] was perfect God and perfect man,[82] and denies that he taught that Christ took his flesh from heaven.[83] These affirmations free Eutyches from the charge of docetism on this count, but why, when he held these beliefs, should he deny that Christ was ἐκ δύο φύσεων?[84]

Draguet notes[85] that even Severus was prepared to say ἐκ δύο φύσεων after the union. He attributes Eutyches' difficulty with the formula to an excessive and unclear fear of Dyophysitism. But why is Dyophysitism seen as such a threat? May it not be seen merely as a guarantee against confusion? We suggest that behind Eutyches' abhorrence of dyophysitism is the idea that φύσις is the equivalent of, or implies a, πρόσωπον, so that to mention two φύσεις is to imply two independent πρόσωπα in Christ. If this is the presupposition behind Eutyches' fear of Dyophysitism, is it a strictly necessary presupposition? Must every concrete φύσις have its own πρόσωπον? This is an ultimate question in Patristic Christology, and we will see it examined by Severus. For the meantime, let us note it, and accept that if one takes the view that all φύσεις (or hypostases) are independent φύσεις, this will have considerable implications for the account of unity which one can give.

Let us turn to Eutyches' account of the ὁμοούσιος ἡμῖν. Again, under pressure, he admitted it, but why was it denied in the first place? His reasons for this are very interesting. Referring to the ὁμοούσιος, he writes, Ἕως σήμερον οὐκ εἶπον· ἐπειδὴ γὰρ σῶμα θεοῦ αὐτὸ ὁμολογῶ (προσέσχες;), οὐκ εἶπον σῶμα ἀνθρώπου τὸ τοῦ θεοῦ σῶμα, ἀνθρώπινον δὲ τὸ σῶμα καὶ ὅτι ἐκ τῆς παρθένου ἐσαρκώθη ὁ κύριος. εἰ δὲ δεῖ εἰπεῖν ἐκ τῆς παρθένου καὶ ὁμοούσιον ἡμῖν, καὶ τοῦτο λέγω . . . .[86]

Thus, originally the formula was denied from the fear that to say that the body of Christ was ὁμοούσιον ἡμῖν implied that it was σῶμα ἀνθρώπου. Were the body of Christ the body of a man, there would be two independent natures in Christ. So again it is because of a fear of Nestorianism that the ὁμοούσιος ἡμῖν was denied. But what did Eutyches say instead? The body of Christ was not σῶμα ἀνθρώπου, but he affirmed it was σῶμα ἀνθρώπινον. We remember that he also affirmed that Christ was τέλειος θεός, τέλειος ἄνθρωπος. So here we have the idea that Christ is τέλειος ἄνθρωπος, but the human element is σῶμα ἀνθρώπινον not σῶμα ἀνθρώπου. We can argue that in intention, anyhow, Eutyches is trying *both* to avoid dyophysitism, *and* to preserve the full integrity of the humanity, but without then making it into an independent centre of activity. If this is really what Eutyches is trying to do, then he is half-way to solving the problem we saw above of the independent status of the human nature, and closer to Cyril and Severus than is often thought.

We can turn now to Sergius. We find with him the same absolute fear of juxtaposition and dyophysitism: if there is no mixture, there is no union.[87] Again, we suggest that behind this fear lies the presup-

position that all natures are independent natures. Unlike Eutyches, there is no questioning as to whether it is the independence or the integrity of the humanity that is important for Christology. This is a lesson which he has to be taught by Severus. Sergius' model of unity succeeds in avoiding Nestorianism by removing the independence of the constituents, but, as we have argued, at the cost of destroying their integrity. To destroy the integrity of the humanity is to ignore the very purpose of the incarnation, for the humanity is preserved so that full humanity may be redeemed and sanctified by God's becoming a man.

There are passages which we have seen in Sergius, particularly in his *Third Letter*, where he seems to state that the humanity is preserved.[88] But we would argue that here it is only "preserved" as an implication of the mode of union (that is, that it is κρᾶσις, not φθορά and γένεσις), and not in its integrity for any clear soteriological import.

In interpreting Sergius' Christology, we have been unable to pass beyond his unification to one ousia and quality.[89] By removing the integrity of identity of the two constituents, he prevents us from understanding the incarnation as the redemption of *man*. If "unity" to Sergius is unity into one ousia in this sense, we can only suggest that it is the wrong model of unity for Christology.[90]

Notes

1. To prove this would not be easy: Sergius, besides quoting Severus, merely quotes Aristotle once, Cyril through Severus, and refers twice to Gregory Nazianzen.

2. cf. H. H. Joachim, *Aristotle on Coming-to-be and Passing-away: A Revised Text, with Introd. and Commentary* (Oxford, 1922). All references to *De Gen. et Corr.* will be to the Greek of this edition.

3. The Aristotelian and Stoic concepts of mixture have been a popular topic with the commentators. Joachim has an excellent article, to which I am indebted, "Aristotle's Conception of Chemical Combination" in the *Journal of Philology*, 29 (1903), pp. 72–86. cf. also H. A. Wolfson, *The Philosophy of the Church Fathers* (Cambridge, Mass., 1964), especially pp. 372–386, "Five Types of Physical Union"; R. A. Norris, *Manhood and Christ* (Oxford, 1963), pp. 68–70; Roberta C. Chesnut, *Three Monophysite Christologies* (Oxford, 1976), pp. 17–20 (on Severus) and pp. 65–70 (on Philoxenus); Henry Chadwick, "Eucharist and Christology in the Nestorian Controversy", JTS, N.S. 2 (1951), pp. 145–164, especially pp. 160–161. For the Stoic side, cf. Robert B. Todd, *Alexander of Aphrodisias on Stoic Physics: A Study of the DE MIXTIONE with Preliminary Essays, Text, Translation and Commentary* (Leiden, 1976). All references to Alexander's *De Mixt.* will be to the Greek of this edition.

4. *De Gen. et Corr.* 327^a33–34.

5. *Ibid.*, 327^a35–327^b2.

6. *Ibid.*, 327^b2–4.

7. *Ibid.*, 327^b4–6.

8. *Ibid.*, 328ᵃ6–7: οὐδὲ σύνθεσις ταὐτὸ καὶ μίξις ἀλλ' ἕτερον.

9. Joachim, "Aristotle's Conception of Chemical Combination", *op. cit.*, p. 75.

10. *De Gen. et Corr.* 328ᵃ10–12: τὸ μιχθὲν ὁμοιομερὲς εἶναι, καὶ ὥσπερ τοῦ ὕδατος τὸ μέρος ὕδωρ, οὕτω καὶ τοῦ κραθέντος.

11. cf. e.g. *ibid.*, 328ᵃ31–33.

12. cf. *ibid.*, 328ᵃ28–29: ὅταν δε ταῖς δυνάμεσιν ἰσάζῃ πως.

13. cf. *ibid.* 328ᵃ24–28. (The example of the drop of wine in 10,000 measures of water.)

14. *ibid.*, 334ᵇ25–30. (Quoted by Joachim, *op. cit.* p. 83 n. 2.)

15. *Ibid.*, 327ᵇ22–26. Though a μιχθέν has resulted, the ingredients are still potentially what they were before. Later Aristotle writes φαίνεται δὲ τὰ μιγνύμενα .... οὔτε φθείρονται, οὔτε θάτερον οὔτ' ἄμφω, σώζεται γὰρ ἡ δύναμις αὐτῶν (327ᵇ27, 30–31).

16. cf. Joachim, "Chemical Composition" *op. cit.*, p. 75 n. 2, commenting on 328ᵇ22, ἡ δὲ μίξις τῶν μικτῶν ἀλλοιωθέντων ἕνωσις, "Unless the components are preserved *in some sense* in the μιχθέν, we should have simply φθορά of the components and γένεσις of the ὁμοιομερές."

17. cf. Alexander of Aphrodisias, *De Mixtione*, *op. cit.*, 216.14–217.1.

18. *Ibid.*, 220.29–34.

19. *Ibid.*, 216.28–31.

20. R. A. Norris, *op. cit.* pp. 69–70.

21. cf. e.g. Alexander, *De Mixtione*, *op. cit.*, 213.2–13; 220.23–29. The Stoic account of κρᾶσις relied on the principle of σῶμα διὰ σώματος χωρεῖν. This is strongly criticised by Alexander: cf. e.g. 218.15–24; 218.24–220.23; 227.10–228.4.

22. cf. *ibid.*, 220.26–221.7.

23. cf. *ibid.*, 221.7–11.

24. *Ibid.*, 230.22–26.

25. διὰ τὴν τῶν δυναμένων ἰσότητα (*ibid.* 230.29–30).

26. *Ibid.*, 230.32–34. μίαν ἐξ ἁπασῶν τῶν δυνάμεων γεννήσει ποιότητα, ἑνωθείσης καὶ μιᾶς γενομένης τῆς ἀμφοτέροις ἢ πᾶσιν αὐτοῖς ὕλης ὑποκειμένης.

27. EM p. 100.16–19. For similar statements, cf. p. 99.15–16; p. 99.21–24; p. 100.20–23; p. 100.30–31.

28. cf. EM p. 99.14–15.

29. EM p. 149.15–18.

30. EM p. 146.15.

31. EM p. 147.13.

32. cf. EM p. 149.17–18; p. 153.27–28; p. 154.1–3.

33. cf. EM p. 100.15–16; p. 150.23–24. We are justified in translating ܡܫܘܕܥܘܬܐ as ποιότης by the marginal note to the Syriac of EM p. 109.1, which states that where there is ܡܫܘܕܥܘܬܐ, it is ποιότης (ܦܘܝܘܛܣ). Only two of the occurrences of ܡܫܘܕܥܘܬܐ in these letters can be checked against extant Greek: at p. 95.7 it translates ποιότης; at p. 95.10 it translates ἐνέργεια (cf. *Appendix A*).

34. cf. e.g. EM p. 134.26–31.

35. cf. Joachim, "Aristotle's Conception of Chemical Combination", *op. cit.*, p. 75.

36. Alexander, *op. cit.*, 230.22–34 (especially 32–34).

37. cf. EM p. 102.9–10. This is certainly reminiscent of Aristotle's μέσον, and Alexander's ἰσότης. One wonders if this is how Sergius understood Christ as Mediator.

38. cf. EM p. 151.17–18. (Sergius omits saying "incarnate", but does not, by this, dissolve the composition); EM p. 151.26 (Aristotle calls a man an ousia, but he does not acknowledge that a man is a composite). By "not dissolving" the composition, Sergius means that the constituents are preserved in a sense. There is not a φθορά and an αὔξησις: cf. EM p. 146.26–27 (the addition (ܬܘܣܦܬܐ) of purified gold to pure gold is not a composition).

39. cf. Aristotle, *De Gen. et Corr.*, *op. cit.* 327ᵇ22–26.

40. That Sergius so understood Christ, see his *First Letter* (esp. EM p. 71.16–28; p. 72.17–26).

41. EM p. 179.24–30.

42. *Anacephalaeosis* 29, in H. Lietzmann, *Apollinaris von Laodicea und Seine Schule* (Reprinted, New York, 1970), pp. 245–246.

43. Lietzmann, *op. cit.*, p. 229.

44. *Fr. 81*, Lietzmann, p. 224.

45. PG. 26.1096B7–8. cf. also Apollinaris, *Fragment 92*, in Lietzmann, p. 228.

46. In this sketch, where we are mainly concerned with the nature of the unity proposed, we need not dwell on Apollinaris' reasons for this exclusion. However, he viewed the human mind as a self-determining subject (αὐτοκράτωρ: cf. Lietzmann, *Fr. 150*, p. 247), and two self-determining subjects in one entity would inevitably lead to duality. Apollinaris also viewed the human mind as intrinsically inconsistent, and unable to be allied with the divine will (cf. Lietzmann, *Fr. 151*, pp. 247–248), cf. also C. E. Raven, *Apollinarianism* (Cambridge, 1923), pp. 182, 184; R. V. Sellers, *Two Ancient Christologies* (London, 1940), p. 61; R. A. Norris, *Manhood and Christ* (Oxford, 1963), pp. 113–116.

47. Lietzmann, *op. cit.*, p. 187.9–11 (*De Unione*, 5).

48. cf. Lietzmann, *Fr. 144* (ln 3).

49. cf. *De fide et incarnatione*, 6: .... μίαν ζωὴν τοῦ λόγου καὶ τῆς σαρκὸς .... (Lietzmann, p. 198.16–17).

50. *Fr. 123*, Lietzmann, *op. cit.*, p. 237.19–23.

51. *Fr. 119*, Lietzmann, p. 236.25–27. cf. also, *Fr. 111*, Lietzmann, p. 233; *Fr. 123*, Lietzmann, p. 237; *Fr. 133*, Lietzmann, p. 239 (on σύνθεσις).

52. *Fr. 134*, Lietzmann, p. 239; *Fr. 147*, Lietzmann, p. 246. Both passages are referred to by Norris, *op. cit.*, p. 106. n. 2; and Sellers, *op. cit.*, p. 52 n. 6.

53. *Fr. 10*, Lietzmann, p. 207: ὢ καινὴ κτίσις καὶ μίξις θεσπεσία.

54. *Fr. 9*, Lietzmann, p. 206.27–28: ἀλλ' ἐν μονότητι συγκράτου φύσεως θεϊκῆς σεσαρκωμένης.

55. *Fr. 127*, Lietzmann, p. 238.14–16.

56. R. A. Norris, *op. cit.*, p. 106.

57. cf. Alexander, *De Mixtione*, *op. cit.*, 216.25–217.2 for an account of κρᾶσις in Chrysippus.

58. *Fr. 124*, Lietzmann, p. 237. cf. also *Anacephalaeosis* 15, Lietzmann, pp. 243–4; *Fr. 71*, Lietzmann, p. 221.14–15; *De Unione* 6 Lietzmann, pp. 187–188: .... ἄκτιστος θεὸς κτιστῇ περιβολῇ φανερούμενος, κενώσας μὲν ἑαυτὸν κατὰ τὴν μόρφωσιν ⟨δουλου⟩ ....

59. There is no question of "the human nature does this, the divine nature does that". The Logos is the same person before and after the incarnation: cf. *Kata meros pistis* 36, Lietzmann p. 181.7–9 εἷς υἱός, καὶ πρὸ τῆς σαρκώσεως καὶ μετὰ τὴν σάρκωσιν ὁ αὐτός ....

60. *Fr. 137*, Lietzmann, p. 240.19–21. cf. also *Ep. ad Dion.* A. 10, Lietzmann, p. 261. 1–2; *ad Dion.* A. 7, Lietzmann, p. 259.10–14.

61. Apollinaris' account of the unity, in other words, like that of Cyril after him (cf. PG.76.1413C, which was also important to Severus, cf. EM p. 122.18–29, and *Letter 1*, PO 12, p. 183) could make sense of the fact that the Logos incarnate *sometimes* did A, and *sometimes* did B.

62. EM p. 179.26.

63. cf. EM. p. 179.28–30.

64. cf. EM. p. 100.11–16 and p. 150.19–24.

65. We must note as well that Sergius insists that the new being of one quality (which we can understand as a self-consistent being), is different from either of its constituents: cf. *Letter I*, EM. p. 72.17–24. ("And so henceforward, neither is any propriety of God to be recognised in his Logos, nor is any (propriety) of flesh to be seen (in him either), but the entire manner of the economy points towards one propriety, that which is with God incarnate."). One cannot but wonder if this is not to call into question the identity of the Λόγος ἔνσαρκος and the Λόγος ἄσαρκος. The relationship and continuity between them is certainly neither examined nor explained. In what sense is one of the constituents of an Aristotelian mixture *the same* as the new ὁμοιομερές?

66. cf. EM. p. 71.15–26.
67. EM. p. 99.12–13.
68. EM. p. 105.2–7.
69. EM. p. 147.6–8.
70. EM. p. 147.16–17.
71. EM. p. 154.29–155.1.
72. cf. e.g. EM. p. 181.12–20; p. 182.23–30; p. 183.17–22.
73. cf. EM. p. 148.8–9.
74. EM. p. 149.15–18.
75. EM. p. 146.9–13.
76. EM. p. 146.15.
77. EM. p. 179.26–28.
78. *μὴ γένοιτο ἐμὲ εἰπεῖν ἐκ δύο φύσεων τὸν Χριστὸν*, p. 17.26–27 in E. Schwartz, "Der Prozess des Eutyches", in *Sitzungsberichte der Bayerischen Akademie der Wissenschaften*, Philos.-histor. Abt., 1929, fasc. 7 (Munich, 1929). See also R. Draguet's excellent article, to which I am greatly indebted, "La Christologie d'Eutychès, d'après les actes du Synode de Flavien (448)", in *Byzantion*, 6 (1931), pp. 441–457.
79. *καὶ ταῦτα λέγων ὡμολόγει τέλειον θεὸν εἶναι καὶ τέλειον ἄνθρωπον τὸν γεννηθέντα ἐκ τῆς παρθένου Μαρίας μὴ ἔχοντα σάρκα ὁμοούσιον ἡμῖν*. See Schwartz, *op. cit.*, p. 15.8–10.
80. *Ibid.*, p. 17.26–27.
81. *Ibid.*, p. 15.9.
82. *Ibid.*, p. 15.8–9.
83. *Ibid.*, p. 14.30 ff.
84. We should note that when pressed, Eutyches was prepared to allow *ἐκ δύο φύσεων* before the union, but not after it: *ὁμολογῶ ἐκ δύο φύσεων γεγενῆσθαι τὸν κύριον ἡμῶν πρὸ τῆς ἑνώσεως, μετὰ δὲ τὴν ἕνωσιν μίαν φύσιν ὁμολογῶ*. *Ibid.*, p. 25 no. 527.
85. Draguet, *op. cit.* p. 453.
86. Schwartz, *op. cit.*, p. 25 no. 522.
87. cf. e.g. EM. p. 99.15–17; p. 100.16–19, 30–31.
88. cf. e.g. EM. p. 147.6–8; p. 148.9–10; p. 149.1–2, 17–18, 21–22.
89. cf. EM. p. 100.15–16; p. 150.23–24.
90. This, essentially, is a criticism which Severus makes of Sergius, showing him that he confuses the kind of unity there is in the incarnation, for the kind of unity there is in the Trinity, cf. EM. pp. 125–128.

V Introduction to the Letters of Severus to Sergius

The letters of Severus to Sergius are repetitive, highly involved and inter-related. But when digressions and Severus' misunderstandings with Sergius are weeded out, it can be seen that he is expressing something quite simple: an intensely Cyrillian vision of the unity and being of Christ. But this vision, though simple in itself, is so far beyond our expression of it, that we can only point towards it from a number of angles. St Cyril rightly said *κινδυνεύσει γὰρ ἀπιστεῖσϑαι τὸ Χριστοῦ μυστήριον, διὰ τὴν τοῦ ϑαύματος ὑπερβολήν.*[1]

Because of the inter-involvement, and disjointed yet cumulative description of virtually all the concepts Severus uses in these *Letters*, we propose to begin by describing in general terms how they inter-relate. This is simply intended to give the reader a background framework against which subsequent detailed and documented explanations may be placed, as the various concepts occur in the *Letters*.

It will be remembered that when in his *First Letter* Sergius tried to identify and describe Christ, he spoke of him having "one propriety from two",[2] and later, in his *Second Letter*, he spoke of Christ having "one ousia and quality".[3] We have already tried to explain what Sergius meant by a "propriety", and how he was misunderstood by Severus. Sergius, understanding "propriety" as "defining property", could see only one in Christ. We suggested that Severus did not approach the question of the unity of Christ in the same way as Sergius, and in understanding Christ as God the Word become a man, wanted to affirm the permanence and the reality of the divinity and the humanity in Christ. This led him to assert that one could see two "particularities" in Christ, and we suggested that by "particularity" he meant *the integrity of the identity* of the elements of divinity and humanity. This concept of particularity, and the affirmation that in the union, the divinity remains divinity, and humanity remains humanity, is the first question Severus takes up in his *First Letter*. We will take that concept as our starting point too.

If to assert two particularities in Christ is to affirm that, though united, somehow the divinity remains divinity and the humanity humanity, why, and against what background, is that insistence

made, and what follows from it? We will show with textual references that behind Severus' (and Cyril's) insistence on preserving the integrity of the humanity and the divinity, is the fundamental soteriological insight that it is only God who can save, and that it is man who is saved, and that salvation for all men is achieved in the person of Jesus Christ.

But what we must understand with Severus is how one concept interlocks with others, so let us consider what his ultimate soteriological presupposition implies both negatively and positively. To insist that in the union God the Word remains who he is, and that the humanity assumed is not done away with, is to rule out any understanding of the union by mixture or confusion. Should the elements be mixed or confused, they would no longer be intact, so it could no longer be truly God who saves, nor truly man who is saved. On the same basis, a union or combination by *συνάφεια* or merely *σχετικῶς* is rejected. This sort of combination would be a denial of real union, and so soteriologically inadequate.

Instead, we will see that Severus describes the union positively as a *σύνοδος*, and a *σύνθεσις*, seeing it as a *κένωσις* or *ταπείνωσις* of the *Λόγος*. There is an emphasis that God the Word is the sole subject throughout, but that somehow two concrete things (*πράγματα*) have come and remain together. The actual mode of union is not stated: it is "inexpressible" or "supreme". Cyril, as we will see, often tries to avoid any descriptive noun, expressing the union in verbal forms: it is a "becoming man" of the *Λόγος*, a "taking flesh".

These verbal expressions of the union, like "becoming man", "becoming flesh", have to be understood hand-in-hand with the insistence on two particularities in the union—though the Word has become flesh, he has not ceased being what he ever was—but this insistence did not prevent them from being seriously misunderstood by the Nestorians. As a result, we will see that certain other explanatory concepts are inter-related. There is a consistent, careful and detailed attack in Cyril and Severus upon any idea that the humanity which was assumed into union with the *Λόγος* had any independent existence prior to the union. Though neither Cyril nor Severus use the systematic terminology of Leontius, we find in both of them an understanding of the importance of seeing that the humanity which is assumed is, to borrow a later term "enhypostatised" in its union with the *Λόγος*. Again we must stress how the concepts interlock and clarify each other: the insistence on two particularities in a *σύνοδος* is only a step away from an understanding of the "enhypostasia" of the humanity.

Following from, and interlocking with, the attack on any idea of the independent existence of the humanity, but also following from the κένωσις doctrine's insistence that the Λόγος is the sole subject in the union, we find in Severus an examination of the concept of possession. If the Λόγος is the subject of the union, all that happens to the incarnate Λόγος belongs to him. He economically makes his own (οἰκείωσις οἰκονομική) all that naturally belongs to the flesh. It will be seen again how this relates to the "enhypostatised" existence of the flesh in the union, and the soteriological insistence that in the union God the Word makes his own what is truly human.

This concept in turn leads to another, that which is often called the *communicatio idiomatum.* The Word becomes tangible and visible by means of the body, and the body shares in the glory of the Word. But in Cyril and Severus, no merely nominal interchange or equal-trading of the properties is taught, but rather, they all belong to the one person of the incarnate Λόγος. Thus, rather than merely seeing an alternation of the properties, we are led to understand the implications of the inseverable possession of the humanity by the Word. The suffering and death of the flesh are not its own suffering and death, but that of the incarnate Word, who is the one subject. The body may rightfully be called divine, but yet not because it is divine independently and in its own right, but because it is the own body of the Word. Here the denial of an independent status to the humanity, the insistence on the Word's being the sole subject, and the idea of the Word's redemptive making his own what is ours all come together.

But the Cyrillian–Severan understanding of the union in Christ does not stop here. Christ did not become man to remain subject to the rule of suffering and death, but to overcome it, ennobling and restoring the human nature to what it was at the beginning. This was not to undo the human nature, to destroy its particularity, but to make it more truly what it ought to be. When the Word united an ensouled human body to himself, making it his own, according to Cyril, he "transelemented" it (μεταστοιχείωσις), using it for his own purpose.

This concept, which we will examine and illustrate in due course, is of the greatest importance in itself, but as our concern here is the overall inter-relation of the concepts in the Cyrillian–Severan scheme, let us go full-circle, returning to the concepts of σύνοδος and σύνθεσις with which we began. Severus and Cyril affirm a σύνοδος, not a κρᾶσις or μίξις. We can now, perhaps, see better what they mean. If the σύνοδος is understood in terms of the economic appro-

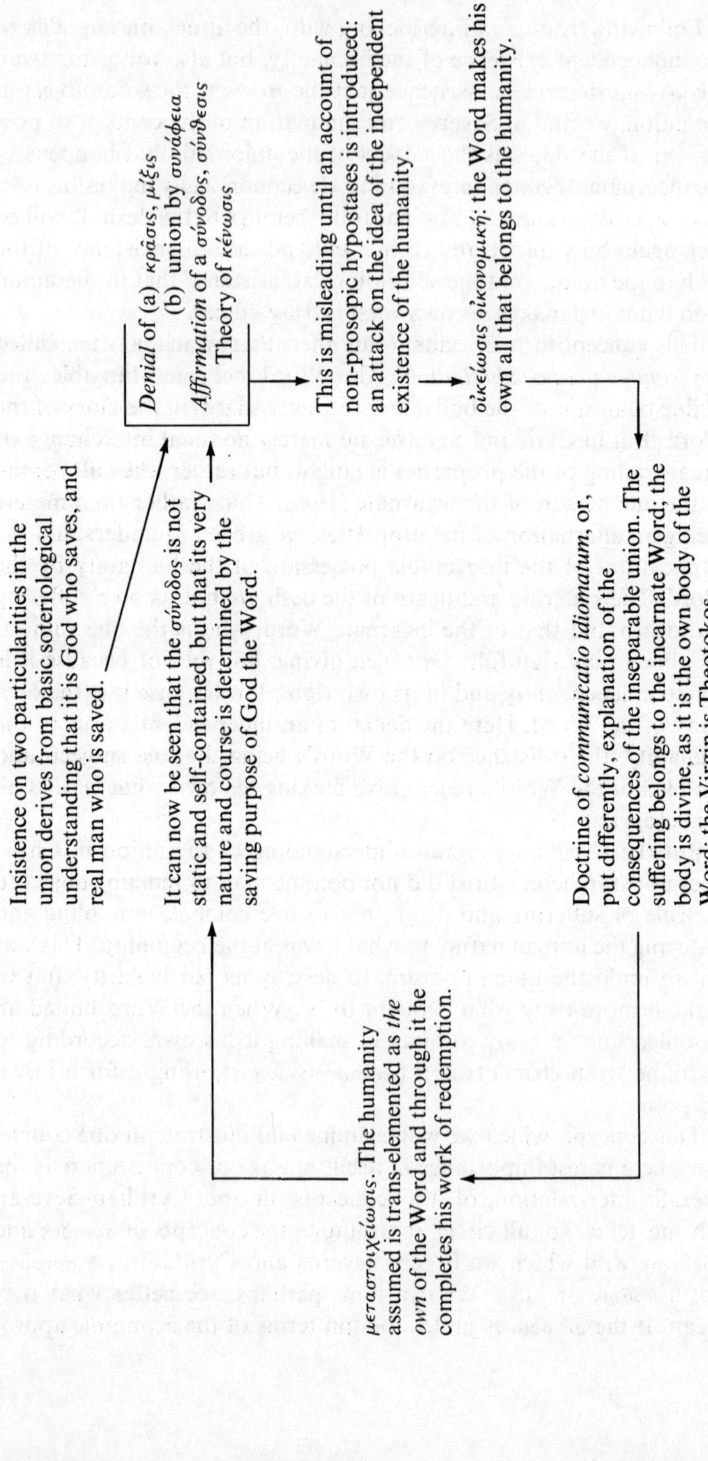
Insistence on two particularities in the union derives from basic soteriological understanding that it is God who saves, and real man who is saved.
It can now be seen that the σύνοδος is not static and self-contained, but that its very nature and course is determined by the saving purpose of God the Word.
Denial of (a) κρᾶσις, μίξις
(b) union by συνάφεια
Affirmation of a σύνοδος, σύνθεσις
Theory of κένωσις
This is misleading until an account of non-prosopic hypostases is introduced: an attack on the idea of the independent existence of the humanity.
οἰκείωσις οἰκονομική: the Word makes his own all that belongs to the humanity.
Doctrine of *communicatio idiomatum*, or, put differently, explanation of the consequences of the inseparable union. The suffering belongs to the incarnate Word; the body is divine, as it is the own body of the Word; the Virgin is Theotokos.
μεταστοιχείωσις. The humanity assumed is trans-elemented as *the own* of the Word and through it he completes his work of redemption.

priation of the humanity by the *Λόγος*, and in terms of a *μεταστοιχείωσις*, it can be seen that it is not merely the concurrence of two *πράγματα*. It is not a static, self-contained union, like a mixture, which could occur and be finished, but a purposive activity, the exact nature of which is governed by something outside of itself. It is a *σύνοδος* in which the Word makes what is ours his own, but not for his sake, because he lacks it, but for the purpose of restoring and saving man, and where the actual course of the *σύνοδος* is determined by that intention. This takes us back to the primary soteriological understanding which we argued underlies Cyril's account of the union. The point of describing the inter-relation of the concepts in the Cyrillian–Severan scheme, as we have done, is to introduce the understanding that the whole scheme is soteriological, and this imports an active and purposive meaning to the concepts. The Cyrillian–Severan *ἕνωσις* is not static or self-contained, and if this purposive element is ignored, the union becomes incomprehensible and inconsistent, as we shall see.

As an illustration, we have set out in summary and diagrammatic form the inter-relation of the concepts which have just been introduced.

Notes

1. Cyril, *QUSC*, PG 75.1269D (= Pusey edn. Vol. 7, p. 347.12–14).
2. EM p. 72.10.
3. EM p. 100.15–16.

VI The First Letter of Severus

In introducing the *Letters* of Severus, we shall follow the same method as before. We will attempt to explain the major theme of a passage, while at the same time picking out the concepts and presuppositions, which we will then examine in greater detail.

It will be remembered that in his *First Letter*, Sergius showed us one of his major presuppositions. This was his idea that every propriety belongs to an underlying nature, and so if we speak of two proprieties, it follows that we are referring to two natures.[1] From this he concluded that there would be one propriety of Christ, in which no-one from those who are invisible or visible shares.[2] His *κεφάλαιον* too, followed from this presupposition: "We do not speak of two natures or proprieties after the inexpressible union".[3] It will also be remembered that Sergius' *κεφάλαιον* was corrected by the Assembly to which he applied, to the form "We do not speak of divided particularities".[4] Sergius, however, took this as "We do not speak of divided proprieties",[5] and, understanding it on the basis of his presupposition that a propriety implies a nature, took it that a duality was being taught, and asked for an explanation.

This is where Severus began, and in his *First Letter* he gives us a careful and quite full account of how he understands the concept of a particularity. In examining this, we must never forget that Severus is not simply explaining a different or alternative terminology, but a wholly different Christology, from which his terminology flows. Severus begins by praising and encouraging Sergius, but turns quickly to the question of what a particularity is. To confess the natural particularity of the natures from which there is the one Christ is not, he says, something new which he has just invented, but is a part of the Cyrillian tradition.[6]

To begin to illustrate this, Severus gives three quotations from Cyril. First, Cyril had argued that even if the Son of God incarnate is said to be one, he is not therefore the result of a confusion, for neither the nature of the Word, nor that of the flesh has passed out of itself into something else, but each continues in the particularity that belongs to the nature.[7] Secondly, trying to explain what "the particularity that belongs to the nature" is, Cyril says that even if the

body born at Bethlehem is not the same in natural quality as the Word from God, nevertheless, it became his, and the Word incarnate is to be considered one Son and Christ and Lord.[8] Thirdly, although the flesh, with regard to particularity, is completely of another nature from the Word, yet it became his. As a result, God the Word is called "the seed of Abraham", when he is incarnate. This does not detract from the Word's still being what he ever was, for although he is God, he became man as well.[9]

What may we deduce from this? The first passage shows us a contrast. Flesh and divinity are completely different, and in the union of incarnation, their difference is retained. That is, they remain what they are, and do not become something else. Severus is pointing us towards the understanding that the particularity of a thing is its being what it is. We may also begin to see that his account of what a particularity is, and insistence that the particularities remain, is brought in to clarify his statement that the Word incarnate is not a confusion. Although the Word has become incarnate, he has not deserted his particularity, his integrity of being, nor has he done away with the integrity of being of the flesh. In his second and third passages, we may see that the union of incarnation is not just a coming together, but involves an aspect of possession. God the Word is the subject of the union, and he has made the humanity *his*, thus becoming the Word incarnate. He remained who he was, and the humanity remained what it was (it kept its particularity), but it then belonged to him, rather than to itself. Though it remained what it was, it was no longer independent. Though he remained who he was, in his incarnate state, he could be called "the seed of Abraham".

We can now draw out the conclusions. First, Severus tries to illustrate for us what particularity is by showing the contrast whereby completely different things differ from each other. But the contrast is just for illustration. One does not need two things to create the particularity of a thing: particularity is the intrinsic otherness of each thing. Secondly, we see that in the union of the incarnation, the humanity, though real and in its particularity, is now "owned", not independent. Its integrity is preserved, but its independence is not. But we can take this further. When Severus tries to explain to us what a particularity is, he is not simply exploring a concept for its own sake, but trying to explain the role and status of the constituent natures in the union of the incarnation. But this itself cannot be understood until it is understood what is the sort and point of the union in the incarnation. This becomes clearer as we proceed.

Severus continues by saying that Sergius should now understand

that particularity implies the otherness of the natures of the things which have come to union.[10] We have seen already that this is an otherness which continues, even when the natures are united.[11] Yet, Severus goes on, this otherness is of such a sort that though it continues and is not blunted by confusion, God the Word, who is totally other than flesh, can be said to have been seen and touched.[12] To say this, that God the Word was seen and touched, is a paradox, and Severus quickly qualifies it by saying that he has not changed from his invisible nature, but has become united to a visible and solid body.[13] He tries to explain himself further: the profession that the Word was seen is not Synousiast,[14] but is demanded by precision and accuracy for the truth.[15] If this is so, what is the truth that we are accurately expressing when we say that *the Word* was seen? Severus asks us to look at the example of a man.[16] A man is made up from body and soul, which are two concrete and different hypostases, yet the man, or one nature who is the union of these hypostases, is called both rational and mortal. This is not because when the union has occurred, we no longer know the difference between the constituent natures. This would be to say that the particularities, the integrities, of the body and soul had been lost, and that man was a sort of confusion. This would be the anthropological parallel to synousiasm. Severus' point is that the unity of body and soul in man is not like that, but that recognising the permanent difference between the constituent natures does not create a division between them, so that we would say that only the body is mortal, and only the soul is rational.

Therefore here, in the case of a man, the unity involved is a different sort of unity from confusion, which parallels Synousiasm, or division, which parallels Nestorian juxtaposition, and the constituents of this unity play a different role: though they are and remain different, they are not exclusive of each other. This is an understanding which we will develop later, but the immediate point is that the union in man, unlike a union of confusion or juxtaposition, is a union where it is appropriate and accurate to say the apparently paradoxical, namely, to call the irrational body rational in the union, or to say that the invisible Word is seen.

Severus turns at once to apply the insights of this example to Christology. First, he refers to Cyril's defence against Andrew over the Third Anathema: it is quite blameless to recognise that the flesh is one thing, and the Only-Begotten another, with respect to their own natures, but to recognise this difference is not to divide the natures after the union.[17,18] Secondly, referring again to the

example of the unity in man, Severus argues that though rational nature is utterly different and distinct from sensible nature, when a single hypostasis is formed by a coming together from a rational nature and a sensible nature, a unity emerges in which the difference of the constituents is not suppressed, as there is no confusion, but they are no longer divided. This, he says, is because the constituents "do not exist independently, but complete one hypostasis from two".[19] We will examine the importance of this shortly.

Thirdly, Severus turns directly to Emmanuel, and the natures of divinity and humanity. Divinity and humanity are totally different, but when a union is professed from them, the difference in natural quality is not suppressed, but division is driven out.[20] He then repeats this, with a quotation from Cyril: though divinity and humanity are different in the mode of how they are, the principle of the union does not ignore their difference, but removes division. This, he adds most importantly, is not from mixture or confusion, "but because the Word of God has shared in flesh and blood".[21] Severus then briefly turns the argument on its head. If one divides Emmanuel after the union into a duality, besides the difference between the natures, which of course remains, a real division is opened up, as each nature in its independence possesses and is a centre for its own properties.[22] If Synousiasm is to be avoided, by the insistence that each of the constituent natures retains its integrity or particularity, Nestorian juxtaposition is also to be avoided, by a denial that the constituent natures in the union have an exclusive independence of each other. To express the sort of union there is in the incarnation, Severus turns back to Cyril: "God is not touchable, but the Word became subject to touch by means of his own flesh".[23] We have seen this idea of the union before, that is, that it is a union because the Word possesses or makes his own the flesh,[24] and we will now examine it more closely.

In going through the first part of this letter, we have already collected a certain number of concepts. Severus began by trying to explain what a particularity is. As we have seen, he tries to illustrate the concept in two main ways. Particularity can be seen in difference: it is the continuing otherness of a thing;[25] it is also explained as being how a thing is "with respect to its own nature"[26], or what it is "according to the mode of how it is".[27] We may summarise this by saying that the particularity of a thing is its integrity of being. But we notice now another thing about particularities: though an individual, independent object of course has a particularity, for it is what it is, and is not something else, a thing can still be concrete, indi-

vidual, in its particularity, and yet not be an independent existent. It is then necessarily a constituent part of a union, and Severus gives the example, though later we will suggest others, of body and soul in the union we call "a man". The body remains what it is, namely flesh and bone, but in the union it is not independent like a leg of mutton in a butcher's shop, but is somehow involved in a union which endows it with qualities beyond itself. It is, for example, alive. It is this aspect of a particularity, that a thing's possession of integrity of being does not imply independence of existence that Severus emphasises when he argues that to acknowledge two particularities in a compound thing is not to see a division in it, or a juxtaposition of two independent things.

We see that Severus puts together these two aspects of what a particularity is, to form what we might call a neutral, illustrative picture of the union of the incarnation. It is a union in which the particularities of divinity and humanity are retained (i.e. there is no confusion), but yet there is no division between them, because retention of particularity does not imply independence in existence (i.e. it is not what he would call a Nestorian juxtaposition). So Severus is left with an unfamiliar sort of unity which is neither a confusion nor a juxtaposition, but which he justifies by pointing to the unity in man: the non-independent but real body and soul have somehow united to make up a man.

This is what we might call his "neutral" account of the union. It is an attempt, as it were, to describe the union from the outside, and just because of this, it is never wholly convincing. But interlaced with it there is a more theological account. We have already seen hints of this in what we called the *aspect of possession* in the union. Though the body is not the same in natural quality as the Word, yet it became his;[28] divinity and humanity are different, and though this difference is preserved in the union, division is driven out, because the Word has *shared in* flesh and blood.[29] In what we called the neutral account of the union, it was stressed that a thing could retain its particularity in a union, but without being independent. The meaning of this lack of independence is now explained: the flesh in the incarnation is not independent, even though it remains flesh, because it is possessed by the Word. It does not belong to itself, but to the Word. It is not closed in on itself, but taken by possession into a union where it is endowed with properties other than its own. But what is this union? It is clearly not a kind of more subtle juxtaposition in which two incomplete things somehow jig-saw together, but it is something active, in which the Word is the subject, or active pos-

sessor, and makes the flesh his. Though we will explore this in greater detail later, this sort of union is more like a process than a mixture which could take place and be completed in a moment. But can we, even now, understand it further?

We began with the concept of a particularity, which expressed the integrity of a thing, without implying its independence. This concept was of importance to Severus because it allowed him to deny that the incarnate Word is a confusion: the difference between the flesh and the divinity is preserved. But why is this important? If we turn the argument round, we see that the concept of particularity allows Severus to affirm that this is a union in which difference is intrinsic: God the Word remains God the Word, and the humanity remains humanity, yet they are one. This is the soteriological root of his Christology, and explains the stress upon integrity of being in the concept of a particularity. But what about the stress upon a denial of an implication of independence? Here we see the role of the concept of possession. God the Word is the subject, and he makes the humanity his own. Because it is owned, it is not independent or divided. Thus we may see that the concept of the ownership of the flesh by the Word sets the stage for understanding the union of the incarnation in a new way, namely as an active process, with the Word as the subject of this activity. On the other hand, the concept of particularity, with its stresses on integrity and denial of independent existence, is a sort of conceptual scaffolding to illustrate the meaning of the owned humanity, and to show its role in the union.

We stated earlier that Severus was not introducing simply an alternative terminology to that of Sergius, but a wholly different Christology. We now have a glimpse of his vision. The union of incarnation is an active possessing, or making his own, of the humanity by God the Word. We will later ask why this is, and what its implications are. The concept of a particularity is brought in and elaborated in an attempt to explain the status and role of the constituents in that sort of active union. Later in his *First Letter*, Severus considers the activities of Christ. Before that he again tries to clarify what sort of union it is that he understands in Christ, and we will examine this next to test out our conclusions.

Severus first reinforces the account of particularity which we have shown him trying to explain. We do not, he says, quarrel about how to name it: what we stress is the difference, or particularity or otherness of the natures from which Christ is, but this is the particularity which lies in natural quality (and he has just defined natural quality as "the principle of how (a thing) is"[30]) and not an understanding of

particularity which would imply things in independent existence.[31] Quoting Cyril, he points to the immediate implication of this: if it is a concept of particularity in natural quality we are dealing with, then affirming two particularities is not to create a division *εἰς ἰδικὴν ἑτερότητα* but to affirm that the Word became flesh.[32] We see reaffirmed here the understanding we have pointed to: the Word is the subject of the union of the incarnation, and the union is one which takes place in his person. As he did before,[33] Severus next shows the implications of this sort of unity by turning the argument on its head and pointing to what would follow if it were not the case. Were Christ divided into two independently existing things, there would be no one subject possessing both natures, so each would belong to itself, claiming its own properties, and perpetuating the gulf between the divinity and the humanity.[34] When, on the other hand, from two natures there is one Christ without confusion, one person and one nature belonging to the Word incarnate, then the Word claims both the properties of his divine nature, which he always had, and the properties of the humanity. What follows from this? A unity of the divine and human natures, in the person of the Word. The Word himself may be seen, through his own visible flesh, and the flesh, being the own flesh of the Word, is rightly understood as divine. It should be noticed here that though there is a *communicatio idiomatum* (the Word is seen, and the flesh takes on the properties of the Word) there is not taught a straightforward alternation of the natures, or that the flesh becomes divine in its own right. It becomes divine, but as the own flesh of the Word, so its exaltation stems from the activity of the Word. So though there is a *communicatio*, it is, in a sense, a one-sided one.[35] This is an aspect of the union we will return to later.

Having established this principle of the one subject in the Word incarnate, Severus puts it to the test. As he does so frequently, the point is made through the mouth of Cyril. Does the earthly Christ lie, when he says that the Son of Man, who is himself, descended from heaven? Cyril answers, "No"; just as the eternal Word, though incorporeal, made his own all that is of the body, and so allowed to be attributed to him statements about the body, so too, he being from above, may truly attribute "he came from above" to himself, while he was man.[36] But what is the force of this argument? Let us ask, "How would it be a lie for Christ to say that?" It would be a lie, if God the Word and the man Jesus were different persons. So the point is to show that the eternal Son and Jesus Christ, the Word incarnate, are one and the same person. He is the one, continuing

subject, and is owner of both his deity and his humanity. Because of this, the one person "will be seen by means of both (sets of properties), both touchable and not touchable, and visible and not visible".[37] This extraordinary paradox can only be made sense of by understanding the Word as the subject, bringing the humanity into union with himself, yet keeping it what it is.

Severus now repeats himself again. Clarity, he obviously feels, must be bought at the cost of any amount of repetition. When we anathematise those who say that after the union Emmanuel has two natures, and then speak of their activities and properties, what is wrong is not primarily recognising two different natures and activities, and the different properties, but the apparent setting up of these natures as if they were independent. If they are independent, they are the centres of their own activities, and exclusively claim their own properties. This is yet again the argument we have been illustrating. The parallel independence of the natures challenges the understanding that the Word is the one subject in the union, who possesses both natures. If this understanding is lost, not only is the union destroyed, but so too is any hope of understanding that union in the specific way that Severus will argue is necessary.[38]

He continues that if it were impossible for him to say that Christ is "from two natures", without implying that the natures were independent, then he would not do so.[39] But as it is, the concept of particularity comes to his rescue. It allows him to refer to the retention of a concrete nature, without implying its independent existence. As we said earlier, the concept is merely a clarifying one, but none the less, it embodies an indispensable distinction: it shows the status of the constituents in a special sort of unity, allowing Severus both to deny their confusion and their independence. He concludes by defining yet again what a particularity is on his terms, distinguishing it from the understanding that it implies a nature in independent existence.[40]

When Severus examines the question of the actions of Christ, we see him considering and working out an implication of his understanding of the union of the incarnation. We will in turn take this application of the concept, and apply it back to extend our original interpretation of Severus. But before doing this, let us widen the understanding of the concept of particularity which we have gained so far. Though the aim of this introduction is quite simply to introduce and explain the letters between Severus and Sergius, in their own terms, it is useful at points where provisional conclusions have been drawn to broaden our outlook, and test and illustrate our find-

ings in this text with examples from some of Severus' other works, from Cyril, and from modern secondary material. For this purpose we will look briefly at some other descriptions of the concept of particularity and its role.

We have seen how important it was to Severus to distinguish the concept of particularity which pointed to the integrity of identity of a thing, from the concept which implied a thing's independent existence. As we might expect, we find this same distinction in others of his letters: for example, ". . . . we mean in the matter of natural quality, and not that those which were naturally united are individually and independently separated and divided from each other, for this is what those who cut our one Lord Jesus Christ into two natures say . . . ."[41] In Severus' *Philalethes* we also frequently find a rejection of the humanity's having any independent status, which in Severus' view led directly to Nestorianism.[42] Behind this, of course, lies Cyril, with his refusal to divide Christ into a man by himself, and the Word by himself.[43]

Though particularity does not imply independence, Severus stresses with equal seriousness that it refers to the perfect integrity of the identity of an object. Though the constituents in the union are not independent, he wants to deny that they are deficient in any way. Thus, he writes as follows in his *First Letter to Oecumenius*, to describe the constituents of the union: "But if Emmanuel is one, (being) from Godhead and manhood which have a perfect existence according to their own principle . . . ."[44] His attempt to clarify the respect in which the constituents are perfect is much clearer and more successful in a letter to Thomas, where, following from a quotation of Cyril, he writes, ". . . . the peculiarity of the natural union is that the hypostases are in composition and are perfect without diminution, but refuse to continue an individual existence so as to be numbered as two, and to have its own person impressed upon each of them, which a conjunction in honour cannot possibly do".[45] This passage is of the greatest importance. It is a paradigm example of what we have called Severus' "neutral" account of the union. It involves all his scaffolding, explanatory concepts like "particularity", "hypostases without persons", but does not show how they interrelate theologically. The hypostases are in composition, and are perfect without diminution, but how, and why, do they refuse to continue an individual existence? We will turn to this later. For the moment let us grasp the point that though particularity refers to the perfection of something which is individual and concrete, for Severus is not talking about a generality, but about the particular human

nature in the union of the incarnation, this is a perfection which has nothing to do with independence. This was an understanding of the perfection of a thing which both Severus' Eutychian and Chalcedonian–Nestorian opponents seemed to find difficult, but one which is vital for his Christology. For the Eutychian side, we remember the argument of Sergius, which was so basic to his position: "Every propriety belongs to an underlying nature, and if we speak of two proprieties, we are obliged also to speak of two natures".[46] Behind this lay his unquestioned presuppositions, that if a thing was uniquely identifiable, it was an independent existent, and if a thing existed independently, it could be brought under a definition. We have already referred to the similar presupposition of Eleusinius.[47] On the Chalcedonian side, the compiler of the Cyrillian florilegium in the *Philalethes* quoted Cyril's letter to John of Antioch, saying that Christ was perfect in divinity and perfect in humanity, but omitted the key word that it was the same one (*ὁ αὐτός*) who was perfect in both natures. Severus very acutely noticed this, saying that the Chalcedonian had cut out *ὁ αὐτός*, thinking that each of the natures was perfect in the isolation of its existence.[48] Severus, following Cyril,[49] understood "perfection" in a very different sense. Thus, behind both the extreme Monophysite, who tried to fuse two independent natures into one, and the doctrinaire Chalcedonian who tended to see an independent sphere of action for each nature, we see a common, ultimately dualist presupposition: namely, that if a thing is concrete and particular, it will possess some sort of independence. It is greatly to Severus' credit that he tried to break with this idea, and, even more importantly, provide an alternative network of concepts.

We find another strand in Severus' network of concepts and theological vocabulary expressed very clearly in his shorter letters. This is an attempted characterisation of the particularity of a thing, in a way very similar to that which we have already seen in his *First Letter to Sergius*.[50] Thus, again in Severus' *First Letter to Oecumenius*, he writes, ". . . . and a particularity is that which exists in the form of a manifestation of natural differences".[51] Severus is more explicit when writing to Eleusinius: "This then is the difference that appears in natural quality,[52] the different principle underlying the existence of Godhead and manhood: . . . . This difference we in no wise assert that the union has removed".[53] Here again, Severus is completely Cyrillian: in Cyril we frequently find emphasis on the permanent and intrinsic difference in kind of the divinity and the humanity which have become united in the incarnation.[54]

These points, that particularity means "integrity of being"; a

denial that particularity implies independence, but an assurance that it refers to a thing in its fullness, can thus all be found in Severus' writings outside of our text. As we have already noted, these points are all components in Severus' "neutral" account of the union. But where does this lead us? Why are they components, and what does this tell us about the nature of the union?

Writing to Eleusinius, Severus says, "Therefore *where we confess the one out of two*, Lord and Son and Christ, and one incarnate nature of the Word himself, *we understand the difference as it were in the natural quality* of the natures from which Christ is".[55] Here we see that particularity (or difference in natural quality) is definitive of the nature of the duality from which the unity in Christ comes.[56] Furthermore, the unity in Christ is a unity in which difference (or duality in natural quality) is intrinsic: Severus writes to Oecumenius, "*Therefore those who confess one nature of God the Word Incarnate*, and do not confuse the (elements) from which he is, *recognise as well the particularity* of those things which came together to union".[57] This again forces us to question backwards for the presuppositions. What sort of union is it, where difference is a permanent factor? How is this a union?

We find an answer by turning to the concept of union by possession which we have already looked at. The union is there understood as something active which the Word does: he makes the human nature his own, and so it is he who holds the union together. This understanding of the union, which Severus calls a σύνθεσις, is something which we will examine in detail in Severus' *Second Letter to Sergius*, and we do not want to anticipate this. We are, besides, concerned at the moment with a different approach, and let us simply point to the understanding that the Word is the one active subject of this union.[58] Where there is one subject or possessor, what happens to the different elements in the union? Again as we follow the text, Severus tells us that the properties of the constituent natures are not distributed out, each to its proper nature.[59] This is because in the union there is just one subject: the constituent natures are no longer independent possessors. The flesh, therefore, becomes the own flesh of the Word. Quoting Cyril against Nestorius, Severus says that as an implication of this union, we do not say that the flesh became Godhead (as if it were independent), but rather it became divine as being his.[60] But what does this mean? Did God the Word lack and need humanity, and simply assume a human nature into himself for his own sake? Were this the case, would it even fit the facts of the Gospel narrative? Jesus could walk on water, as his body

was the body of the Word, but he did so only occasionally; on one occasion he turned water into wine, on another he refused to turn stones into bread. If the union is to be understood as a possession of humanity by the Word, who is the one subject, why is there this apparent inconsistency in his incarnate behaviour?

Let us put this differently. In a union of possession, for example, the union of body and soul, we can understand that the inanimate flesh is endowed with properties beyond itself. This endowment is part of what a unity by possession is. Unlike a mixture or a confusion, which are essentially static, it has an inherently dynamic aspect. But how are we to understand a union where the endowment seems inconsistent or merely occasional? We can see from this that an understanding that God the Word is the one subject, or possessor, in the union of the incarnation, is not by itself enough, and we can here see the limits of the usefulness of the analogy of the union of body and soul. A confusion is a static union in that it yields a new substance which then acts self-consistently with its new properties. Though it has a dynamic aspect, in that the body is endowed with properties beyond its nature, the union of body and soul is still too static to provide real illumination for us. The endowment which the body has is a consistent one.

Let us therefore try to construct a more complex analogy. Let us imagine a man who is totally blind, but who is able to see his way around by touching and probing at things with a stick which he holds in his hand. By means of the stick he can reach out and discover what lies around him. Now, what is the relationship between the man and the stick? He holds the stick in his hand; but he is not primarily aware of this. What he is primarily aware of is the object which the tip of his stick is able to bring into his awareness. The blind man pours out all his concentration onto the object which he discovers through his stick: he disattends as far as possible from the stick, for any concentration on the stick itself would spoil his primary intention, which is to look through, or past, the stick to the object beyond it. The stick then becomes like an extension to his own body. Though alien in material to him, and in itself quite lifeless, in his knowing process it becomes internalised to him, and he becomes quite unaware of it as something external or independent of him. Now, let us call the blind man's activity in knowing the outside world through his stick a "process". It is a process because it is something which is continuing, and active and intentional: it is not an event. In this process, as we have seen, there is a unity between the man and his stick. Let us examine the nature of this unity.

If the blind man is genuinely to throw his attention in knowing beyond the stick, the stick has to become so internalised to him that he is no longer aware that it is there. In this union, then, what happens to the stick? First, it loses its independence: as we have seen, it becomes internalised and possessed within the process of knowing. The blind man is the subject of it, and it becomes an extension to his senses. Second, we see that even so, it remains a stick. Though it is taken up into a process which gives it a role quite beyond itself, it still truly remains what it is. Third, we can develop this: the union of the man and the stick is of such a kind that the stick does not just happen to remain what it is, but its very remaining what it is is what permits it to be taken up into this role. As a stick it remains straight, flexible, resonant, and it is because this is how it is that it can be used in this way. The union is a process in which the retention of identity of the constituents is an inherent part.

Although every analogy can be easily over-worked, we can see that within the process, the stick assumes a role not unlike that of the assumed humanity in Severus' "neutral" model of the incarnation. It is not independent, but internalised or possessed; it remains what it is, even though it is somehow transformed and taken out of itself; its remaining what it is is of intrinsic importance to its place in the union. These are all elements in Severus' neutral account, but in our model there is a further factor. This is the object outside that the blind man is trying to know through his stick. If he were put in a great open space with nothing near him, the stick would no longer be internalised to him. Its unity with him would dissolve, and it would become a mere stick in his hand. This is because there would be nothing beyond the stick, onto which he could project his primary attention, while disattending from the stick. So this unity-in-a-process is not only active and continuing, but it can only occur when it is achieving its goal, which is actually to experience outside objects.

Let us apply this back to the unity in the incarnation. We began by considering the model of union by possession, where the nature possessed into union is endowed with qualities beyond itself. We then raised the question of an apparently inconsistent endowment, which would seem to deny there was any real union. Going back to the analogy of the stick, we saw that if one took away the external objects, and so made futile the blind man's intention, there could be no union between him and the stick. The goal of the incarnation was to redeem mankind, and in his life on earth, God the Word was perpetually fulfilling that goal. But if this goal of the incarnation is

ignored, it at once appears inconsistent, and its constituent elements seem to fly apart.

What does this mean? We could understand the union of the blind man with his stick, by looking at it *from within*, from the point of view of the man pouring his attention onto the external object and looking completely beyond his stick. The blind man himself would not even be aware that the stick was there, but a merely external observer would see no union between them. Similarly, any attempt to understand the union of the incarnation in purely external, neutral terms which ignore the intention of God the Word in becoming man, is bound to find it utterly inconsistent and paradoxical. We noted this in general terms in the introduction to this section. We argued there that the σύνοδος between God and man could not be understood as something static and whose point was contained within itself, but that it was a unity in activity the very nature and course of which was determined by the saving intention of God the Word, who on this occasion walked on water, and on that occasion walked on land, adapting everything he did to his one purpose. It is this adaptation to his goal that underlies what an external eye will call inconsistency. Here finally, though still utterly inadequately, we are reaching a more satisfactory approach to the union: we are realising that it is not static like a mixture, nor even dynamic like the union of living body and soul, but is an ongoing, alive, goal-directed process. Severus rightly marks this by calling it a dispensatory union.[61] The union can only be understood from the inside, that is, in the light of, and along with its actively accomplishing its goal.[62]

How do we know that this is what Severus is trying to express? Because this is how Severus understood the varied activities of the incarnate Word, and it is how we understand the activities that determines how we understand the unity in the person.

Severus now turns to examine the activities of the incarnate Word. He would seem to suspect that Sergius confuses activity and effect. Why is this, and why does it seem objectionable? It will be remembered that on Sergius' account of the union in Christ, the divine nature and the human nature came together to form a new unit, and that this unit was of one quality, and was characterised by one propriety. Why did Sergius see this: what was the problem he was trying to answer? He could see apparently inconsistent elements in the figure of the Biblical Christ: he walked with feet of flesh, which seemed human, but could walk on water, which appeared divine. Thus, against any Dyophysite understanding, he saw Christ as a sort of fusion[63] into a new unit. This new unit, just like a new chemical

compound, would have its own peculiar and new properties, all of which, no matter how strange, could be regarded as consistent members of a new set of properties. Thus, illustrating the activity of the new unit, the Christ, Sergius says that he could walk on the water without being dragged down; he was sealed in the tomb, but not held in; closed doors could not prevent his entrance.[64] But what is the consequence of this? It is to treat the things done by Christ, which were the results of intentional action, as if they were the unintended, or necessary, consequences of an object's simply being itself. Quinine tastes bitter. It always tastes bitter, because this is one of its properties. Sergius, likewise, is treating the things done by Christ as if they were the effects of a thing. To change our metaphor, he is a sort of theological behaviourist: he looks at the Biblical Christ, but only from an external point of view, understanding what Christ does not in the light of his intention, but as if it were the necessary product of the new unit.

Let us refer this back to our example of the blind man and his stick. To the merely external observer, there is no union between the man and the stick. The external eye cannot see how the blind man has internalised the stick to himself, and, as it were, sees through it. Sergius would see both the blind man and the stick, but being both external and yet determined to call them a union, would call them a new unit which acts together in a way different from either a man by himself, or a stick by itself. This is a new stick-and-man action. This position of Sergius' is taken up against what he would see as a Dyophysite position. Putting this in the terms of a caricature, which will be explained shortly, the Dyophysite, who would take an equally external position, instead of seeing the blind man and the stick coming together to form a new unit with a new consistent stick-and-man activity, would see both the stick and the man working together, but would say that now the man, now the stick, was the actor.

Severus very acutely sees that Sergius is treating the consequences of intentional activity as if they were unintended effects. He borrows the anti-Eunomian terminology of Basil, to distinguish between agent (*ὁ ἐνεργῶν*), activity (*ἡ ἐνέργεια*) and effect (*τὸ ἐνεργηθέν*).[65] This enables him to introduce for Sergius the idea that one agent may consciously act in different ways. That is, different sorts of effects, for example mental effects and physical effects, when produced by a conscious agent, need imply neither as many independent agents as there are effects (which would be the Dyophysite view), nor that the effects, if they are the product of one source, must be all of one sort, or self-consistent, and so without variety (which is the

apparent view of Sergius). What the external eye would see as mutually inconsistent acts (now building a boat, now reaching a decision) may be understood as the intentional acts of one agent. Let us see this by quickly going over the text of Severus' letter.

As we have already said, Severus first distinguishes between agent, activity and effect. This was a distinction which Sergius did not make, and it means that discussion of what is done is immediately placed in the realm of what is intended and voluntary. Having drawn the distinction in the abstract, Severus tests it on the example of a man. Some of the things done by a man are intellectual, while some are bodily, but though there is this diversity in the things which a man accomplishes, there is just one agent, and one activity.[66] The stress is upon the *diversity* of the things done by the one agent, in distinction to Sergius' idea that the effects are without diversity, being all of one new sort.

Having made his case with the example of a man, Severus turns to show that Emmanuel too is an agent, whose actions are the results of intentions. There is again diversity in the things that are done, but there is one Word who was incarnate, and there is one activity which performed them all.[67] We have argued that Sergius would view the actions of Christ as if they were the necessary fused effect of a new compound. His presupposition would be: "One unit yields one sort of effect". This presupposition will also be shared by the Dyophysite, who, on seeing two different sorts of effect, will argue that there are two units working together in tandem. Against both Sergius, the extreme Monophysite, and against the supposed Dyophysite, Severus poses his account of agency. To Sergius he stresses the variety of the utterances of the incarnate Word, to the Dyophysite he insists that these may not be separated out to two agents.[68]

Severus, Sergius, and his imagined Dyophysite opponent, all recognise human and divine aspects in the activity of the incarnate Word. Sergius fuses these aspects into a new divine–human effect, the Dyophysite separates them out between two agents, but what exactly is Severus' answer? We know that he argues that the Word incarnate is one agent, acting in different ways, but what does this mean? We can understand his own position more clearly as he turns to criticise not Sergius, but Leo.

He claims that what Leo writes in the Tome directly contradicts what he believes. Leo, he quotes, wrote "For each one of the forms does what belongs to it; the Word doing what belongs to the Word, and the body fulfilling those things which belong to the body, and the one of them is radiant with wonders, but the other falls under in-

sults".[69] Against this, Severus argues that if each nature performs only those things which are *its* own, they have not come to a union, but only to a sort of partnership.[70] Jesus Christ would not be God the Word become a man, but only a man "clothed with God",[71] making use of a power which is not his own.[72] In contrast to Leo, Severus teaches that Jesus is one subject: "he is seen using his own power as God inhominate".[73]

Severus' position against Leo is clearer and more developed in his *First Letter to Oecumenius*. There, after quoting the same passage from Leo, he refers to the teaching of Cyril in Section IX of the *Scholia*.[74] Cyril argued there that God the Word was united to the manhood without ceasing to be that which he is, "but rather changed what had been assumed or united into *his* glory and his operation".[75] Cyril pursues the parallel of fire taking hold of wood: it does not make it cease being wood, but changes it into the appearance and force of fire, "and performs all *its own* acts in it".[76] Similarly, when God the Word was united with manhood, "he is reckoned as one with it, appropriating its qualities to himself, but he also carried on the operation of his nature in it".[77] Severus then, as so often after a quotation from Cyril, sums up the passage and interprets it. "If .... the things which clearly belong to the flesh have come to belong to the Word, how shall we allow that each one of the forms performs its own acts?"[78] Christ is then one subject, one agent, who performs *his* actions with what he has made his own. But with an eye to the position of Sergius, we have to ask what sort of subject or unit this is. What happens to that which the Word has made his own, and what is the action he does with what he has made his own?

We can again answer this from Severus' criticism of Leo: in his Tome, Leo not only wrote that each form did that which belonged to itself, but also said that "Each of the natures preserves its own property without diminution".[79] Against Leo, Severus suggests that God the Word did not permit his flesh in all things to undergo the passions proper to it.[80] He quotes Cyril against Theodore, saying that the Word incarnate "feared by dispensation, inasmuch as he *sometimes* allowed his flesh to suffer the things that belonged to it, in order that he might make us strong".[81] Commenting as before on Cyril, Severus concludes: "If he *sometimes* allowed his flesh by dispensation to suffer the things which belonged to it, he did not preserve its propriety undiminished:[82] for it is seen in many cases not to have suffered the things which clearly belong to its nature, for it was united to the Word, the Maker of nature".[83] We can conclude that

in Severus' understanding of the union, the human nature and the divine nature are not independent. The human nature is a "possessed" nature.[84] It only sometimes undergoes the passions proper to it: and this is the nature of its union by possession to God the Word. If the humanity is divided from the Word, Severus, in a vivid phrase, says it will "walk in its own ways, following its nature".[85]

But what is the meaning of this "sometimes",[86] and what governs it? To the external eye, it could seem as if the incarnate Word were behaving in a merely haphazard way. To understand Severus' account of this, we can look at the use he makes of Gregory Nazianzen and Cyril. He quotes Gregory: "For he is purity itself, and did not need purification, but he is purified for you .... for he himself was a warden to himself of what he should suffer".[87] In a remarkable and creative adaptation, Severus extends this: "He was a warden to himself of hungering, and of being tired after a journey, and of accepting the other human sufferings .... in order to demonstrate the inhomination truly and without illusion".[88] Thus, the "sometimes" is governed by an internal intention. The union of God and man in the incarnate Word is continually adapted to a certain point. This *adaptative* nature of the union is very clear in Cyril: he speaks of Christ being baptised, *τῆς κατὰ σάρκα οἰκονομίας τὸ μυστήριον διὰ τῶν αὐτῇ πρεπόντων διοικούμενος τρόπων*.[89] Christ, Cyril writes, *ἰέναι γε μὴν τὴν τῷ πράγματι πρέπουσαν οὐκ ἀπαξιώσας τρίβον, τὴν καθ' ἡμᾶς γέννησιν ὑπομεῖναι λέγεται, μεμενηκὼς ὅπερ ἦν*.[90] Severus picked out from Cyril this picture of the union as being adaptative and voluntary, and we can see it in his *First Letter to Sergius*. After his criticism of Leo, which we have seen, Severus says that the Word incarnate acted in certain ways and said certain things, "because it was suitable to the economy".[91] Earlier in the same letter, he had quoted Cyril writing against Nestorius, and saying that the Word incarnate took for his own all that belonged to his body, "for the sake of that which is proper to the emptying".[92]

But what is this adaptative union of the economy? Why does the Word incarnate adapt himself now to this, now to that? The reason is the redemption of man. The soteriological dimension and purpose of the inhomination of the Word is spelled out with great emphasis by Cyril. He spoke of the Word incarnate *ἀναμορφῶν εἰς τὸ ἐν ἀρχαῖς τὴν ἀνθρώπου φύσιν*.[93] He wrote, *ἀπεφάνη γὰρ ἡμῖν Θεὸς ὢν κύριος, ἵνα τὴν καθ' ἡμῶν τυραννήσασαν ἀνέλῃ φθόραν, οὐχ ἵνα φθορᾶς μέτοχον τὴν οἰκείαν αὐτὸς ἀποφήνῃ φύσιν* ....[94] Cyril understood the incarnation as not a single event, but an active, restorative interplay. Again, he wrote that the Word *πλήρης ὑπάρχων καὶ ἐξ ἰδίου πληρώματος πᾶσι*

διδοὺς, ἀνθρωπίνως δέχεται, τὴν ἡμῶν πτωχείαν οἰκειούμενος ....[95] To recognise this immense emphasis upon the soteriological activity of the Word is of fundamental importance in understanding the Cyrillian–Severan account of the union in Christ. What they understood is that it is not a self-contained fusion, like that taught by Sergius, nor a series of alternate, parallel, and ultimately independent actions, as on the model of the Dyophysites, but a union of such a kind that its nature and course can only be understood in terms of its goal. It is a union in which there is an intrinsic inter-relation between what the Word incarnate does, and who he is. Where this redemptive purpose is ignored, what before, to use a metaphor, was three-dimensional and had depth, collapses into something flat. Each nature, as Severus so graphically put it, will walk in its own way. There would be no kenosis of the Word, no possession of the humanity. An understanding of the union in its soteriological dimension, so that its course is intrinsically inter-related with its point, is, very simply, Severus' vision, and virtually all that he sets out to impart in these letters with Sergius. All his criticisms of Sergius follow from this understanding.

Let us now return to the argument of the text. The end of Severus' *First Letter* is less of a connected argument, and Severus, on the basis of what he has just explained, tries to tidy up a few points raised in Sergius' letter. First, he chooses to criticise the terms in which Sergius expressed the union. It will be remembered that in his *First Letter*, Sergius, following what we have seen was one of his basic presuppositions, namely that a propriety identifies and implies an independent nature,[96] and trying to express and identify the unity he saw in the Biblical Christ, suggested that, "just as we believe Christ is one from two natures, so also we (should) accept one propriety from two".[97] By this Sergius meant, as we have suggested, that the new unit, if it actually was a unit rather than some sort of Dyophysite junction of two continuing natures, would be marked by one propriety, not two. Severus seems completely to misunderstand Sergius' point.[98] He takes ܕܝܠܝܘܬܐ in the sense of "properties",[99] and ridicules Sergius, asking him if he thinks a man is composed of two properties, perhaps "thinking" and "whiteness" or "blackness". He cannot yet understand that for Sergius, starting as he does from the enigmatic figure of the Biblical Christ, the problem of Christology is one of identification, while for himself, starting with the Word, the eternal Son, the question is to understand the saving purpose behind the Son's becoming a man.

Following this, Severus rather dangerously introduces the writ-

ings attributed to Julius of Rome, in an attempt to substantiate and sum up his own conclusions against Leo. Like Apollinaris, and very much against any Dyophysite tendency, Julius stresses that the Word incarnate is one subject. He writes, "There is one nature, one hypostasis, one activity, one person, entirely God, entirely man, the same".[100] This is very much to Severus' liking. But lest it be thought that Julius encourages the idea that Christ is a fusion along the lines understood by Sergius, Severus adds a caution: though Julius confesses one nature incarnate of God the Word, he also recognises the properties of the natures from which the one Christ is, and the difference between them.[101] He quotes Julius again: the flesh, far from having changed to what is not bodily, possesses "both what is its own, which is from us by the birth from the Virgin, and that which is above us, by the mixture or union of God the Word".[102] Quoting Julius again, Severus suggests that "one nature is established from the two parts".[103] Though Severus is merely trying to substantiate his case, these references to Julius do not help him to explain himself to Sergius. As we have seen, Sergius had the idea that Christ is the product of two nameable, and therefore identifiable and independent natures. Against any idea of what he understood as dyophysitism, these natures were understood to have come together to form a new unit. We have described this earlier as an understanding in which "incarnation" or "the uniting" is an operation performed on two inert, pre-existing entities.

We have argued that Severus, following Cyril, moved away from this static account of the union, seeing it instead as the act of the Word. We have already pointed to Cyril's use of verbs to show the activity of the Word, who "became man"; "makes a body his own"; "empties himself", and how this means that the incarnation is understood not as an event, but as a dynamic process. Though in this *First Letter* Severus has made considerable headway in explaining these categories of thought to Sergius, these references to Julius bring back the static language of Apollinaris: it does not help Sergius to tell him that the union is from two (as if independent) *parts*, implying, as that model does, that the union is like a jig-saw, or that the flesh keeps *what is its own*, as if it were an independent subject. It was this kind of language which provoked Sergius' correspondingly static account of the union, which we saw so clearly in his *Second Letter* to Severus.

Severus now takes up another point from Sergius' *First Letter*. At the end of his letter, having given his argument for there being one propriety from two, Sergius had gone on to characterise this pro-

priety. As the propriety of God identifies and implies the nature of God, and the propriety of flesh implies the nature of flesh, and the new unit, Christ, is truly new and different, neither of these proprieties apply to it.[104] Consequently, just as "laughter" is a defining characteristic, which belongs only to man, so too there will be "one propriety of Christ, in which no-one from those who are visible or invisible shares".[105] Severus, again very acutely, understood this as implying that according to Sergius, Christ, being different from men in that he was born from the Holy Spirit and the Virgin, did not truly possess human properties.[106] In his attempt to refute him, he again appeals to the anti-Eunomian distinctions of Basil. According to Eunomius, the Father, the Son and the Spirit should be considered different in ousia, in that the Father is unbegotten, the Son is begotten, and the Spirit is by procession.[107] Severus, with Basil, produces an argument from what he considers evident fact. Difference in origin of existence does not imply difference in ousia, or not even men would be the same in ousia. Adam, Eve, Abel and Jesus all came to be in different ways, but share the same ousia. If then these four, who all came to be in different ways, share the same ousia, how does it not follow that each possesses the properties of the ousia?[108]

Is this argument against Sergius apt? On Sergius' scheme, the divine nature and the human nature have in Christ come together to form a new unit, with one new self-consistent quality. Therefore this unit, being new and different, does not possess genuinely human properties. Severus has correctly diagnosed this. However, he does not seem to appreciate that this denial of human properties to Christ follows consistently from Sergius' presuppositions, and that until these presuppositions have been undermined, his own objections cannot make sense. Sergius, as we have argued, was concerned with a problem of unification and identification at the expense of, or certainly without due consideration for, soteriology. Severus' Christology, like that of Cyril, is deeply soteriological, and his stress that the Word took upon himself real humanity, with true human properties, can, in Sergius' eyes, only seem Dyophysite. To Sergius, the retention of truly human properties will imply a *complete*, and thus, lacking as he does the concept of particularity (*ἰδιότης ὡς ἐν ποιότητι φυσικῇ*), an independent, ununited human nature.

This is the depth of the misunderstanding between Severus and Sergius. But Severus' objections to Sergius illustrate for us again the adaptative, redemptive and voluntary nature of the union, which we have just tried to describe. The Word incarnate does not renounce in everything the human laws of nature, because his conception and

birth from the Virgin is a wonder.[109] This is stressed by quotations from Gregory and Cyril to emphasise that the Word underwent a real incarnation. The Word did not flow through the Virgin as if through a pipe, but was formed in her in both a human and a divine way.[110] Severus places enormous weight upon this: *unless* the Word became flesh and was inhominate, he would not have become a curse when he suffered the cross on our behalf;[111] *unless* the flesh could receive what belonged to it, he could not endure death.[112]

We tried earlier to explain Severus' understanding that the union is intrinsically redemptive. God the Word became man, but to restore man. Therefore as it was humanity which he willed to restore, real humanity was precisely what he willed to make his own. We pointed to the Cyrillian background for this, and it is very clear in Cyril. In the *Thesaurus* he wrote, *καὶ ἐφ' ἑκάστῳ τῶν ἀνθρωπίνως γεγονότων τὸν αὐτὸν ἐφαρμόζων λόγον, εὑρήσεις ἐν Χριστῷ τὰ τῆς σαρκὸς πάθη κεκινημένα, οὐχ ἵνα κρατήσῃ, ὥσπερ καὶ ἐν ἡμῖν, ἀλλ' ἵνα κινηθέντα καταργηθῇ τῇ δυνάμει τοῦ ἐνοικήσαντος τῇ σαρκὶ Λόγου, πρὸς τὸ ἄμεινον μεταποιουμένης τῆς φύσεως.*[113] In the light of these presuppositions—that it was precisely by taking on humanity that Christ restored humanity—Severus draws his conclusions against Sergius. He objects to him: "How do you completely remove him from human properties, which the Word incarnate receives willingly?"[114] But, as we have argued, there is a complete impasse between Severus and Sergius. That what the Word took upon himself was assumed in an intentional process has simply not been taken into consideration by Sergius: instead, we have argued that he sees the union as self-contained, and so the nature of the union is not, and cannot, be understood in the light of its intention. Thus, the Word's involvement with suffering is robbed of its soteriological purpose. But when this is removed, it becomes pointless and inexplicable. Thus, insofar as Sergius' Christ tends to become a third entity, neither really divine nor really human, there is a tendency for soteriology and true involvement with humanity to be less stressed. Though Sergius is an extreme Monophysite, in its implications, his thought involves as deep a dualism between God and man as that in the worst Nestorian.

Sergius, as we have seen, wanted to deny that Christ, as a consequence of the union, had real human properties, and we have tried to show why he was committed to this view. Yet, what Sergius says can seem to have an element of truth in it: Christ did walk on the water, heal the sick and know the thoughts of men's hearts, so how is this reconcilable with truly possessing a human nature? If one under-

stands that Jesus Christ was God the Word become a man, he was different from all other men. In what way is this difference to be characterised? Both Sergius and Severus recognise this difference, and we come again to their different viewpoints. Sergius, from his external viewpoint, as it were freezes the difference, and sees it in static terms: Christ is become neither like God nor man. Severus also faces this question, but expresses himself more subtly, and in dynamic rather than static categories. He understands the being of Christ as a process rather than as an event. He touches on this again in his *Second Letter*, where we will examine it at greater length, but before considering what he says here, let us try to illustrate his way of thinking from the model we used before.

Before, we looked at the relationship of union there is between a blind man and his stick, as he uses it to explore the world around him. Of the fact that they are united, there is no doubt. As the man focuses his attention upon an object which he feels, he becomes totally unaware of the presence of the stick. But what is the nature of this union? It is not a mixture. It is not a merely external conjunction. It is not the mere event of a moment, but something which intrinsically extends over time. Earlier, we called it an active process. But in this process, what happens to the stick? Undoubtedly, it remains a stick, but as it is involved in the process, it is somehow lifted out of itself into a higher level activity. It is endowed with properties beyond itself,which, though it does not possess them independently, do belong to it, as it is a part of the compound process. The stick remains a stick, but it is transformed, and this transformation is able to be described in active, dynamic terms. Let us now think in these terms of the transformation undergone by the humanity assumed by the Word.

Thus, describing the assumed humanity, Severus says that it was not able to be downtrodden as far as sinning is concerned, but that it was capable of receiving the cutting of iron and other torments, since the incarnate Word allowed that it should suffer this when he wished.[115] Then, dwelling more clearly on the nature of the transformation, he twice refers to Cyril's *De Recta Fide ad Theodosium*. There Cyril argued that just as the flesh, because it became the flesh of the Word, was above the grasp of death and corruption, so too the soul, because it became the soul of him who knew not how to sin, possessed an established and unchanging position in all good things.[116] As we have said, we will return to this, in the examination of Severus' *Second Letter*. But it is not a new point, only an unfolding of what we have already seen. The issue is the implication for the

humanity of being possessed by the Word, and as we have already tried to argue, possession by the Word, in Severus and Cyril, is something which is active, intentional and soteriological.

Severus' intention in this section has been to stress the real humanity assumed by the Word. The Word remained who he was, even though he became flesh,[117] and he brought no rejection of the flesh, or transformation of the human ousia.[118] However, in a final quotation from Cyril's *De Recta Fide*, he inadvertently spoils much of the progress he might have made with Sergius. Though Cyril's intention is to teach an active, soteriological union, there is at times a tension in his language between more dynamic and more static forms of expression. On this occasion, Cyril spoke of Christ as being "composed so as to become one in the middle from human properties and from those which are above man",[119] and as we have already seen from our examination of Sergius, he picked upon this phrase, seeing it as an encouragement for his idea that Christ, as the product of the union, is some kind of new, third entity.[120] In fact, no impression could have been further from what Severus intended. Severus at least twice[121] quoted Cyril's letter to Valerian of Iconium, explicitly denying that God and man came together to make up a "Christ"; rather the Word, being God, partook of flesh and blood like us, *ἵνα Θεὸς ἐνανθρωπήσας νοῆται, καὶ τὴν ἡμετέραν σάρκα λαβών, καὶ ἰδίαν αὐτὴν ποιησάμενος.*[122]

One sees the same dangerous language in Gregory Nazianzen, who was, of course, a source to both Sergius and Severus.[123] The product of the union is not a "Christ", one of a new class,[124] and in consequence his activity is not something monolithic of a self-consistent quality, but something adaptative, involving an interplay of giving and receiving, as we have argued.[125]

We can deal with the remaining points of the letter quickly. If Sergius has absorbed all Severus' points, he should, Severus claims, confess Emmanuel from two natures, and not deny difference and particularity with respect to natural quality of the natures from which the one Christ is brought to union.[126] He again denounces all duality after the union, and denies that instead of a duality he introduces "two united natures".[127] He also, and unfortunately, quotes another instance of Cyril's more static uses of language, in this case from the *Second Letter to Succensus*: *δι' ἀμφοῖν δὲ τὸ ἕν ἀποτελεῖσθαι ζῶον.*[128] Sergius is warned as well not to think that only bodily things can have natural quality.[129]

In a final word of advice, Severus suggests Sergius leaves doctrinal matters to those who are more mature, and that if he is ever com-

pelled to make a pronouncement, he only lay down the Nicene Creed.[130] Severus ends the letter by blessing Sergius and praying for him.

Notes

1. cf. EM p. 71.28–72.1.
2. cf. EM p. 72.22–24.
3. EM p. 71.1–3.
4. EM p. 71.4–7.
5. Lebon, *Chalkedon*, p. 548 notes that Sergius' position is like that of Timothy Aelurus (cf. p. 545) and Philoxenos (cf. p. 546). All three, according to Lebon, saw in the preservation of "la propriété des natures" not the safekeeping of the permanent distinction of the reality of the divinity and the humanity after the union, but the mark of the division of Christ into two individual subjects.
6. cf. EM p. 74. cf. also Lebon, *ibid.*, p. 537, and p. 549 n.44, where Severus' reliance on Cyril is noted.
7. cf. EM p. 74.19–20.
8. cf. EM p. 74.29–75.5.
9. cf. EM p. 75.6–18.
10. cf. EM p. 75.20–21.
11. cf. EM p. 74.19–20, 24–26.
12. cf. EM p. 75.25–27.
13. cf. EM p. 75.29–31.
14. *συνουσιαστής*. The name was given to the exaggerated Monophysites who were supposed to follow Apollinaris, in asserting that Christ's flesh in the union had become of one *οὐσία* with the Godhead. It is then, essentially, to teach a loss of the integrity of the Godhead and the humanity in the union. Severus' point is that if the Synousiast were to say that God the Word is seen, this might be taken as saying that the Word is somehow seen in his Godhead, and this is the position of confusion of the natures which Severus wants to show he is avoiding. Diodore of Tarsus used the word as a term of abuse for the Apollinarians, and wrote *Contra Synousiastas* (cf. *Fragments*, PG 33.1560Aff., and ap. Leontius B. *Nest. et Eut.*, PG 86.1385Dff.). Cyril of Alexandria also made it clear that he taught no confusion of the natures, writing *Contra Synousiastas* (see extensive *Fragments*, Pusey edn., Vol. 5, pp. 476–91). For modern notes, see R. V. Sellers, *Two Ancient Christologies*, p. 53, note 2; C. E. Raven, *Apollinarianism*, p. 123, note 1; p. 274. Also cf. G. W. H. Lampe, *A Patristic Greek Lexicon*, s.v.; J. Quasten, *Patrology*, Vol. 3, p. 400 (on Diodore).
15. cf. EM p. 76.5–6.
16. cf. EM p. 76.7 ff.
17. cf. EM p. 76.17–21.
18. To defend himself against accusations of Synousiasm from the Chalcedonians, Severus develops this insight of Cyril's, that it is possible *to recognise* two natures in Christ after the union, but *ἐν θεωρίᾳ μόνῃ*. The expression and argument occur chiefly in his anti-Chalcedonian works. It is discussed extensively by Lebon, *op. cit.* pp. 501–509. For example, cf. *Philalethes* (CSCO 133 (Syr. 68)), p. 223.3–12; p. 261.13–23.
19. EM p. 77.8–10.
20. cf. EM p. 77.11–17.
21. EM p. 77.26–27.
22. cf. EM p. 77.28–78.3.
23. EM p. 78.5–7, and PG. 76.105A (= *Adv. Nest. Lib. II.* Pusey edn. Vol. 6, p. 128.25–27).
24. cf. e.g. EM p. 75.3–4, 9.

25. cf. e.g. EM p. 75.20–22.
26. cf. EM p. 76.20.
27. cf. EM p. 77.22–23.
28. cf. EM p. 75.3–4, 9.
29. cf. EM p. 77.26–27.
30. EM p. 78.16.
31. A particularity which implied the independent existence of the thing it characterised would be very similar to Sergius' understanding of "propriety". As we noted above, when we discussed Sergius' *Apology* and eventual conversion to Severus' point of view, the concept of "particularity as to independent existence" was one which Severus specifically rejected: cf. EM p. 80.26–81.1 and p. 158.26–27. There is a useful discussion of this in Lebon, *op. cit.* pp. 535–536. Lebon shows Severus' avoidance of what he calls "la propriété quant à l'existence".
32. cf. EM p. 78.24–30.
33. cf. EM p. 77.28–78.3.
34. cf. EM p. 79.3–5.
35. This aspect of the *communicatio idiomatum* in Cyril is excellently put by Dr. Constantine Dratsellas: "By *communicatio idiomatum* Cyril asserts that the two natures are, as we have seen, inseparably united in the One Person, not being confused, and that they both transfer and communicate their properties, their Idiomata, to the One Person which is their centre, and in which they are united, and not to each other". "Questions on Christology of St Cyril of Alexandria", *Abba Salama* (Athens), 6 (1974), p. 222.
36. cf. EM p. 78.19–80.5 (especially p. 80.1–5).
37. EM p. 79.12–14.
38. cf. EM p. 80.9–16.
39. cf. EM p. 80.17–18.
40. EM p. 80.23–81.1: "And we call this a particularity and name it: (that is) that which (lies) in difference of natural quality, which (definition) I will not cease repeating many times, and not that (which lies) in (independent) parts, and natures in independent existence are implied".
41. *To Oecumenius, Collected Letters*, p. 177.3–6.

The text is edited by E. W. Brooks, who supplies an English translation. I have departed from Brooks' translation, to bring the terminology into line with that which I have used in the letters between Severus and Sergius. As an aim of this study is to introduce the Christology of Severus to the reader without Syriac, I have quoted the extract in English. However, the reference is to the lines of the Syriac text, and this is the practice which will be followed. cf. also *To Eleusinius*, *ibid.*, pp. 201–203. Eleusinius did not want to recognise difference between the natures in Christ, since he held as a presupposition that difference implied division. Severus has to wean him from this view, which is not unlike that of Sergius, showing that in a "natural union" division ceases, but "the difference and particularity, as it were in the natural quality of the elements which have come together into one, is preserved" (p. 203, lines 5–6).

42. For example, cf. *Philalethes*, *op. cit.*, p. 323.2–3, where Severus quotes Nestorius, to show that Nestorius understood that the natures in their independence were retained; pp. 326–328, where Severus tries to show the divisive implications of granting an independence to the humanity, and diagnoses this error in the Tome of Leo, and the Chalcedonian definition.
43. For example, cf. Cyril, *Scholia XXXVII*, Pusey edn. Vol. 6, p. 574. 15 ff; *Adv. Nest. Lib. V*, PG 76.224 C–D = Pusey edn. Vol. 6, p. 220.28–221.3; *QUSC*, PG 75.1289C = Pusey edn. Vol. 7, p. 364.2–5.
44. *Collected Letters*, p. 178.11–12.
45. *Ibid.*, p. 210.8–12. I have here quoted Brooks' translation. These letters which Brooks collected and translated, though little referred to, are a store-house of interesting material, and at times are quite beautiful in their expression of Severus' Christology.

46. EM p. 71.28–72.1.

47. *Collected Letters*, pp. 201–203.

48. cf. *Philalethes*, *op. cit.*, p. 215.11–13, for Severus' comment.

49. cf. Cyril, *Ep. II ad Succ.*, PG 77.241B = ACO I, 1, 6a, p. 159.18–160.2.

50. cf. EM p. 78.21–23; p. 80.23–81.1.

51. *Collected Letters*, p. 177.14–178.1. I have followed Brooks' translation, except that where he says "property", I have translated "particularity". The Syriac noun underlying "manifestation" is ܦܘܪܫܢܐ.

52. The Syriac underlying "quality" is ܦܘܪܫܢܐ, not ܡܦܪܫܘܬܐ which we might expect. For a similar use of ܦܘܪܫܢܐ see *Collected Letters*, p. 182.9. However, ܡܦܪܫܘܬܐ is used as we might expect from the pattern in the Severus–Sergius *Letters* in the *First Letter to Oecumenius*, *ibid.*, p. 177.1 and p. 177.3. See EM p. 109, marginal note to ܡܦܪܫܘܬܐ.

53. *Ibid.*, p. 204.6–10.

54. cf. e.g. Cyril, *Adv. Nest. Lib. II*, PG 76.61A6–12 = Pusey edn. Vol. 6, p. 94.16–22; *Contra Diod. Tars. Episc.*, *ibid.*, Vol. 5, p. 493.24 ff; *Contra Syn.*, *ibid.*, p. 476.11 ff; *Scholia II*, *ibid.*, Vol. 6, p. 504.4–9.

55. *Collected Letters*, p. 201.3–5.

56. It is worth referring here to Severus' very interesting comment to number 181 in the Cyrillian florilegium in the *Philalethes*. If one only recognises diversity of the natures in difference in natural quality, then one will not attack the "unattackable diversity" (ܠܐܚܪܢܘܬܐ ܗܝ، ܠܐ ܡܬܟܬܫܢܘܬܐ), and will not divide the one Christ. *Philalethes*, *op. cit.*, p. 343.6–18.

57. *Collected Letters*, p. 177.12–14. It is Severus' basic soteriological concern that underlies his insistence that the incarnation is a union in which difference is intrinsic. This is clearly brought out in his *Letter to the Emesenes*: ". . . . in the dispensatory conjunction (ܢܩܝܦܘܬܐ) he is not without flesh . . . . but he kept (the Godhead) sublime and pure and unmixed . . . . as also he did not change the manhood. . . . ." *ibid.*, p. 233, lines 1–2; 5–7. Severus similarly stresses that the unity in Christ is a unity of such a sort that it preserves the soteriological difference in *Philalethes*, *op. cit.*, p. 344.18–28. cf. Cyril, *οὐκοῦν τὸ ἀσύγχυτον . . . . εὖ μάλα τετηρηκώς, φησὶν ἐν ἡμῖν ἐσκηνωκέναι τὸν Λόγον*. *Scholia XXVII*, Pusey edn., Vol. 6, p. 548.24–5; *Ep. II ad Succ.*, PG 77. 241 C1–4 (= ACO I, 1. 6a, p. 160.4–7). cf. also Sellers, *op. cit.*, p. 93, where Sellers emphasises the anti-Eutychian stand in Cyril.

58. cf. e.g. the way Severus quotes Cyril: *To Oecumenius*, *Collected Letters*, p. 177.9–12; p. 178.10–11; *To the Emesenes*, *ibid.*, p. 231.9–12. cf. also Cyril, *Adv. Nest. Lib. II*, PG 76.64A.6–8 (= Pusey edn. Vol. 6, p. 105.19–21); *Contra Diod. Tars. Episc.*, Pusey edn. Vol. 5, p. 494.11–14.

59. *To Oecumenius*, *Collected Letters*, p. 194.5–7: "It is not confessing the particularity of the natures from which Emmanuel comes that we avoid . . . . but distributing and dividing the properties to each of the natures". (Brooks' translation).

60. *To the Emesenes*, *ibid.*, p. 232.7–8.

61. *To Oecumenius*, *Collected Letters*, p. 178.13; p. 183.7; *To the Emesenes*, *ibid.*, p. 233.1–2.

62. In this model I have tried deliberately to show Severus' Christology as something in which the inter-relation and interdependence of concepts can be shown to be alive, as the understanding of the unity is seen to be dependent upon the motive for the unity. When it is understood that the *σύνοδος* is not merely the event of Christ's conception, but the whole course of his redemptive life, this yields an illumination which passes back to, and enriches, the other concepts. My model is based upon the analysis of action by Michael Polanyi (cf. *The Tacit Dimension*, London, 1967). Any compound action could have served equally well as an example: in typing, for example, the typist is involved in a union with the typewriter, insofar as he disattends from it, letting it be internalised to himself, and pours his attention onto the message that he is typing.

63. The suggestion that Sergius teaches a fusion, which is an illuminating idea, is

made in passing by N. Zambolotsky: "The Christology of Severus of Antioch", in *Ekklesiastikos Pharos*, 58 pts. 3–4, (1976), p. 380.

64. cf. EM p. 72.12–16.

65. cf. EM p. 81–82 (esp. p. 82.8–16). cf. also Lebon, *Chalkedon*, pp. 554–555.

66. cf. EM p. 82.17–31.

67. cf. EM p. 83.1–11.

68. cf. EM p. 83.14–19. That Severus, following Cyril, allowed one to recognise variety in the utterances, but refused to separate them out, cf. *Philalethes*, *op. cit.* pp. 201.14–202.7. The Nestorians, he held, introduced the idea of two agents: cf. p. 203.19–27. In Cyril, for example, see *QUSC*, PG 75.1328C (=Pusey edn. Vol. 7, p. 395.30–396.8). cf. also Lebon, *Chalkedon*, pp. 543–4; 552–3.

69. EM p. 84.24–28; PL 54.767A–B. It is worth noting that in his quotation Severus omits the words, "*cum alterius communione*", and so makes the Tome appear more Nestorian than it actually is.

70. cf. EM p. 84.28–85.2.

71. EM p. 85.6.

72. cf. EM p. 85.7.

73. EM p. 85.12. This passage was almost certainly misunderstood by Dr. Chesnut, who, in her *Three Monophysite Christologies*, *op. cit.*, translated it as follows: ". . . . it appears that he used the strength of his soul as God incarnate . . . ." (p. 34).

74. *Περὶ τοῦ ἄνθρακος*. See Pusey edn., Vol. 6, pp. 514–517.

75. Severus, *To Oecumenius*, *Collected Letters*, p. 180.12–13. Cyril, *Scholia IX* (Pusey edn. Vol. 6), p. 516.3–5. The Greek *μεταστοιχειώσαντα* is rendered by ܫܚܠܦ in Syriac.

76. Severus, *ibid.*, p. 181.1–2. Cyril, *ibid.*, p. 516.8.

77. Severus, *ibid.*, p. 181.5–6. Cyril, *ibid.*, p. 516.12–14. The Greek *οἰκειούμενος* is translated by ܡܕܒܪܬܐ.

78. Severus, *ibid.*, p. 181.6, 8–9.

79. Severus, *ibid.*, p. 182. Leo, *Ep. XXVIII*, Section 3. PL 54.765A. Severus refers to this passage in his *Second Letter to Sergius*: cf. EM p. 122.13–29. Selective quotation again exaggerates the Nestorian appearance of the Tome.

80. cf. Severus, *To Oecumenius*, *ibid.*, p. 182.13–14.

81. Severus, *ibid.*, p. 183.5–6. Cyril, *Apol. contra Theod.*, PG 76.441B–C (=Pusey edn. Vol. 6 p. 476.11–12). There is a similar idea in Cyril's *Adv. Anthropomorphitas*, though "often" is used instead of "sometimes": ". . . . *διὰ τῆς ἰδίας αὐτοῦ σαρκὸς πολλάκις ἐνήργει ὡς ἰδίαν ἔχων αὐτην* . . . . ." PG. 76.1117C.

82. Severus may appear ambiguous here. He is not claiming that once united to the Word, the human nature ceased to be human nature, but that it did not have an independent existence. See Severus, *To Thomas*, ". . . . the peculiarity of natural union is that the hypostases are in composition and are perfect without diminution, but refuse to continue an individual existence so as to be numbered as two . . . .", *Collected Letters*, p. 210.8–10.

83. Severus, *To Oecumenius*, *ibid.*, p. 183.6–9.

84. This is a concept which will be illustrated in Severus' *Second Letter to Sergius*.

85. Severus, *To Oecumenius*, *ibid.*, 184.9–10. Brooks' translation.

86. *ἔσθ' ὅτε*.

87. Severus, *ibid.*, p. 185.4–5, 7; Gregory Nazianzen, *Or. XL*, *In Sanctum Baptisma*. PG 36.400C: . . . . *αὐτὸς γὰρ καὶ τοῦ παθεῖν ἦν ἑαυτῷ ταμίας* . . . .

88. Severus, *ibid.*, p. 185.7–9.

89. "ordering the mystery of the economy with flesh *through the ways that* beseem it." *Adv. Nest. Lib. IV*, PG 76.177B 10–12 (=Pusey edn. Vol. 6, p. 185.5–7).

90. *QUSC*, PG 75.1261B 11–14 (= Pusey edn. Vol. 7, p. 340.20–22). For other examples where Cyril stresses this aspect of the union, cf. *Adv. Nest. Lib. III*, PG 76.137C (=Pusey edn. Vol. 6, p. 153.26–7); 153B–C (= Pusey, p. 166.5–8); 153D (=Pusey, p. 166.22–24).

91. EM p. 85.20.

92. EM p. 80.1. (Cyril, *Adv. Nest. Lib. III*, PG 76.137C 4–5 = Pusey edn. Vol. 6, p. 153.26).

93. Cyril, *QUSC.*, PG 75.1337 B10–11 (= Pusey edn. Vol. 7, p. 404.5–6).

94. Cyril, *Contra Syn.*, Pusey edn. Vol. 5, p. 479.17–19. For a similar stress that the inhomination is inherently restorative, cf. *QUSC.*, PG 75.1320D (= Pusey edn. Vol. 7, p. 389.14–19); 1304D–5A (= Pusey, p. 376.6–10); 1268D (= Pusey, p. 345.14–16).

95. "being full, and *giving* to all from his own fulness, in human wise *receives*, making his own our poverty". *QUSC.*, PG 75.1320C (= Pusey, p. 389.7–9). For another example of this interplay, cf. PG 75.1268C (= Pusey, p. 345.3–7).

96. cf. EM p. 71.28–72.1.

97. EM p. 72.9–11.

98. cf. Lebon, *Chalkedon*, pp. 549–50. Lebon agrees (cf. p. 550 n. 47) that Severus has perverted the thought of Sergius to refute him.

99. This is evident from EM p. 86.18–21, where he writes, "How is it not absurd to speak of (just) two properties or two activities? For there are many properties and not just two, of every nature".

100. EM p. 87.17–19.

101. cf. p. 88.5–8. For an account of the Monophysite stress upon the formula ἐκ δύο φύσεων, cf. Lebon, *op. cit.*, pp. 514–15. Lebon shows how Cyril adopted the expression to defend himself against the charge of being an Apollinarian or Synousiast (Lebon, *op. cit.*, pp. 515–516).

102. EM p. 88.11–14.

103. EM p. 88.18–19.

104. cf. EM p. 72.17–20.

105. EM p. 72.23–24.

106. cf. EM p. 88.28–89.3.

107. cf. EM p. 89.6–9.

108. cf. EM p. 89.11–23.

109. cf. EM p. 90.4–6.

110. cf. EM p. 90.8–12, and Gregory Nazianzen, *Ep. CI* (*I ad Cled.*) PG 37.177C. Severus again stresses an actual incarnation, by immediately continuing the same quotation from Gregory in his *Second Letter to Oecumenius*, *Collected Letters*, p. 190.6–8: "Whoever says that the man was formed, and afterwards God crept in, is condemned: for this is not a birth of God, but an escape from birth".

111. cf. EM p. 90.15–19, and Cyril, *QUSC*, PG 75.1264B (= Pusey edn. Vol. 7, p. 342.6–10).

112. cf. EM p. 90.23–27.

113. Cyril, *Thesaurus XXIV*, PG 75.397C. This remarkable passage is quoted by Dratsellas *op. cit.*, p. 209, note 2.

114. EM p. 90.21–23. For Severus' insistence that the Word's sharing in humanity is voluntary and intentional, cf. EM p. 91.3–4; *Collected Letters*, p. 184.13–185.2; *Philalethes*, *op. cit.*, p. 186.7–16; p. 340.22–27.

115. cf. EM p. 91.14–18.

116. cf. EM p. 92.9–15, 18–24. The question of the nature of Christ's sinlessness is excellently discussed by Dratsellas, *op. cit.*, pp. 224–226, within the context of his account of the *communicatio idiomatum* in Cyril.

117. cf. EM p. 93.2–3.

118. cf. EM p. 93.11–12.

119. EM p. 92.28–30. Cyril, *De Recta Fide ad Theod.*, PG 76.1193B (= Pusey edn. Vol. 7, p. 134.13–14): ἀνθρωπίνοις τε αὖ καὶ τοῖς ὑπὲρ ἄνθρωπον ἰδιώμασιν εἰς ἕν τι τὸ μεταξὺ συγκείμενος.

120. cf. EM p. 102.8; p. 121.2 ff; p. 161.6 ff.

121. *Collected Letters*, pp. 230.14–231.4; *Philalethes*, *op. cit.*, p. 305.9–13. This point is picked out by Lebon, *op. cit.*, p. 488: "Il est donc clair que, dans l'expression μία φύσις σύνθετος, la μία φύσις est celle du Λόγος ἄσαρκος, la divinité, et que σύνθετος,

elle n'est pas combinée avec l'humanité en une essence spécifique de caractère mixte, mais elle a attiré l'humanité dans l'union et l'unité de son existence individuelle".

122. PG 77.257D.

123. In his *First Letter to Cledonius*, Gregory wrote of the natures: τὰ γὰρ ἀμφότερα ἓν τῇ συγκράσει PG 37.180A; and in his *Fourth Theological Oration*, εἰ γὰρ καὶ τὸ συναμφότερον ἕν, ἀλλ' οὐ τῇ φύσει, τῇ δὲ συνόδῳ τούτων. Τί ἂν γένοιτο γνωριμώτερον; PG 36.113B. As Sellers' notes (*op. cit.*, p. 76. n. 6), with ἀλλ' οὐ τῇ φύσει Gregory rejects Eutychianism, but he could have been clearer, and εἷς would have been better than ἕν.

124. cf. John of Damascus, *De Fide Orthodoxa*, Bk. 3, Ch. 3 (PG 94.993A). As John so clearly sees, there is no predicable form of Christlihood, and Christ is not an individual (one of a class).

125. This is one point where some questions may be levelled at the judgement of Sellers. Sellers contends (*op. cit.* pp. 251–252) that Severus *adopts* the expression μία ἐνέργεια σύνθετος from Pseudo-Dionysius, and that it is expressive of what both the Alexandrine and Antiochene teachers were meaning to say. This may be so, but one might suggest that what Severus means is quite different from what Dionysius meant. In his very puzzling Letter 3 to John the Hegoumenos (pp. 309–310 in Franz Diekamp: *Doctrina Patrum de Incarnatione Verbi*, Münster, 1907), Severus quotes from the Fourth Letter of Ps-Dionysius, "ἀλλ' ἀνδρωθέντος θεοῦ καινήν τινα τὴν θεανδρικὴν ἐνέργειαν ἡμῖν πεπολιτευμένος". (Diekamp, *op. cit.*, p. 309.19–20; Ps-Dionysius, PG 3.1072C). Lebon, surely convincingly, writes, "ce n'est pas de son propre mouvement, mais sur l'invitation venue d'ailleurs, que Sévère cite et examine ici le texte dionysien". (Lebon, "Le Pseudo-Denys L'Aréopagite et Sévère d'Antioch", RHE, 26 (1930), p. 894.) So it is as a consequence of citing the Pseudo-Dionysian passage that Severus, in this Letter to John the Hegoumenos, uses the expression ἐνέργεια σύνθετος (Diekamp, *op. cit.*, p. 310.4). In the same article (RHE, 26, p. 895), Lebon writes that "l'épithète θεανδρική s'appliquant soit à la nature, soit à l'hypostase, soit à l'activité du Verbe incarné, n'appartient nullement, si l'on en juge par les textes, à la terminologie de la dogmatique christologique de Sévère". When faced with the Dionysian phrase, he concludes that Severus "ne peut comprendre cette activité *théandrique* que comme une activité *composée* mais *unique*" (*op. cit.*, pp. 894–895). We have already shown the stress on the *human* activity of Christ in both Severus and Cyril. This stress on the human activity is quite lacking in Ps-Dionysius. Of the Christ of Ps-Dionysius, René Roques writes, "La communication des idiomes est poussée si loin qu'il n'y a plus de distinction réelle entre les vocables du Sauveur. *Jesus* n'est plus le nom de l'homme, mais un doublet du *Verbe*. Il possède en effet l'attribut de la simplicité (ὁ ἁπλοῦς Ἰησοῦς), l'unité et le caractère caché qui conviennent à Dieu". And, "Si les caractères de la personne divine du Verbe sont facilement reconnaissables dans l'ensemble de l'oeuvre, nous y chercherions vainement une doctrine sur l'humanité du Christ". (René Roques: *L'Univers Dionysien: Structure Hiérarchique du Monde selon le Pseudo-Denys*, Lyon, 1954, pp. 310 and 312). Because of this lack of attention to the soteriological role of the humanity in Christ, we would argue that what Ps-Dionysius means by ἐνέργεια θεανδρική must be quite different from what Severus could mean. Lebon devotes two articles in RHE to disputing the claim of P. J. Stiglmayr that Ps-Dionysius was, in fact, Severus of Antioch. (Vol. 26, 1930, pp. 880–915 and Vol. 28, 1932, pp. 296–313).

126. cf. EM p. 93.24–28.

127. cf. EM p. 93.28–94.8. The Chalcedonian defence, under Nephalius and John the Grammarian, claimed to avoid Nestorianism, in teaching two united and not separated natures. On this, and Severus' reaction to this move, see Lebon, *Chalkedon*, p. 503 ff.

128. EM p. 94.15–17 and PG 77.245B (= ACO, I, 1, 6a, p. 162.8–9).

129. cf. EM p. 94.18–95.11. cf. also Lebon, *op. cit.*, p. 538 (and note 15), where this is briefly commented on.

130. cf. EM p. 95.16–96.1.

VII The Second Letter of Severus

Severus' *Second Letter to Sergius* is rambling and repetitive. It deals with little that has not at least been touched upon already. Our aim in the introduction to Severus' *First Letter* was to give the reader an entrance into Severus' system and vision. Now that we have that outline, we can deal with his argument more briefly. As this *Second Letter* is also more relaxed and far less cryptic, the argument will be presented in outline, and Severus' points will be referred back to the structure which was explained earlier, while notes are added to new aspects as they arise.

Severus begins by saying that from his previous letter, Sergius should know that he should confess particularity as to natural quality of the natures from which there is the one Christ. He emphasises that in Christ, there is one person and one hypostasis: that is, there is just one subject, one nature belonging to the Word, meaning incarnate.[1] He praises Sergius for his honesty in questioning, saying that he welcomes a man with an enquiring mind, who does not merely agree with him. For his part, he is very ready to enter into discussion, provided this discussion remains within reasonable limits.[2]

Severus re-opens the discussion by requoting for Sergius a passage from Cyril, which he had quoted earlier in his *First Letter*.[3] Cyril wrote: *Παρενηνεγμένου γε μὴν εἰς μέσον ἡμῖν μυστηρίου τοῦ κατὰ Χριστὸν, ὁ τῆς ἑνώσεως λόγος οὐκ ἀγνοεῖ μὲν τὴν διαφορὰν, ἐξίστησι δὲ τὴν διαίρεσιν· οὐ συγχέων [τὰς φύσεις] ἢ ἀνακιρνῶν τὰς φύσεις.*[4] The point of this quotation was that though differences between the natures is maintained (for good soteriological reasons), division is removed (again for soteriological reasons),[5] but not through confusion or mixture. Sergius had shown in his own *Second Letter* that he could not understand a (category of) union other than confusion or mixture, and he insisted that the natures be understood as mixed, claiming that in this he was merely following Gregory Nazianzen.[6] The real problem, as we again have seen, is that Sergius understands the problem of the union in a way which is different from Gregory, Cyril or Severus. He is trying to understand and express some kind of internal union.

Severus now urges Sergius to apply himself, and make real efforts to understand.[7] He shows that the quotation from Cyril does not merely deny mixture and confusion, but does in fact give an account of the union, but in active terms, in terms of the agency of the Word. The Word partook of flesh and blood, just as also the children participated in the same things.[8] Severus now picks upon this metaphor: our own construction as men is neither a mixture nor a juxtaposition (and thus it can be seen that the alternative "mixture or juxtaposition" does not form a total monopoly upon modes of union), but it is inexpressible, and even so it is less wonderful than the union in Emmanuel. Thus, why should we be obliged to apply these categories of mixture, juxtaposition or confusion to Emmanuel?[9] He presses this point home by referring to Cyril: the fact of union may be accomplished in many ways, for example by *παράθεσις*, *μίξις* and *κρᾶσις*. But the union of God the Word to our nature is not one of these, but is above our comprehension. But incomprehensibility and inexpressibility are not unfamiliar: our own construction is beyond our comprehension, and even if this is utterly inferior to the truth, the union of Emmanuel may be understood as being not unlike this.[10] We have already, earlier, had reason to consider the value of the picture of the union in man as an illustration of the union in Emmanuel. It is a useful illustration, in that the union in man is a dynamic rather than a static one, but it is still a self-contained union. Severus now turns back to Sergius. How can Sergius not see that here there is a union which is neither Eutychian (involving mixture or confusion) nor Nestorian (relying on juxtaposition)?[11] Can Sergius not see that something else is involved?[12] Severus' point is that here we have a union which can only be understood in the light of its external, soteriological point. But Sergius, seeing the union as being self-contained, is committed to looking for an internal unity: to him, we are obliged to speak of two natures unless we can confess that at one time Christ had one ousia and quality. While this is Sergius' position, Severus suggests it is merely a deception for him to claim that he agrees with Severus in confessing difference and particularity in natural quality of the natures.[13]

Thus, Sergius thinks it is impossible to say that Christ is one (that is, internally and self-consistently) unless he passes to one ousia. Severus now asks him what "mixture without confusion" is: the category of union that Sergius seems to make use of.[14] He provides an answer of his own from Cyril: the word "one" is not reserved only for things which are simple, but may also be applied to units which come together by composition. Thus, "one" may be applied

not just to things which are internally simple, and of one quality, but may also be applied to single agents.[15] The elements which make up a man are different and not consubstantial, but they complete one *man*: that is, these non-consubstantial elements do not maintain independence, but make up one active subject.[16] Similarly, the *one* nature of God the Word incarnate does not imply confusion or mixture (simply because there is one nature), nor that the human nature is removed or stolen away. It is sufficient to say that the Word was "incarnate", to show that the human nature is not diminished or removed.[17] The point which Severus is trying to make through Cyril is perhaps more clearly made for us in Cyril's *Quod Unus Sit Christus*. There it is put to Cyril that if the nature of the Word incarnate is one, surely one needs to say that some mixture and confusion took place, with the nature of the man being lost? For what is the nature of man, compared with the glory of the Godhead?[18] Cyril's answer is typical, and truly remarkable: it is not impossible for God who loves man to make himself endurable to the measures of humanity.[19] He pointed to God coming in fire onto the bush in the wilderness: yet how is a tree not a thing that has no alliance with fire? The point is that, for those with eyes to see it, here is a union of such a type that the humanity, far from being eliminated, is specifically and intrinsically upheld. Once again we see the absolute necessity for recognising the soteriological dimension to the union. This point raises in a very acute form the question of the status of the humanity in the soteriological union. It is not independent; it is not diminished, so what is its role? Severus comes to this question shortly. First he rounds off the argument at this stage.

He gives us an additional quotation from *Quod Unus Sit Christus* that not only what is simple is called "one", and then from *De Trinitate ad Hermiam*, that God the Word, without damage in any way, and preserving the glory of his nature, took up manhood, being understood one Son from two natures.[20] He then turns back to the attack: if, as Sergius has heard so often, composition is above reason and inexpressible, why does Sergius resort to mixture and confusion to understand the union? If the inhomination were like a mixture, and one of the constituents ceased being what it is, there would be nothing remarkable in that.[21] Severus now refers to Athanasius. We have already suggested that Sergius viewed the union of the incarnation as it were from the outside. He was a kind of theological behaviourist, refusing to understand the purposive dimension to the union. He began, according to our picture of him, with two pre-existing and inert natures, and his problem was how to unite them.

As such, his questions were "How?"; "In what way?". The incarnation became a problem needing only a technical solution. The question of "How?" blinded him from the questions "Why?" and "Who?", which could have taken him inside the intention of the Word. This is Athanasius' point: by asking the wrong questions, the heretics have thought of a dwelling place instead of an incarnation, and a human activity instead of union and composition.[22]

Severus now develops the argument by returning to the question of the status of the humanity in the soteriological union he is describing. He again turns to Sergius: how can Sergius confuse what he says with the teachings of Nestorius? That is, how can Sergius not see that with him, the humanity in the union has a different role and status from that which it has on Nestorius' understanding? If we say with Severus that God the Word himself assumed our composition and participated like us in flesh and blood, we do not say that first of all an independent infant was formed in the womb, and then through the love of friendship the Word dwelt in him, and gave him the title and rank of Son.[23] To prove that this is the Nestorian view of the role of the humanity Severus quotes a fragment[24] in which Cyril quotes Diodore. In this, it is alleged that it is Diodore's opinion that while our Lord was in the womb of the Virgin, he did not have the rank of Sonship, but when he was formed and became the temple to God the Word, which receives the Only-Begotten, he took up the rank of the name, and participated also in the rank itself.[25] Against this view, Severus quotes Cyril: in the first beginnings of the body's becoming firm in the womb, it was holy as the body of Christ, and one sees no time in which it did not belong to him.[26] Now, what is the importance of this difference of approach, and what does it mean?

We have said that Severus is trying to explain the role and continuing status of the humanity within the union. He insists here that the humanity at no point had an independent status: at no point did it not belong to the Word. But if it was never independent, what, precisely, was its status? Severus makes himself clear in his very remarkable *Second Letter to Oecumenius*, which he wrote during his episcopacy.[27] Oecumenius seems to have thought that the two natures from which Emmanuel consists were generalities, covering many hypostases. To get him out of this false opinion, Severus asks him a series of questions. Does Oecumenius call the flesh which God the Word voluntarily united to himself a specimen or a generality: that is, one soul-possessing hypostasis, or the whole human generality?[28] One soul-possessing body. Thus, Severus says, it was a union

not of generalities, but of "special hypostases".[29] We knew this much, and have met this terminology before. But Severus now adds: "And do not think that hypostases in all cases have a distinct person assigned to them, so that we should be thought, like the impious Nestorius, to speak of a union of persons".[30] Severus rams home the theological point: he quotes the letter attributed to Athanasius, to Jovian: *Ἅμα γὰρ σὰρξ, ἅμα Θεοῦ Λόγου σὰρξ .... ἐν αὐτῷ γὰρ καὶ τὴν ὑπόστασιν ἔσχεν*[31], and Cyril's *Second Letter to Nestorius*: *οὐ γὰρ εἴρηκεν ἡ γραφὴ, ὅτι ὁ Λόγος ἀνθρώπου πρόσωπον ἥνωσεν ἑαυτῷ, ἀλλ' ὅτι γέγονε σάρξ*,[32] but it is the implication of the point that is important in our context. The humanity that is assumed is not independent, but it is nevertheless real and concrete. It is an hypostasis, but it is non-prosopic. Severus has found a way of expressing that the humanity is both concrete and yet not independent. It is because he has this concept that he can on the one hand deny that he is teaching a juxtaposition, and on the other hand refuse to admit that union brings about a mixture or confusion. It is this concept, that the humanity is real, but only comes into existence in the ownership of the Word, that he has to teach to Sergius. This concept, that the humanity in the union is a non-prosopic hypostasis, which is given a prosopon as it is owned by the Word, is not a substantive Christological concept in itself. Like the concept of *ἰδιότης ὡς ἐν ποιότητι φυσικῇ* which we examined earlier, it is like a rule of theological grammar, or part of the conceptual framework, which allows Severus to express his substantive Christological vision. The concept is very similar to that of enhypostatos which was later formally developed by Leontius of Byzantium.[33] This will become clearer as we see how the concept is used.

To return to Severus' *Second Letter to Sergius*, Severus now contrasts Diodore's account of union, with the role for the humanity which it involves and presupposes, and hypostatic union.[34] He understands Diodore's union as a merely external relation between two persons,[35] while on his account, the flesh had existence in very union with the Word,[36] so that the Word himself is believed without change to have become a child, while he remained what he was, and did not change that which he took up, but humbled himself to gradual growth, and exit and full conception.[37] How, then, Severus asks, can anyone say that he is two (independent) natures or hypostases? We see no time, after the time when the Word "rested" on the Virgin, in which the body did not belong to him.[38] Earlier, we went to great trouble to try to show that Severus' vision of the union in Christ is of something active and purposive which God the Word

does. The understanding we have now of the status of the humanity in the union further helps us to grasp this. It is not a union between two pre-existent and inert things, but a union which is inherently dynamic, as the humanity is brought both into existence and union at the same time. The humanity is only brought to personhood in God the Word: it is thus a *personalising* union. Severus is trying to give us a framework in which we can think of the becoming man of God, of God *as* man.

Severus now returns to the question of the meaning of the word "incarnate", when it is applied to God the Word.[39] God the Word himself, who had existence before the ages, and is simple in ousia, became composite in the economy. The word "incarnate" thus means that the flesh existed in relationship to the Word himself[40] (that is, "*enhypostatically*"), and was not independently completed in its own hypostasis.[41] At the risk of being repetitive, let us ask again what is the nature of this union: what is Severus showing Sergius? The humanity, he tells us, undergoes gradual growth, but it does not exist independently, but is rooted in the person of the Word. The union is thus something which is an on-going process. For all its obvious inadequacies we would refer back to our illustration of the dynamic on-going relation between the blind man and his stick and the sort of unity that is created there.

It is a union in which there is one continuing and active subject. Severus reinforces this, by adding two quotations from Cyril to stress the identity of the eternal Son and the incarnate Word.[42] We have already seen that this is an important part of Cyril's Christology and soteriology: there has saved us not an elder, not an angel, but the Lord himself, not with another's death and the mediation of a mere man, but with his own blood.[43]

Severus next turns to consider Sergius' use of the concept of "mixture" (*κρᾶσις*),[44] which Sergius claimed to borrow from Gregory Nazianzen. As we have noted earlier, Sergius understood this as a mingling to produce one image (ܦܘܪܐ = *εἰκών*) and hypostasis,[45] later describing the resultant unit as "one ousia and quality".[46] Severus allows that Gregory used the word, but denies that he understood it as producing a union of Sergius' type: in Gregory the word is used as a way of trying to express the supreme union, but without there being implied any of the *σύγχυσις* or *μίξις* which occurs between fluid bodies.[47] To substantiate his point, he refers to Cyril, and then to the usage of Gregory himself. According to Cyril, though some of the Fathers used the word *κρᾶσις*, there is no need to fear that this implied an *ἀνάχυσις* as is the case with liquids. The Fathers did not

think in this way, but used the word illustratively, in an attempt to point towards the supreme union. Cyril goes on to show that even the Scriptures use the word metaphorically and illustratively.[48] Gregory does indeed refer to the union as a *μίξις* and *κρᾶσις*,[49] but, and this is Severus' point, he also shows beyond any doubt that whatever his terminology he understands the union of God the Word to the flesh endowed with a soul as a composition, not as a fusion along Sergius' lines. This can be seen from the fact that he attributes the things that are lowly (the sufferings) to the composite one.[50] The point Severus is trying to get across to Sergius is that Gregory's understanding of the union, no matter how misleadingly it is expressed in literal terms, involves an intrinsically soteriological recognition that the lowly things are real, and really belong to the Word, but to the Word *become man* so as to bear and overcome them.[51] There is no question here of a literal mixture to something which is static and in-between, but a real understanding that the Word incarnate is the Word who has assumed humanity to redeem it, *τῷ ὁμοίῳ τὸ ὅμοιον ἀνακαθαίρων*.[52] As Gregory says, in the passage Severus quotes, *Ὃ μὲν ἦν, διέμεινεν· ὃ δὲ οὐκ ἦν, προσέλαβεν*.[53]

Severus sums up from this: Gregory soteriologically recognised the incarnation as a *σύνθεσις*, not as a *κρᾶσις* and *σύγχυσις*, even if he should happen to use the word *κρᾶσις* to illustrate the supreme union.[54] If we were going to look for, and make a literalist exploitation of Gregory's more exaggerated language, we could draw from him utterly contradictory positions: on the one hand he says, *τὸ μὲν ἐθέωσε, τὸ δὲ ἐθεώθη*,[55] which might seem to imply that the flesh was deified, being changed into the ousia of the divinity, and on the other hand he says, *οὐδὲν δὲ χεῖρον εἰπεῖν, καὶ ἀνθρωπισθέντι*,[56] which might seem to imply that God the Word fell to the ousia of humanity. Even the Nestorians can claim verbal support from Gregory, for he wrote, *Ἀπεστάλη μὲν, ἀλλ' ὡς ἄνθρωπος· διπλοῦς γὰρ ἦν*.[57]

The question of the meaning of *διπλοῦς* here is one which Severus will soon return to. For the moment, he hastily assures Sergius that Gregory is not in fact a Nestorian: he does not recognise the Son as being double in natures and hypostases, but understands him as God inhominate, one from two.[58] The point which it is more urgent to explain to Sergius is the meaning of *τὸ δὲ ἐθεώθη*.

We have already touched on this question in Severus' *First Letter*, when we began to consider the implications for the humanity of being "the own" of the Word. The human nature remains a human nature, and the divine nature remains divine, but the human nature, being hypostatically united with the divine, as Dratsellas puts it, "is

elevated as far as it is possible for human nature to be".[59] In terms of our own crude model of the blind man with his stick, while the stick is actually caught up into union with the blind man, it is endowed with properties beyond itself, which it possesses not in its own right, but in virtue of being involved in the active process. Here, Severus tries to explain the word by saying that the flesh shone out with the glory proper to God, and not because it had fallen into the nature of divinity.[60] Gregory himself rejects the idea that the flesh is laid down, while the divinity is stripped of the body.[61] Severus continues that, however it is expressed, the concept does not imply a change of ousia, but that the flesh shares in the glory proper to God.[62] He then refers to Cyril's *First Letter to Succensus*, where it is denied that the body was changed into the nature of divinity, but affirmed that the body of Christ is divine, because it is the body of God.[63]

This gives us, and Sergius, the documentation, but does little to explain the issue. We would maintain that this is a further unfolding of the implications for the humanity of being "the own" of the Word, which lets us see in yet another way that the union, as understood by Cyril and Severus, is an *active*, on-going *process*. To understand this, let us look at the background of the concept in Cyril.

We saw above that Cyril considered the objection that if we say the nature of the Son is one, surely we must say some mixture and confusion took place, for what is the nature of man, compared to the Godhead?[64] Against this, Cyril said it was not impossible for God to make himself endurable to the measures of manhood, and pointed to the bush in the wilderness, which God made able to make support the fire.[65] As a second step, Cyril shows that fire may warm matter, and make it warm, even though it is not warm of its own nature.[66] Similarly, if visible fire can change water, which though itself is cold by nature, into what is contrary to its nature and hot, how can one disbelieve that God the Word made the flesh which was united to him, and was his very own, life-giving?[67]

If this gives the principle, let us now consider the specific case. What, exactly, is the change, if change it is, that the humanity undergoes in union with God the Word? In his fragments *Contra Synousiastas*, Cyril writes of Christ: *Οὐκ εἰς φύσιν θεότητος τὴν ἀτρέπτως τε καὶ ἀσυγχύτως σάρκα μεταστοιχειώσας ὁρᾶται, δόξῃ δὲ μᾶλλον ἰδίᾳ καταφαιδρύνας αὐτὴν νοοῖτ᾽ ἂν εἰκότως καὶ θεοπρεπῶν ἐμπλήσας ἀξιωμάτων.*[68] The humanity, as the own humanity of the Word, is endowed with properties beyond itself. It should, though, be noticed that Cyril does not call this a "change", but a "transelement-

ing" or "transformation" (μεταστοιχείωσις). Cyril wrote in a very similar way in his *Scholia*: ἑνωθέντα μὲν τῇ ἀνθρωπότητι τὸν τοῦ Θεοῦ Λόγον, οὐ μὴν ἀποβεβληκότα τὸ εἶναι ὅ ἐστι, μεταστοιχειώσαντα δὲ μᾶλλον τὸ προσληφθὲν, ἤγουν ἑνωθὲν, εἰς τὴν ἑαυτοῦ δόξαν τε καὶ ἐνέργειαν.[69]

However, what happens to the humanity in the person of Christ did not take place for his sake, but in the light of his soteriological purpose. So this specific μεταστοιχείωσις of the human nature only took place for the sake of its implications for all who believe in him. This general μεταστοιχείωσις is equally clear in Cyril. Against Nestorius, he wrote: πεπονθέναι δέ φαμεν οἰκονομικῶς ἰδίᾳ σαρκὶ τὸν θάνατον, ἵνα πατήσας αὐτὸν, καὶ ἐγηγερμένος, καθὸ πέφυκεν εἶναι ζωὴ καὶ ζωοποιὸς, μεταστοιχειώσῃ πρὸς ἀφθαρσίαν τὸ θανάτῳ τυραννούμενον.[70] In consequence of this, ὡς ἐν ἀπαρχῇ δὲ Χριστῷ, μετεστοιχειώμεθα καὶ ἡμεῖς εἰς τὸ εἶναι καὶ φθορᾶς καὶ ἁμαρτίας κρείττονες.[71]

Earlier, when we examined Severus' understanding of the union, we showed how he saw the humanity as being "non-prosopic" in itself, but "enhypostatised" in the person of the Word. We suggested that Severus was trying to find words to express his understanding that the humanity comes to personhood in the person of the Word: the union is consequently a dynamic, personalising act. We now see, from this examination of μεταστοιχείωσις, another dimension to this: as the humanity is personalised, it is transformed. But this transformation is inherently soteriological. He is transformed, so that we may be also. Yet again we can see that the vision which underlies the position of Cyril and Severus, could hardly be more removed from the picture of the union as a static event, as it is portrayed by Sergius. In Sergius' terms, as we saw in his *First Letter*, Christ can only be described as being like neither God nor man.[72] Like Severus, he sees the figure of the Biblical Christ: the Christ whose face shone on the mountain, and who was nailed to the cross, who turned the water into wine, but refused to make bread out of stones. Unlike Severus, he does not have an adequate apparatus of theological concepts to describe this.

Severus now returns to the question of Christ being "double". Why did the Fathers call Christ διπλοῦς? Severus quotes Cyril, quoting Athanasius, in the Letter *Ad Monachos*: it is the aim of scripture to recognise two sides to Christ; that our Saviour is God the Word who is, and remains, the eternal Son, but who yet became man for our sakes.[73] It is this recognition of the two sides which allows one to see the preservation of the human nature, which is the all-important soteriological dimension to the union. God the Word suffered

not in his divinity, but in his own human nature, to overcome suffering. In consequence, some things are said about him in a human way, and some things as is proper to divinity.[74] Then, injecting a note of greater caution, Severus again refers to Cyril: to say this is not to attribute the human words to another, independent, person, but to attribute them to the Word in his humanity.[75] The form of the words is two-fold, but Christ himself is not double in natures or hypostases. There is again reference to Cyril: Christ *οὐ γάρ τοι διπλοῦς ἐστιν· ἀλλ' εἷς τε καὶ μόνος Κύριος καὶ Υἱὸς, ὁ ἐκ Θεοῦ Πατρὸς Λόγος, οὐ δίχα σαρκός*.[76]

Then, in an interesting comment, Severus refers Sergius to Cyril rather than Gregory, as a builder and establisher of divine teaching, if one is going to resist the Nestorian faction accurately.[77] In comment on Gregory, he quotes St Peter's remark on the letters of St Paul: "There are in them things which are hard to understand, which unlearned and unstable men pervert, as also the rest of scripture, to their own destruction".[78] The Eutychians, as well as the Nestorians, have corrupted Gregory's meaning. They picked upon his phrases, *ὁ Λόγος παχύνεται*[79] and, *πτωχεύει τῷ σὰρξ παγῆναι*[80] understanding the incarnation on this basis as a sort of internal change, like water changing to ice, undergone by the Word, and not as the assumption of something new.[81] Against this distortion, Severus argues that Gregory's point was to teach a real incarnation brought about for a soteriological purpose: *ὕστερον γέγονε δι' αἰτίαν. Ἡ δὲ ἦν, τὸ σὲ σωθῆναι τὸν ὑβριστὴν, ὃς διὰ τοῦτο περιφρονεῖς θεότητα, ὅτι τὴν σὴν παχύτητα κατεδέξατο.*[82] The Word thus united an *οὐσία*, not a *φαντασία* to himself.[83]

In a final comment in this section, Severus notes that even Cyril has been perverted so as to be made to appear an advocate of the doctrine of two natures after the union. It was because of this distortion of Cyril that Severus published his own *Philalethes*.[84]

Severus now returns to his consideration of Sergius' doctrine. From Cyril's statement, *ἀνθρωπίνοις τε αὖ καὶ τοῖς ὑπὲρ ἄνθρωπον ἰδιώμασιν εἰς ἕν τι τὸ μεταξὺ συγκείμενος*[85] Sergius drew the conclusion that the Word incarnate united both the natures and the properties, becoming one from every side, both nature and particularity.[86] Severus interpreted this by referring to Sergius' earlier account of the nature of the union: there became one ousia and quality. He confesses himself astonished at this interpretation of Cyril: Cyril distinguished between the properties of divinity and humanity, and difference in properties is a consequence of the difference in natural quality between the two natures. He affirms, as we have seen, that

difference in natural quality of the natures stands firm: the divinity remains divinity, and the humanity remains humanity, but because the Word was united in hypostasis to visible flesh, *the Word himself* was seen and touched.[87] Thus, the properties of the flesh became properties of the Word, and the properties of the Word became properties of the flesh, but this is not because there is a new unit of an amalgamated type, but because there is one active subject who voluntarily made what is human his own.[88]

We have seen all of this before. But Severus presses his attack: Sergius is contradictory even on his own terms. Cyril described Christ as εἰς ἕν τι τὸ μεταξὺ συγκείμενος so how can Sergius claim he is following Cyril, when he interprets the result of this composition as having one ousia and one quality, or being one in both nature and particularity?[89] An object of one ousia, one quality, and one particularity would be simple, not composite, and Sergius is in fact contradicting Cyril. Furthermore, Sergius affirmed that in Christ there is one particularity. Severus reminds him that we have already seen in his own *First Letter* to Sergius that Leo, in his efforts to avoid a confusion, taught that "Tenet .... sine defectu proprietatem suam utraque natura",[90] which, as we have seen, implied that each nature remained master of itself, and consistently went in its own way. There would be no kenosis of the Word and no being possessed of the humanity. In place of this, Severus had given the teaching of Cyril. When one has the concept of particularity in natural quality, the divinity could remain divinity, and the humanity could remain humanity, but this *duality* in natural quality (against Sergius) does not imply the independent existence of the natures (as Severus understood was taught in Leo). But the union is now neither one of alternate action (in which now the divine nature would act, and now the human nature, again as Severus understood Leo), nor a static union in an event (as in Sergius), but something dynamic and purposive, involving an apparent discontinuity. The flesh sometimes suffers what belongs to it.[91] This "discontinuity", far from being an inconsistency, is, as we have seen, intrinsic to the type of union Severus and Cyril teach: it is an active union, the very course and nature of which is governed by its purpose. Thus, too, intrinsically, the human nature is preserved: "How will anyone with a God-fearing mind, and (who) cleaves to the teachings of the Apostles believe that the body which is subject to being seen, and so was seen, and is expected to be seen, was changed to the divine ousia?"[92]

Severus now presses home his point by referring to Cyril's treatise *Contra Synousiastas*. This merely emphasises what we have seen

before: the intrinsic importance of the preservation of the humanity. From Cyril he shows that if one says that the flesh of the Word was changed to the nature of divinity, it must be understood that the Word renounced his wish that he should become man.[93] If the Word renounced his wish to become man, the redemptive aspect of the incarnation falls away, and the union which we have called purposive and active would become static.

After this insistence on the soteriological retention of the humanity, with all the implications this has for the nature of the union, Severus returns to his point as to whether Sergius' account of the union can qualify as "a composition". But now he tries to understand why Sergius argued in this way. As so often, this gives us further insight into Severus' own position. Did Sergius argue that in the union composition ceased, as the unit was reduced to a thing of one ousia, so that the Trinity should remain a Trinity, and not receive a fourth person? Against the reduction of the unit in the incarnation to being a thing of one ousia, Severus appeals to the witness both of scripture and the Fathers: the Word ascended to heaven endowed with a body. Against the fear that this implies a quaternity in place of the Trinity, he shows how this point has already been answered in terms of the conceptual apparatus of the humanity being a non-prosopic hypostasis, personalised in the person of the Word. Severus' teaching of duality in natural quality is thus not equivalent to Nestorius' account in which a man complete in his own hypostasis adheres to the Word only benevolently. On his, the Cyrillian account, even if the Word was incarnate and inhominate, the Trinity remains a Trinity, for the Word is only one person.[94]

In his *Second Letter*, Sergius had, Severus notes, borrowed the concept of *συμφυΐα* from Gregory Nazianzen, in an attempt to bring to one ousia two concrete things which were different in natural quality.[95] We have already dwelt at considerable length on the fact that Sergius and Severus understood the union in different ways, and so saw it as involving different aims. Because Severus' vision of the union was of something active and soteriological, the preservation of the integrity of the humanity was an intrinsic part of the union. On Sergius' static model of union, unity would not be achieved until there was internal self-consistency. We need not go over that ground again, but let us state the point in this issue as simply as possible. Severus takes Sergius as seeing *συμφυΐα* (in Gregory Nazianzen) as a category for bringing two concrete individual hypostases to one ousia, in such a way that there will be one ousia, one person, and quality and one propriety. Against this, in a difficult but quite mas-

terly argument, Severus shows: first, in Christology, Gregory used the term συμφυΐα to describe σύμβασις φυσική and ἕνωσις ὑποστατική: that is, the coming of two hypostases to be one hypostasis (but where there is still a difference in ousia between the two uniting hypostases). Secondly, in Trinitarian thought, Gregory used the term συμφυΐα to describe the interrelationship of consubstantiality possessed by the three hypostases of the Trinity. Here, though there is one ousia, there are three hypostases. Thirdly, Severus shows that these two uses of συμφυΐα are not interchangeable, for, if the Trinitarian use were ever to be applied to the incarnational ἕνωσις, though there would be one ousia, there would still be two hypostases, and the Trinity would then indeed be made into a quaternity. Severus then shows us that in the incarnation, Gregory does *not*, in fact, use the word in its Trinitarian use: that is, though Gregory calls the incarnational union a συμφυΐα he does not see this as a union to consubstantiality, and consequently, we should not be so foolish as to think that the term συμφυΐα implies unity both of hypostasis and ousia. Are we so stupid as to think that because of the term συμφυΐα the body and the soul of a man together complete one ousia?! Again, Severus' real point—though it is now one we have seen so often before—is to try to show to Sergius that an internal unity of this sort to one ousia and quality is neither the only sort of unity nor the sort that is appropriate in Christology. Gregory, he continues, describes the composition of man, at various times, as a κρᾶμα[96] as well as a συμφυΐα. He also uses the term θεοποίησις:[97] none of these implies a change in the ousia or identity of a man, so why should they in the case of the inhomination of God the Word?

Severus now returns to Sergius' argument that the humanity must come to form one ousia with God the Word, so that the Trinity should not be turned into a quaternity. He very neatly borrows and applies the argument of Athanasius' *Letter to Epictetus*, to repeat the point he has himself just made. Though the Son (and the Spirit) are consubstantial with the Father, they are not the Father, for their consubstantiality does not destroy their distinction as persons. Similarly, if one considers the assumed humanity to be consubstantial with the Word, the flesh would nevertheless be other than the Word, and so the Trinity would still be made into a quaternity.[98] Now, how fair is this argument? Does it in fact apply to Sergius, or only to a man of straw?

We saw earlier that on Sergius' account of composition, the constituent parts, once united, were not afterwards adjudged according to the principle of duality,[99] since one ousia and quality had come

into being. We may take it from this that Sergius understood union through *συμφυΐα* to bring about not merely consubstantiality in the ousia of the uniting elements, but also unity in person. On that count, it would be unjust to accuse him, along the lines of the Athanasian argument, of making the Trinity a quaternity. But Sergius' thought is heterodox nonetheless. We must remember as well how he described the Christ figure, the product of this union. No propriety of God is to be seen in the new entity, nor any propriety of flesh either.[100] Thus, though the two constituent natures do indeed come to form a "one", this new one would seem to be different in propriety, and so in identity, from the eternal Son. If one is to take Sergius unsympathetically—and it is hard not to—one is inclined to say that his problem is more one of reducing the Holy Trinity to two, than of increasing it to four.

Severus sums up this part of the letter with a warning: do not bring the flesh to consubstantiality with the Word, on the pretext of the literal usage of those Fathers who have applied the word "mixture" in a non-contentious way to the union.[101] Even Cyril used the word without, because of this, raising up the flesh to the divine ousia, and confusing the difference in ousia of the natures which have come to union. Severus confirms this by giving a long quotation from Cyril, ending with Cyril's statement that the Virgin bore *ἐκ δυοῖν μέν, πλὴν ἄνθρωπον ἕνα, μένοντος μὲν ἑκατέρου τοῦθ' ὅπερ ἐστίν, συνδεδραμηκότων δὲ ὥσπερ εἰς ἑνότητα φυσικὴν, καὶ οἷον ἀνακιρνάντων ἀλλήλοιν, ὅπερ ἂν ὡς ἴδιον ἑκατέρῳ προσῇ.*[102]

Cyril's statement that the two natures "as it were mix with each other that thing which each one of them has as its own" is, of course, a statement of the *communicatio idiomatum*, as we have seen before. With the illustration of the human person, which Severus once again uses, the whole living creature is called "rational", and the whole living creature is called "mortal".[103] We have, again, argued earlier that what is involved here is not a merely verbal interchange of properties between the two natures, but that because the humanity has actually become *the own* of the Word, the properties of the humanity now actually belong to the Word. The properties are not interchanged between the natures, but they all belong to the one subject. In terms of the theological and soteriological concept of "transelementing" which we have just examined, or in terms of our own model of the stick which is lifted out of its own sphere as it is put to use by the blind man, we may say that the humanity is endowed with properties beyond itself, but it nevertheless remains humanity. Severus uses quotations from both Julius and Cyril to illustrate this.

But what is his point? Why does he emphasise this to Sergius? He is trying, we suggest, to highlight two basic ideas in his understanding of the union. The first is that the constituent elements in the union are not consubstantial, and do not become consubstantial. The second is that these elements do, however, come together to form a unit of such a kind that there is a *communicatio idiomatum*: there is *one* active subject, to whom belong the properties of both natures. These two ideas, which are so essential to the Cyrillian–Severan account of the union, cannot be reconciled or make sense to Sergius. There is an utter incompatibility between his kind of union and any kind of duality. By confronting him, as Severus now does, with the *communicatio idiomatum* in one subject, Severus is compelling Sergius to begin to question his presuppositions, and to re-think his understanding both of the unity and of the status and role of the constituents in that unity.

Severus' tactics must by now be becoming quite clear: we have seen from his *Second Letter to Oecumenius* that though he understood the humanity as an hypostasis, he saw it as being non-prosopic. We also saw above[104] how he interpreted the word "incarnate" as it is applied to God the Word: it meant that the flesh existed in relationship to the Word (it was "*enhypostatised*" in the person of the Word) and was not independently completed in its own hypostasis. We described this earlier as *a personalising union*: the God who loves man preserved and built up the humanity in the union, just as he made the bush in the wilderness able to support the fire without being destroyed. It is against this background that Severus now returns again to the meaning of the word "incarnate",[105] this time to correct Sergius' usage and misapprehensions. The claim of the extreme Monophysite (Synousiast) faction that when one says "One nature of God the Word", and adds "incarnate", one is introducing the other nature as an independent entity is just nonsense.[106]

Against the Synousiast understanding that the Word was simple[107] after the union, the word "incarnate" specifically indicates the composite nature of the Word after the union, and that he is one hypostasis from two.[108] Severus again quotes from Cyril's *Quod Unus Sit Christus*, that it is not the case that only what is simple may be called "one":[109] his point, yet again, being that Synousiast fusion and Nestorian separation do not form an exclusive disjunction, but that the Cyrillian vision of an active soteriological union in the person of the Word is a third alternative, but an alternative which involves re-thinking both the nature of the union, and the continuing role of the constituents within it.

Severus now develops this point in a rambling, almost circular argument. Very simply, its structure is as follows: first, it is not the case that only what is simple may be called "one". Second, it is, therefore, utterly stupid to run to the Nestorians[110] to avoid the position of Cyril, who does not teach simplicity, but what is one-but-not-simple. Third, one must now take care not to confuse what is one-but-not-simple for an aggregate of independents: for it would be stupid to be driven to hold a union of simplicity, so as to avoid Nestorian duplication, when all the time it is not the case that only what is simple is unitary.[111]

Of this argument, the first step is already familiar to us, and the second step is an obvious consequence of the first. For the third step, Severus borrows lengthy quotations from the debate between Cyril and Andrew of Samosata.[112] Andrew's argument is very literalistic: Cyril wrote that the Son sat with (συνήδρευσεν) the Father, along with (μετά) his flesh. How then can Cyril anathematise the person who would say that the man and God the Word are worshipped together (συμπροσκυνεῖσθαι), when σύν and μετά have the same meaning?[113] Mercifully, Cyril is no literalist, and in putting his finger on the issue makes the point Severus wants to teach Sergius.[114] There is an important difference between being able to refer to the continuing constituents out of which a thing is naturally composed, for example the body and soul which together compose a man,[115] and naming the individuals forming an aggregate, perhaps Peter and John, who are together called men.[116] Severus' point is that in just the same way, it is as silly to shy away from calling the Word "incarnate" for fear of introducing an independent nature, as it would be to avoid mention of the soul or body of a man, for fear of dividing him into two men. Consequently, it would be very silly to take refuge in a union of simplicity, so as to avoid Nestorian duplication, when duplication is not what is taught by Cyril, and simplicity is not the only form of union.

Severus concludes this section by making a fair point against Sergius, which we have remarked upon before. If the union has produced a unit of one ousia and quality, how can Sergius maintain that there remained a difference in ousia of the natures which have produced Christ? If there is only one quality and ousia, the difference between the constituent natures has vanished.[117]

Severus now moves from the central argument of the *Letters* concerning the nature of the union and its constituents, to pick up a number of side issues raised by Sergius' *Second Letter*. Though these points are neither unimportant nor uninteresting in themselves, they

are outside the main strand of the argument, and we will deal with them more briefly. Severus begins by returning to his debate with Sergius, as to whether it makes sense to say that Emmanuel was composed from two properties or activities.

It is as well that we understand the issue at stake, so we will quickly summarise the points raised earlier. In Sergius' *First Letter*, from his basic presupposition[118] that a propriety identified and implied an independent nature, he tried to express the uniqueness and identity of the Biblical Christ, by saying "just as we believe Christ is one from two natures, so also we (should) accept one propriety from two, of God incarnate".[119] In Severus' *First Letter*, we suggested earlier that he misunderstood Sergius at this point. He took the Greek underlying ܕܝ̈ܠܝܬܐ to mean "properties", and ridiculed Sergius, asking him if he considered that a man is composed from two properties (and why just two?[120]), perhaps "thinking"[121] and "whiteness" or "blackness".[122] Thus, he missed the point of what Sergius was trying to do. He did not see that Sergius' concern was simply an attempt to describe and identify the uniqueness of Christ, an attempt somehow to bring him under a definition as "Christ", rather than to understand him as God the Word incarnate.

Sergius, in his *Second Letter*, allowed that it was foolish to speak of a coming together of properties:[123] we do not say that a man is constituted from "being rational",[124] and "blackness". But then he adds that "being rational" and "blackness" are not properties of equal weight. "Being rational" completes an ousia so that it should be one: a man is a *rational*, mortal, living thing.[125] If one removes the "being rational" one spoils the man.[126] "Blackness", on the other hand, is not in the hypostasis, but is merely a "sign" of what is there. If it fades, it leaves the thing just as it was.[127] Now, what is the point of this argument? In his *First Letter*, Sergius' concern was to coin a new definition (a propriety) for Christ, from the (two) defining properties of the two natures which united to produce him. His pointing to the difference between "being rational" and "blackness" is a kind of half-defence for this line of approach: he is suggesting that "being rational" is a more fundamental property, that for man it is a *sine qua non*. The implication is that if we could find something which was an absolutely fundamental property, we would have something which was epistemologically important.

We now come to Severus' *Second Letter*. Severus summarises the earlier argument, but then shows Sergius that while he, Severus, said "from understanding",[128] which is the verbal form, indicating the activity or faculty of a rational mind,[129] Sergius had distorted his

meaning, quoting him as having said "from 'being rational'".[130] Severus notes that Sergius also took "blackness" as a contingent property.[131] Sergius may have done this because he already understood "being rational" as the single *defining* property of man, but Severus now claims that he meant "blackness" as an inseparable accident, like the blackness of the Ethiopian.[132] Presumably he also understood the faculty of "understanding" as an inseparable property of a mind, and so his point is that we would not define "man" as the product of even two inseparable properties, but as the union of two natures, those natures in which these properties inhere.[133]

This argument now gives Severus the opportunity to warn Sergius not to think he can make headway in Christology with the aid of philosophical definitions or proprieties.[134] Even if, philosophically speaking, it were the propriety of the human body to be moulded in a particular way, we would not say that a man is composed from learning and remembering, and a fashioning of the body in a particular way.[135]

Severus pursues this vein of argument against Sergius' approach. In the case of the divine nature, one can only speak metaphorically,[136] and not in any precise way, of propriety.[137] He quotes Evagrius: the Holy Trinity cannot be brought under genus, or species, or difference, or property, or accident: rather, we must worship in silence what is inexpressible.[138] This is to contradict Sergius' definitional approach utterly, and as so often, Severus substantiates his own argument by referring to Gregory Nazianzen and Cyril. From Gregory, he quotes: *Τὸ γὰρ πρῶτον, καὶ ὑπὲρ τὴν φύσιν*[139] and from Cyril: *ἔσται δὲ πάλιν καὶ ὑπὲρ τοῦτο Θεὸς, ἅτε δὴ καὶ ὑπερούσιος ὤν, καὶ τὸ ἄκρως προσεοικὸς οὐκ ἔχων ἐν γενητοῖς.*[140] Severus concludes that we do not know what God is, in ousia or nature.[141]

Consequently, neither in Trinitarian nor in incarnational theology can terms be used in their strict, philosophical senses.[142] Strictly speaking, a propriety is that which is possessed by something uniquely: it is not a shared property.[143] All living creatures, not just men, suffer hunger, thirst and weariness, but in Christology, and speaking imprecisely, we say it is the propriety of the humanity to hunger or to thirst. This imprecise usage is allowable, because what is at stake is not the exact characterisation of the human nature, but the more fundamental contrast between human nature and divine nature. It is in the light of this contrast that we may loosely call hunger, thirst, and so on, "the properties of humanity".[144] And even if these are naturally properties of humanity, because of the economy, they became properties of God the Word, so that he him-

self can be said to have hungered, and thirsted, and been weary from a journey.[145] We have seen earlier Severus' arguments that the preservation of the human nature forms an intrinsic part of the union:[146] the repetition of the point in this context is to stress, against Sergius' definitional approach to the person of Christ, both the reality of the human properties, and the reality of their possession by God the Word himself. Sergius' account cannot allow for this, and Severus is again compelling him to question his presuppositions.

As a final prong to his attack on what we have called Sergius' "definitional" approach to Christology, Severus warns him not to turn to the *τύποι* of the Old Testament, as if one could hope from there to find *literal* expressions and models for the union of the incarnation: these things are only partial and obscure suggestions of the truth.[147] As so often before, he refers to Cyril, this time telling us first the inferior and partial nature of examples as illustrations of what is true,[148] and secondly, and deliberately going against a literal typological model, taken perhaps from the fastening of the curtains in the Tabernacle,[149] telling us again that God the Word *made his own* the body taken from the holy Virgin.[150]

This really concludes the theological content of the letter. Severus writes that he has heard that some people who have read his *First Letter* to Sergius do not much agree with the theology of Cyril.[151] He takes it on himself to quote a testimonial on Cyril's behalf, written by Dioscorus to Domnus of Antioch.[152] For those who would oppose the Council of Chalcedon, the theology of Cyril is their very battle-armour, and he urges Sergius to remain in this armour and lay low the enemy.[153] The letter ends with a word of encouragement, and a final plea to Sergius to leap clear from the foolish doctrine which brings to one ousia the elements from which there is without confusion the one Lord and God and our Saviour Jesus Christ.[154]

Notes

1. cf. EM p. 103.18–27.
2. cf. EM p. 103.27–104.16.
3. cf. EM p. 77.23–26.
4. Cyril, *Adv. Nest. Lib. II*, PG 76.85 A–B (= Pusey edn. Vol. 6, p. 113.11–14).
5. cf. Cyril writing against those who *ἀναβοθρεύουσι τῆς σωτηρίας ἡμῶν τὴν ῥίζαν: Οὐ γὰρ γεγονότος σαρκὸς τοῦ Λόγου οὔτε τοῦ θανάτου κατεσείσθη τὸ κράτος, κατήργηται δὲ κατ' οὐδένα τρόπον ἡ ἁμαρτία*. cf. *QUSC*, PG 75.1268D (= Pusey edn. Vol. 7, p. 345.17, 19–21). For Severus' account of composition, cf. Lebon, *Chalkedon*, pp. 474–7.
6. cf. Sergius: EM p. 99.11–27. We have already seen that it is not the case that Gregory teaches a fusion: cf. *Or. XXX*: *εἰ γὰρ καὶ τὸ συναμφότερον ἕν, ἀλλ' οὐ τῇ φύσει,*

τῇ δὲ συνόδῳ τούτων. PG 36.113B. The language of the Cappadocians, which is undoubtedly misleading, is well explained and defended by Sellers, *Two Ancient Christologies*, *op. cit.*, pp. 75–8.

7. cf. EM p. 104.27–105.2.
8. cf. EM p. 105.4–11.
9. cf. EM p. 105.12–17.
10. cf. EM p. 106.9–20.
11. cf. Severus, *Philalethes*, *op. cit.*, p. 326.22–26. Confusion and separation do not form the only alternatives: the elements which are not confused are not necessarily divided.
12. cf. EM p. 106.21–27.
13. cf. EM p. 106.27–107.1.
14. cf. EM p. 107.6–11; and p. 100.16–17.
15. cf. EM p. 107.18–21. Severus' reference here is to Cyril's *Ep. XLVI* (*Ep. II ad Succ.*), PG 77.241B (=ACO I, 1, 6a, p. 160.2–4). In a similar and important passage in *QUSC*, Cyril argues that a man like us is one, and has one nature, though not simpleness: καίτοι τὸ μονοειδὲς οὐκ ἔχοντος PG 75.1292A (=Pusey edn. Vol. 7, p. 365.3). Simplicity is not the only criterion of unity: cf. *QUSC*, PG 75.1289B–C (=Pusey, p. 363.19–28), where Cyril denied that the consubstantiality of the natures was required for there to be union. (To require this would be to ask the wrong question.)
16. For Severus' stress on the non-consubstantiality of the elements, cf., for example, *Philalethes*, *op. cit.*, p. 240.3–4. For the stress in Cyril on the ἕτερον .... ἕτερον of the elements, cf. *Adv. Nest. Lib. III*, PG 76.160D (=Pusey edn. Vol. 6, p. 171.10–12); *QUSC*, PG 75.1292A (=Pusey, Vol. 7, p. 364.17–21).
17. cf. EM p. 108.1–5.
18. cf. *QUSC*, PG 75.1292C (=Pusey, Vol. 7, p. 366.1–5).
19. cf. *QUSC*, PG 75.1293A (=*ibid.*, p. 366.17–18) Pusey's translation.
20. cf. EM p. 108.5–24.
21. cf. EM p. 108.25–109.4.
22. cf. EM p. 109.5–23.
23. cf. EM p. 109.25–110.2.
24. It is preserved only in Syriac: cf. *Philalethes*, *op. cit.*, p. 140.2–12. Latin only in Migne.
25. cf. EM p. 110.7–11.
26. cf. EM p. 110.16–19. Again, the fragment is preserved only in Syriac: cf. *Philalethes*, *op. cit.*, p. 140.14–21.
27. *Collected Letters*, pp. 186–194.
28. *Ibid.*, p. 188.7–9.
29. ܩܢܘܡܐ ܕܡܠܬܐ *ibid.*, p. 188.13. cf. p. 189.4–5.
30. *Ibid.*, p. 189.5--7. (The English is Brooks' translation.)
31. PG 28.532A, and *Collected Letters*, p. 191.2–4.
32. T. H. Bindley and F. W. Green, *The Oecumenical Documents of the Faith*, (London, 1950) p. 96.88–90 (=Pusey edn. Vol. 6, p. 10.2–4).
33. R. V. Sellers in *The Council of Chalcedon* (London, 1961), p. 319, and p. 319 note 4, notes that Leontius' *enhypostasia* was merely summing up in a formula a Christological assertion which had been made long before his day. He notes also that, while it is not developed, this idea is found in Severus of Antioch. Dr. Constantine Dratsellas finds the same idea in Cyril's insistence that the body united to the Only-Begotten was his own body: cf. Dratsellas, *op. cit.*, pp. 226–227.
34. cf. EM p. 110.21–111.22.
35. cf. EM p. 111.1–4.
36. cf. EM p. 111.6–7.
37. cf. EM p. 111.10–14.
38. cf. EM p. 111.17–22.
39. cf. above, EM p. 108.1–5.

40. EM p. 111.29–31.
41. EM p. 111.31.–112.1.
42. cf. EM p. 112.1–29.
43. cf. Cyril, *QUSC*, PG 75.1340 C (= Pusey edn. Vol. 7, p. 406.13–15). For Cyril's insistence that in the union, God the Word is the sole subject, apart from the quotations given by Severus, cf. *Scholia*, Pusey edn. Vol. 6, p. 526.12–17; p. 526.26 and p. 528.1–11. cf. also, Lebon, *Chalkedon*, p. 483.
44. cf. EM p. 113.1 ff, and cf. Sergius, EM p. 99.11–27.
45. EM p. 99.24.
46. EM p. 100.15–16.
47. Severus makes the same point about Gregory's terminology in his *First Letter to Oecumenius*, *Collected Letters*, p. 179.8–10. He adds the point that where there is a union of something incorporeal with a body, there is no risk from κρᾶσις/ܡܘܙܓܐ.
48. cf. EM p. 113.11–114.5.
49. cf. EM p. 114.11–12, and PG 36.325B–C.
50. EM p. 114.24, and PG 36.97C: τῷ συνθέτῳ.
51. As Sellers, *op. cit.*, p. 66, put it so well: "Behind all their (the Cappadocians') teaching is the conception of an ethical God, who Himself stoops down to bring man to Himself".
52. Gregory Nazianzen, *Oratio XXXVIII*, *In Theophania*, PG 36.325 B. cf. also the great Cappadocian principle of τὸ ἀπρόσληπτον, ἀθεράπευτον *Ep. C1*, PG 37.181C. The "like for like" principle, which of course presupposes the preservation of the humanity, can be seen again in the same letter: PG 37.188 B.
53. EM p. 115.3–4, and Gregory, *Oratio XXIX*, PG 36.100A.
54. cf. EM p. 115.5–8.
55. Gregory, *Oratio XXXVIII*, *In Theophania*, PG 36.325 B/C, and EM p. 115.12.
56. Gregory, *Oratio XXIX*, PG 36.97C, and EM p. 115.14.
57. Gregory, *Oratio XXXVIII*, *In Theophania*, PG 36.328C, and EM p. 115.22–24.
58. cf. EM p. 115.25–28. Severus is undoubtedly right in his interpretation of Gregory. In his *First Letter to Cledonius*, Gregory would call the elements from which Christ comes ἄλλο καὶ ἄλλο, but not ἄλλος καὶ ἄλλος (cf. PG 37.180A). There is the same idea of a continuing, but not personal, difference, in Severus' ἰδιότης ὡς ἐν ποιότητι φυσικῇ.
59. Constantine Dratsellas, *op. cit.*, p. 222.
60. cf. EM p. 116.5–7.
61. cf. EM p. 116.10–11.
62. cf. EM p. 116.25–27.
63. cf. EM p. 117.1–14. cf. also Severus' *Letter to the Emesenes*, *Collected Letters*, pp. 237–8, where, discussing the same question, Severus again refers to Cyril's *First Letter to Succensus*, and Gregory's *First Letter to Cledonius*, as he does here.
64. cf. Cyril, *QUSC.*, PG 75.1292C (= Pusey edn. Vol. 7, p. 366.1–5).
65. cf. Cyril, *QUSC.*, PG 75.1293A (= *ibid.*, p. 366.21–26). This passage is quoted by Severus: cf. *Philalethes*, *op. cit.*, p. 242.23–243.16.
66. cf. Cyril, *QUSC.*, PG 75.1360D–1361A (= *ibid.*, p. 423.2–9).
67. cf. Cyril, *Adv. Nest. Lib. IV*, PG 76.189D–192A (= Pusey edn. Vol. 6, p. 194.29–195.6).
68. Cyril, *Contra Syn.*, Pusey edn. Vol. 5, p. 484.19–22.
69. Cyril, *Scholia IX*, Pusey edn. Vol. 6, p. 516.1–5 (= PG. 75.1380A). Severus quotes this passage in his *First Letter to Oecumenius*, *Collected Letters*, p. 180.11–13. It is worth noting that in the Syriac version, the verb ܫܚܠܦ renders μεταστοιχειώσαντα while a few lines later (p. 181.1), ܡܫܚܠܦܐ renders μεθίστησι, so the nuance of the Greek is lost. For a similar use of the concept of μεταστοιχείωσις to describe the implication for the humanity of being "the own" of the Word, cf. *Contra Syn.*, Pusey edn. Vol. 5, p. 488.14–17 (ἀναστοιχειώσας), and *Adv. Nest. Lib. II*, PG 76.61C (μεταστοιχειοῖ) (= Pusey edn. Vol. 6, p. 95.18–22).
70. Cyril, *Adv. Nest. Lib. V*, PG 76.212D–213A (= *ibid.*, p. 212.6–11).

71. Cyril, *QUSC.*, PG 75.1269B–C (= *ibid.*, Vol. 7, p. 346.21–23). cf. also *Adv. Nest. Lib. III*, PG 76.125C–D (μεταστοιχειούμενοι) (= *ibid.*, Vol. 6, p. 144.27–145.1); *Adv. Nest. Lib. III*, PG 76.128B–C (μεταστοιχειούμεθα) (= *ibid.*, p. 146.3–4); *QUSC.*, PG 75.1353A (ἀναστοιχειουμένης) (= *ibid.*, Vol. 7, p. 416.13–17).

72. cf. EM p. 72.17–26.

73. cf. EM p. 117.20–26 (Athanasius, *Or. III*, *Contra Ar.*, PG 26.385A, and Cyril, *Ad Monachos*, PG 77.13C–D = ACO I, 1, 1a, p. 12.5–8). Severus could equally well have referred to Cyril, *Adv. Nest. Lib. III*, PG 76.145B (= Pusey edn. Vol. 6, p. 159.17–21) which is an echo of Athanasius.

74. cf. EM p. 117.15–17. On Severus' treatment of διπλοῦς, cf. Lebon, *Chalkedon*, p. 490.

75. EM p. 117.29–118.6.

76. EM p. 118.22–24, and Cyril, *Adv. Nest. Lib. III*, PG 76.85A (= Pusey edn. Vol. 6, p. 113.6–7).

77. cf. EM p. 119.1–13.

78. 2 Peter iii. 16, and EM p. 119.16–18.

79. Gregory Nazianzen, *Or. XXXVIII*, *In Theophania*, PG 36.313B.

80. Gregory Nazianzen, *Or. XLIV*, *In Novam Dominicam*, PG 36.612B.

81. cf. EM p. 119.19–120.

82. Gregory Nazianzen, *Or. XXIX*, *Theologica III*, PG 36.100A. And cf. EM p. 120.4–7.

83. cf. EM p. 120.9.

84. cf. EM p. 120.17–30.

85. Cyril, *De Recta Fide ad Theod.*, PG 76.1193B (= Pusey edn. Vol. 7, p. 134.13–14).

86. cf. EM p. 121.8 (cf. p. 121.1–8).

87. cf. EM p. 121.21–22.

88. cf. EM p. 121.23–28.

89. cf. EM p. 122.3–7.

90. PL 54.765A, and EM p. 122.14.

91. cf. EM p. 122.22–23.

92. EM p. 123.3–6.

93. cf. EM p. 123.17–25.

94. cf. Severus, *To the Emesenes*, *Collected Letters*, pp. 230–4, where the same question is discussed.

95. cf. EM p. 125.5–13. For Sergius' *Second Letter*, cf. EM p. 99.19–27. Sergius seems to be referring to Gregory's *First Letter to Cledonius* (*Ep. CI*), PG 37.181C. This passage is also referred to by Severus: cf. *To Oecumenius*, *Collected Letters*, p. 179.7–8.

96. EM p. 127.23, and Gregory Nazianzen, PG 35.865C.

97. EM p. 127.27, and cf. Gregory Nazianzen, PG 36.324A (θεούμενον).

98. cf. EM p. 128.15–129.14.

99. cf. EM p. 100.14–15.

100. cf. EM p. 72.17–18.

101. cf. EM p. 129.15–17.

102. Cyril, *Ad Monachos*, PG 77.21D (= ACO I, 1, 1a, p. 15.31–33) and EM p. 131.2–6.

103. cf. EM p. 131.12–15.

104. cf. EM p. 111.29–112.1.

105. cf. EM p. 132.9–23.

106. cf. EM p. 132.9–13.

107. cf. EM p. 132.14–15.

108. cf. EM p. 132.15–16.

109. cf. EM p. 132.19–23.

110. I.e. "those who divide Emmanuel"; EM p. 132.25–26.

111. cf. EM p. 132.15–134.25.

112. cf. EM p. 132.28–134.16.

113. cf. EM p. 133.7–12, and Cyril, *Apol. pro XII Cap. contra Orient.*, PG 76.352C (=Pusey edn. Vol. 6, p. 322.11–16).

114. cf. EM p. 133.22–134.2.

115. cf. EM p. 134.2–9.

116. cf. EM p. 134.9–14.

117. cf. EM p. 134.26–31.

118. cf. EM p. 71.28–72.1.

119. cf. EM p. 72.9–11.

120. cf. EM p. 86.18–21.

121. ܗ̇ܘ, ܕܢܬܚܫܒ: EM p. 86.12–13; cf. EM p. 86.10.

122. cf. EM p. 86.7–17.

123. cf. EM p. 101.23–24.

124. ܡܠܠܐ EM p. 101.25.

125. cf. EM p. 101.27–29.

126. cf. EM p. 101.29–102.1.

127. cf. EM p. 102.2–4.

128. ܗ̇ܘ, ܕܢܣܬܟܠ: EM p. 135.18–19.

129. cf. EM p. 135.27–28.

130. cf. EM p. 135.23–26. Lebon, in the short summary he gives of these letters in *Le Monophysisme*, on p. 547 says in his apt French that while the Patriarch had spoken of "*la faculté* de penser", Sergius had misquoted this as "*l'élément intelligent*".

131. cf. EM p. 136.1–5.

132. cf. EM p. 136.5–10.

133. cf. EM p. 136.17–21.

134. cf. EM p. 136.22–31.

135. cf. EM p. 137.12–20.

136. cf. EM p. 137.23.

137. cf. EM p. 137.22.

138. cf. EM p. 137.26–138.2.

139. Gregory Nazianzen, *Or. XXXIV*, PG 36.248D, and EM p. 138.10.

140. Cyril, *In Ioannis Evangelium, Lib. I*, PG 73.85A (=Pusey edn. Vol. 3, p. 72.5–7) and EM p. 138.13–15.

141. cf. EM p. 138.17–18.

142. cf. EM p. 138.19–23.

143. cf. EM p. 138.29–139.2.

144. cf. EM p. 139.2–5.

145. cf. EM p. 139.5–8.

146. cf. EM p. 123–124.

147. cf. EM p. 140.1–14.

148. cf. EM p. 140.17–18.

149. cf. EM p. 141.1–8.

150. cf. EM p. 141.13–15, and Cyril, *Adv. Nest. Lib. II*, PG 76.84C (=Pusey edn. Vol. 6, p. 112.14–16).

151. cf. EM p. 141.16–18.

152. cf. EM p. 141.26–142.18.

153. cf. EM p. 142.21–24.

154. cf. EM p. 144.2–5.

VIII The Third Letter of Severus

Severus' final letter adds very little to what we have seen already. Indeed, Severus spends much of it recapitulating the argument of the earlier letters, and himself tells us that it is a letter he would rather not have written.[1] However, he does reply, even in this time of flight,[2] quoting the proverb that he who reproves openly makes peace.[3]

Severus begins by referring to Sergius' *First Letter*. Sergius had seemed disinclined to confess the particularities of the natures from which there is the one Christ. Severus had replied by trying to teach him the Cyrillian doctrine of difference in ἰδιότης ὡς ἐν ποιότητι φυσικῇ, as a concept of limited duality which did not imply the independence of the constituent natures.[4] Not to confess this difference, he states, is to invite confusion of ousiai.[5] As so often, this last statement is substantiated by quotations from Cyril: not to confess otherness of the natures, and particularity, and difference as far as natural quality is concerned, does not fall outside the folly of those who confuse ousiai.[6] Equally, Severus notes, those who divide Emmanuel make this natural difference a pretext for division.[7]

Severus' making these points did not amount to his accusing Sergius of heresy, as he now appears to think.[8] When Sergius, in his *Second Letter*, claimed that he could only see a juxtaposition, unless the two natures were mixed unconfusedly, Severus again replied in a kindly way, showing that mixture and juxtaposition are not the only possible alternatives, but that hypostatic union unites into one composite hypostasis[9] things which are, and remain, different in ousia from each other. This is a union totally different from Sergius' mixture to one ousia and quality.[10]

Expressly against Severus' advice and a great deal of evidence from the Fathers, Sergius persisted in defending the description of Emmanuel as being of one ousia and quality and particularity, from the mistaken idea that unless the Word incarnate is one in ousia and quality, a fourth person will be added to the Trinity.[11] It was in this context that Sergius introduced the term and concept of συμφυΐα. Against this, Severus showed that in Trinitarian theology the term συμφυΐα properly marked the consubstantiality of three hypostases,

while in incarnational theology it marked the union in hypostasis of things which differed, and continued to differ, in ousia. In neither case does it abolish all difference in both ousia and hypostasis, which is what Sergius would seem to want from it.[12]

Sergius, Severus now tells us, has taken these more or less theoretical points too much to heart, and as if he were under personal attack, has himself chosen to become an advocate of expressions which introduce the confusion of ousiai![13] Severus, accordingly, turns to consider the terms of Sergius' defence.[14] Sergius has said that he says "one ousia", in preference to saying "one nature";[15] he chooses to omit the word "incarnate";[16] and he speaks of there being "one quality", on the grounds that the quality of the ousia of the Word had a share in bodily activity.[17] Severus asks: Is this tolerable? Are these proper beliefs for Christians?[18] He takes the points in turn.

First, where in Athanasius and Cyril has Sergius ever found Emmanuel called "one ousia and quality", or "one ousia incarnate"?[19] He allows that one can easily find evidence in the Fathers of "*οὐσία*" being used instead of "*μία φύσις*" or "*ὑπόστασις*"—and he supplies examples—but he claims that none of the Orthodox Doctors of the Church ever called the Word "one ousia" when it was composed with the flesh.[20]

Second, quoting the famous passage in Athanasius' *Ad Afros*, he allows that *φύσις* and *οὐσία* (and *ὑπόστασις* and *ὕπαρξις* as well) can all mean "being",[21] but equally he quotes Basil saying: *οὐσία δὲ καὶ ὑπόστασις ταύτην ἔχει τὴν διαφορὰν, ἥν ἔχει τὸ κοινὸν πρὸς τὸ καθ' ἕκαστον*.[22] Consequently, Severus writes, in incarnational theology, the Fathers rightly distinguish between these terms (i.e. *οὐσία* and *ὑπόστασις*). He refers to the usage of Cyril: Cyril, realising that the word *φύσις* may be used for the signification of a kind (*γένος*), as well as an individual, used the words *πρόσωπον* and *ὑπόστασις* as well as *φύσις* to refer to the Word incarnate.[23]

Rather than following the usage of the Fathers, Sergius has chosen to appeal to Aristotle. We remember Sergius' point in his *Third Letter*: he quotes Aristotle giving *ἄνθρωπος* and *ἵππος* as examples of *οὐσία*,[24] and then added, "But it is not the case that he does not acknowledge the composition of the living creature because of this",[25] asking how it could then be the case that he defrauded the truth, if he called the incarnate Word (one) ousia?[26] Severus now gives us his answer: "none of those who think that the human soul is rational and intelligent and not mortal says this, that it is one ousia and quality along with a mortal and sensible body",[27] and similarly,

no intelligent person says that the nature of God the Word and flesh endowed with a soul and with a mind, which was united hypostatically to him, has become one ousia and quality.[28] This is an interesting point: what Severus says is true, but unfair to Sergius, who is correct in his own way, even if only trivially correct. Once again we may see quite clearly their radically different presuppositions, and understandings of the nature of the Christological unit. We can allow Sergius his trivial point: the Biblical Christ was one person, one thing, and consequently he could be called "one ousia" in the trivial and obvious sense. But though the Biblical Christ was one, he was not a "one" in the sense in which every other "one" is: he was not a member of any class at all. Though single, he was not one-of-a-type, and thus he is not repeatable, definable or self-contained. We have tried very hard in this introduction to show that, for Severus, *who* Christ was was inter-related with *what he did*. The course and nature of the union was determined by the purpose of the union. Thus, to define him as if he were self-contained, or one of a class, would be to knock out his soteriological activity, and that was precisely *not* the kind of unit the Fathers understood Christ to be. Sergius, in his terms, cannot understand a "one" which is not one of a class.

Concluding his examination of the points of Sergius' defence, Severus simply dismisses Sergius' claim that the quality of the Word has shared with the quality of the body. How can Sergius distinguish qualities from natures?[29] We remember that to Severus, natural quality is the principle of how a thing is (*ὁ λόγος τοῦ πῶς εἶναι*): to separate this from a nature would just be nonsense.

Severus now rebukes Sergius for the use he makes of philosophy: this is outside the law of the Church. The Fathers do not accept pagan philosophy as a leader in their studies of terms, but only as a handmaid, subsequently.[30] To substantiate his opinion here, Severus quotes from Basil at some length.[31]

The letter now becomes more personal. Why is Sergius indignant at this correction?[32] Why does Sergius say he has been wounded, when all Severus has done is remind him of the teaching of the Fathers?[33] Does he not see that in his arguments he merely wounds himself? For example, when in his *Second Letter*, Severus said, from Cyril, that God is *ὑπερούσιος*,[34] Sergius took *ὑπερούσιος* as introducing that which is without being,[35] and attempted on Biblical grounds to defend calling God "*οὐσία*".[36] Similarly, after Severus had denied that one could apply a propriety with any precision to God, and had quoted Evagrius[37] to confirm this, Sergius, in a last

ditch defence of his definitional approach, has seized upon Severus' statement that properly speaking a propriety "is that thing which belongs to something alone, and without sharing with another".[38] He then quotes St Mark's Gospel: "Why do you call me good? No-one is good, except one, God",[39] claiming that Severus has defined, and very clearly, that the propriety of God is goodness, for it belongs to God alone to be good.[40] Severus finds this defence utterly futile and self-defeating. Is goodness to be the official propriety of God, as laughter is supposed to be of man?[41] He turns the tables on Sergius: let him take note of the verse: "To the only wise God".[42] Are there, on Sergius' foolish approach, to be two proprieties for God?!

Severus concludes the letter by telling Sergius severely to cease his foolishness, to let him alone, and to learn humility.

Notes

1. cf. EM p. 157.14–15.
2. cf. EM p. 158.6–7.
3. Prov. x. 10.
4. cf. EM p. 158.22–27.
5. cf. EM p. 158.27–29.
6. cf. EM p. 159.24–28.
7. cf. EM p. 159.29–160.2.
8. cf. EM p. 160.3–9.
9. EM p. 160.30.
10. cf. EM p. 161.1–4.
11. cf. EM p. 161.11–21.
12. cf. EM p. 161.21–162.4.
13. cf. EM p. 162.12–13.
14. cf. EM p. 162.21–22.
15. cf. EM p. 162.22–23 and p. 151.7–16.
16. cf. EM p. 162.23–24 and p. 151.16–17.
17. cf. EM p. 162.24–26 and p. 152.3–4.
18. cf. EM p. 162.26–27.
19. cf. EM p. 163.16–19.
20. cf. EM p. 164.9–13. Severus makes clear his dislike of this usage in his *Second Letter to Oecumenius*, *Collected Letters*, p. 193.6–9: "But saying that Emmanuel is from two ousiai also, as we confess him to be from two natures, even if one understood the ousiai as hypostases, we avoid, as being something imprecise, and not said in so many words by any of the God-clad Fathers". For Severus' terminological distinctions and preferences, cf. *To Eusebius*, *ibid.*, p. 195, and *To Maron*, *ibid.*, p. 196. cf. Lebon, *Chalkedon*, pp. 512–3.
21. Lebon, *ibid.*, p. 455, puts this by saying that the three terms *οὐσία*, *ὑπόστασις* and *ὕπαρξις* all indicate "l'être même, l'être réel, ce qui est, ce qui existe".
22. EM p. 166.17–18, and Basil, *Ep. CCXXXVI*, PG 32.884A.
23. cf. EM p. 166.22–31, and Cyril, *Adv. Nest. Lib. II*, PG 76.60D (=Pusey edn. Vol. 6, p. 94.10–11); *Ep. XVII*, PG 77.116C (=*ibid.*, p. 28.21–3).
24. Aristotle, *Categories*, 4.1b.27.
25. EM p. 151.26.

26. cf. EM p. 151.28–152.1.
27. EM p. 168.4–7.
28. cf. EM p. 168.9–12.
29. cf. EM p. 168.13–14.
30. cf. EM p. 169.9–13.
31. cf. EM p. 170.1–171.8.
32. cf. EM p. 171.17–20.
33. cf. EM p. 172.24–26.
34. cf. EM p. 138.11–18; Cyril, *In Ioannis Evangelium*, *Lib. I*, PG 73.85A (= Pusey edn. Vol. 3, p. 72.5–9).
35. cf. EM p. 173.8.
36. cf. EM p. 155.9–16.
37. cf. EM p. 137.21–138.2.
38. EM p. 138.29–139.2.
39. Mk. x. 18.
40. cf. EM p. 155.16–22, and p. 173.15–174.1.
41. cf. EM p. 174.2–4.
42. Romans xvi. 27.

Part Two

THE LETTERS BETWEEN SEVERUS OF ANTIOCH AND SERGIUS THE GRAMMARIAN

Letter I of Sergius

The Letters to each other of Sergius the Grammarian and of Severus, Patriarch of Antioch (*Lebon p. 70*).[1]

The First Letter of Sergius the Grammarian to the venerable Severus, Patriarch of Antioch, in which he asks how those who think Christ is from[2] two natures are to be reconciled, who have used the name of Antoninus, Bishop of Aleppo. The letter is as follows.

To my Lord who is holy in all things, and venerable spiritual Father, Bishop Antoninus: Sergius a humble Grammarian: Greetings in our Lord.

When just now I looked out upon these divine matters, my faculty of sight cringed back, as if I (were) looking directly into the rays of the sun. And the promises of the ship[3] are awaited by me anxiously, because I have no clear opinion, but rather I look to "The depths of the navigation[3] of the wisdom and of the knowledge of God".[4] And as I was thrust out from this with diverse reasonings, I read the law of the one who sings, which says "Ask your Fathers, and they will inform you".[5] Now is the time of uncertainty: I shall speak now with the (rest of the) city.[6]

I made a request from your holy gathering: for we are asking for the eradication of the confession from those who fell and returned to themselves, while you make enormous concessions. I stammered as much as I was able about matters of the rule of the faith, (and) I wrote as much as I understood.[6] (*Lebon p. 71*)

But the summing up of it all was: "We do not speak of two natures or proprieties after the inexpressible union". But this, which did not seem to be expressed in accordance with reason, was corrected as follows by you: "We do not speak of divided proprieties". And my mind is shaken by this, and though I turned my reasoning up and down, even now I am unable to ascend to comprehension of the proposition.

What then? Shall we speak of two proprieties, so that we may remove the foolishness of the metousiasts, flesh being understood as flesh, and divinity not descending to confusion? But this is to keep (two) ousiai, and by no means just proprieties. For God and flesh are ousiai, but it is the [propriety][7] of God to be eternally, but of flesh to

become and to be corrupted. But if we should say that the proprieties persist how will we find them, when we enquire about the facts in question? For the propriety of God, to be sure, is that he is not seen or touched:—yet God came visibly, and "was seen on earth, and had dealings with men",[8] and "we saw him, and his appearance was not honourable, and was despised by men",[9] .... "that which was from the beginning, which we have heard and seen, and our hands have touched, concerning the Word of Life...".[10] But it is the propriety of flesh that it is brought forth from two parents, and when once it is brought forth, that it should also be corrupted. But where are these things in the case of the flesh of Life? For no man was father of Christ, for without the bush being burned,[11] and the door being still sealed,[12] the Lord went forth endowed with a body. Hence because he was not born in accordance with the propriety of the flesh, neither did his flesh see corruption. But every propriety belongs to an underlying nature, and if we speak of two proprieties, (*Lebon p. 72*) we are obliged also to speak of two natures. But if we suppose that the proprieties are undivided, neither do those (Dyophysites) divide the natures, but everywhere proclaim to us (natures) which are undivided. And this is the summing up of the sickness of Chalcedon and the madness of Leo, which, while it divides the activities with the natures, says (each form does what is proper) undividedly "in partnership with the other".[13] Therefore how shall we escape from such frenzy, we who teach one nature of the Word incarnate after the union, unless, just as we believe Christ is one from two natures, so also we accept one propriety from two of God incarnate, of him who out of kindness undertakes to be seen, but transcended the human propriety by means of the supreme union: thus he walked on the waters without being dragged by the burden of the flesh into the depth of the sea. And when they sealed the sepulchre, he was not held in, and closed doors were unable to prevent his entrance.

And so henceforward, neither is any propriety of God to be recognised in [his][14] Logos, nor is any (propriety) of flesh to be seen (in him either), but the entire manner of the economy points towards one propriety, that which is with God incarnate. For just as laughter is the propriety to "man", and none of the other animals is like him in this, so also there is one propriety of Christ, in which no-one from those who are invisible or visible shares. For only God who was incarnate is born from the Virgin, and performed everything and suffered on our behalf, and from where he descended, there again he ascended, endowed with the flesh.

Good Fathers, let it be your concern that I should emerge from this grievous doubt. And enquire by yourselves into my contemptible thoughts, and correct and raise them to your own, and do not reject my smallness and youth, being like Christ, the chief of shepherds, who (*Lebon p. 73*) did not reject the children when they came near. But as you are high priests of his, you plan by all means to offer pure sacrifices; now this is the sacrifice of him who was inhominated on our behalf: a pure mind fulfilled in the knowledge of the Spirit.

The First Letter of Sergius the Grammarian to the holy Patriarch Severus has ended.

Notes

1. "*Lebon p. 70*" refers to the pagination of Lebon's edition of the *Letters*, CSCO 119 (Syr. p. 64).
2. ܕܟܝܢ ܬܪ̈ܝܢ Lebon notes that the text should probably be emended to read ܕܒܬܪ̈ܝܢ ("in two natures"), i.e. the Chalcedonian formula ἐν δύο φύσεσιν.
3. Lebon notes that the Syriac translator seems to have taken the word πλούτου to be the genitive of πλοῦς.
4. cf. Rom. xi. 33.
5. cf. Deut. xxxii. 7. All OT references are to LXX.
6. The text of these two paragraphs is particularly obscure.
7. Reading ܕܡܠܬܐ for ܕܡ̈ܠܬܐ (cf. lines 17 and 22, below).
8. Baruch iii. 38.
9. Is. liii. 2–3.
10. 1 Jn. i.1.
11. cf. Ex. iii.2–3.
12. cf. Ezek. xliv.1–2.
13. PL 54.767B. *Ep. XXVIII, ad Flavianum* ("*The Tome*").
14. Reading ܕܡܠܬܗ for ܕܡܠܬܗ̇. ܡܠܬܐ is translated by "Logos". An easier meaning might be given if it is translated by "condition": "in [his] condition . . .".

Letter I of Severus

A copy of the Letter of holy and blessed Severus, Archbishop and Patriarch of Antioch, to chaste Sergius the Grammarian, who was asking about particularities and activities and about the sufferings which bring salvation.

I praise your Chastity, who wanted to explain the problem expressed in the letter logically and at the same time in the fear of God. For there is, furthermore, the prophetic saying which permits that we should make enquiry, along with the fact that enquiry should be restrained by an anchor of the fear of God, saying as follows, "If you enquire, enquire, but dwell with me",[1] and (The Book of) Proverbs introduces this instructively, when it defines, "Unchastened education goes astray".[2] [And I admired][3] your coming to me in humility, which bears witness to your wisdom. For the same (Book of) Proverbs may be heard, which says: "Wisdom is meditated upon in the mouth of the humble".[4] And the writings of the law order priests to resolve what is uncertain, and to expound those things which would otherwise be anywhere unclear, and to distinguish what is good from what is not good, when it says to them as follows: "The law is for ever for your generations, that you should distinguish between what is holy and what is profane, and between what is pure (*Lebon p. 74*) and what is not pure, and that you should teach the children of Israel all the laws which the Lord has spoken to them".[5]

It is recognised through these things that you have asked well, and that we ought to (give an answer) to the question. But since questions of doctrine are considered hard to comprehend and hard to express, I shall write as regards the question so far as I can grasp (the matter), looking towards him who gives a word of knowledge and a word of wisdom. For the word of the Proverbs says again: "The desire of the heart belongs to man, but the answer of the tongue comes from the Lord".[6]

Know, therefore, that professing the natural particularity of the natures from which there is the one Christ is not just recently determined by us. Far from it—for we remember that holy Cyril wrote as follows in the Second Letter to Succensus: (CYRIL): "For even if

the Only-Begotten Son of God, incarnate and inhominate, is said by us to be one, he is not confused[7] because of this, as he seems to those people; nor has the nature of the Word passed into the nature of the flesh, nor indeed has the nature of the flesh (passed into) that which is his, but while each one of them continues together in the particularity that belongs to the nature, and is thought of in accordance with the account which has just been given by us, the inexpressible and ineffable union shows us one nature of the Son, but as I have said, incarnate".[8] Observe, therefore that when the Doctor has confessed one nature of God the Word, who is incarnate, he says that each one of them continues together and is understood in the particularity that belongs to the nature.

But the same (Cyril) elucidates what the particularity that belongs to the nature is, by writing again as follows in the Treatise against Diodore: (CYRIL): "Therefore let us recognise that even if the body which was born (*Lebon p. 75*) at Bethlehem is not the same, that is, as far as natural quality is concerned, as the Word which is from God and the Father, yet nevertheless it became his, and did not belong to another man beside the Son. But the Word incarnate is to be considered one Son and Christ and Lord".[9]

And after other points, as he sets out this very matter, he adds these as well: (CYRIL): "Because we say too that, with respect to particularity, flesh is completely of another nature from the Word which sprang from God and the Father: nevertheless it became his, in an inseverable union, with the result that the Word who shone forth from the ousia of God and the Father, is also named "seed of Abraham" in the flesh; when the economy calls him this, it in no way detracts from his being what he is. For although he is God by nature, he became in truth Son of man as well, and he is also Son of God and the Father, not in a spurious way nor with a false name, but he is he who ineffably and inexplicably is born from him, even though he is not thought of without the flesh after the union".[10]

It is therefore already made known for your Chastity from these things that particularity (implies) the otherness of natures of those things which have come together to union, and the difference (lies) in natural quality. For the one is uncreated, but the other created. And the one is not seen, but the other is seen, and the one is not touched, but the other is subject to touch. Nevertheless, while this difference, and the particularity of the natures, from which (comes) the one Christ, still remains without confusion, it is said that the Word of Life was both seen and touched, and the Gospel says that those theologian Disciples were spectators and ministers of the Word[11];

not that he[12] changed from his invisible nature, devoid of flesh, but he was united to a visible and solid body, not denying touch. (*Lebon p. 76*)

Therefore do not ascribe the folly of the Synousiasts to this exact profession of the faith. For we are not ignorant in accordance with their madness, and cure evil with evil, and, as the saying is, thrust out a nail with a nail. But know quite clearly that precision and an accuracy for the truth demand this. For we say as well that a man like us is a living being, rational, mortal, capable of reason and knowledge, (and) because there is one nature and hypostasis from two, the whole living being is said to be mortal, and the whole is called rational, and we do not say that we do not know what (part) is living, and what (part) is rational; No, the fact that we know this does not divide the composition from which the one living being is constituted. For holy Cyril too, while making a defence against Andrew who found fault (with him) viciously in the Third Chapter, says as follows about the study of Emmanuel: (CYRIL): "There is no share in any blame that one should recognise, for example, that the flesh is one thing[13] in its own nature, apart from the Word which sprang from God and the Father, and that the Only-Begotten is another again, with respect to his own nature. Nevertheless, to recognise these things is not to divide the natures after the union."[14]

And your Chastity will recognise that it is of necessity that rational nature all has a difference with regard to everything apprehended by sense, and not a difference only, but also a distinction: for these things are also removed from each other in quality of nature and in that they stand apart (*Lebon p. 77*) in place. And they are removed distinctly from each other, and with the difference is yoked entire distinctness and remoteness. But when a single hypostasis is completed by a coming together in natural union from a rational nature and from a sensible one, we see that the difference of those things which have come together to be one, (the difference that is) which lies in natural quality, has not been suppressed, because there is no confusion of the union; but the division has been removed, because those things which were different in natural quality do not exist independently, but complete one hypostasis from two.

Well then, let us transfer this to the study of Emmanuel, and let us make an enquiry of the divinity and the humanity. They are not only different in everything but they are removed from each other and distinct as well. But when union is professed from the two of them, the difference, again, in the quality of the natures from which there is the one Christ is not suppressed, but in conjunction by hypostasis

division is driven out. And look how wise Cyril clearly teaches this, in the Second Volume against the blasphemies of Nestorius. (CYRIL): "For I too allow that there is a great difference or distinction between humanity and divinity. For these things which were named are seen to be other, according to the mode of how they are, and they are not like each other in anything. But when the mystery which is in Christ has come for us into the middle, the principle of union does not ignore the difference but it removes the division; not because it confuses with each other or mixes the natures, but because the Word of God has shared in flesh and blood, thus again the Son too is understood and named as one."[15] But if someone should wrongfully divide Emmanuel with a duality (*Lebon p. 78*) of natures after the union, there also occurs a division at the same time, along with the difference of the natures, and the properties are divided in every respect to suit the (two) natures. And wise Cyril again learnedly explained this in the same volume, when he said as follows after other things: (CYRIL): "God is not touchable, but the Word became subject to touch by means of his own flesh; he is invisible by nature, but he became visible by means of the body. But you again, in making distinctions in every way, play craftily with the truth, in that on the one hand you keep distinct the natures, but on the other hand you unite, so you say, the worship. But if you keep distinct the natures, the properties of each one of them naturally go with them as well. Then the principle of difference occurs in everything, (and) thus two are confessed."[16]

It is clearly established, therefore, from these things which have been quoted, that natural quality is the principle of how (a thing) is, for the Doctor said: with respect to how they are, these things which are named are seen to be different and are unlike each other in anything. And so we confess the difference and the particularity and the otherness of the natures from which Christ is, for we do not quarrel about names, but (we confess) the particularity which (lies) in natural quality and not that which will be set in parts,[17] each one existing independently. For holy Cyril writes as follows too, in the Treatise of question and answer *That Christ is One*: (CYRIL): "Therefore, as I have said, it is not right that we should make a division into an independent diversity, so that they should become separate and apart from each other; rather we ought to bring (them) together to [undivided][18] union. For the Word became flesh, according to the word(s) of John."[19] (*Lebon p. 79*)

For we do not refuse to confess the difference, God forbid, but we flee from this, that we should divide the one Christ in a duality of

natures after the union. For if he is divided, the properties of each one of the natures are divided at the same time with him, and what is its own will cling to each one of them. But when a hypostatic union is professed, of which the fulfilment is that from two there is one Christ without confusion, one person, one hypostasis, one nature belonging to the Word incarnate, the Word is known by means of the properties of the flesh, and the properties of the humanity will become the properties of the divinity of the Word; and again the properties of the Word will be acknowledged as the properties of the flesh, and the same one will be seen by means of both (sets of properties), both touchable and not touchable, and visible and not visible, and belonging to time and from before time, and we shall not attribute the properties of each nature, dividing them up.

And the clear and astute words of wise Cyril will again teach and instruct us clearly (in) these things, for he writes as follows in the Third Volume against the blasphemies of Nestorius: (CYRIL): "Does he then lie, when he said that the Son of Man, who is himself, descended from heaven? Far from it! For he is himself the truth. Therefore how may 'the Son of Man from above' be understood rightly? Because although he is God the Word and from the ousia which is above every (ousia), it is said that he descended and took the form of a servant, and then speaks with us, not, from then on, as the naked Word, but as a man like us, and as one who is understood already as one with flesh united to him. (*Lebon p. 80*)

Just as, for the sake of that which is proper to the emptying, he takes for his own all those things which are of the body, even though he is incorporeal by nature, so too, he, being from above and from heaven, attributes (the words) 'he came from above' to himself, while he was man, even though he was in the flesh with us from woman. Therefore the properties of the Word became properties of manhood, and those of manhood, properties of the Word. For thus one Christ and Son and Lord is understood."[20]

Therefore when we anathematise those who say Emmanuel has two natures after the union, and (speak of the) activities and properties of these, we are not saying this as subjecting to anathema the fact of speaking of, or naming, natures, or activities or properties, but speaking of two natures after the union, and because consequently (those natures) attract their own activities and properties which are divided along with the natures completely and in everything, whether we say (this) or not. For if this were not so, it would be right for us not to profess Emmanuel even to be "from two natures", if the word "natures" were to be shunned. But now, when we say

"from two natures", and acknowledge one God who was immutably incarnate and inhominate, and believe that there was an unconfused union, we are obliged to acknowledge as well the particularities of the natures from which Emmanuel is. And we call this a particularity and name it: (that is,) that which (lies) in difference of natural quality, which (definition) I will not cease repeating many times, and not that (which lies) in (independent) parts,[21] and natures in independent existence are implied, (*Lebon p. 81*) for to say this belongs to those who mutilate (Christ) with a duality after the inexpressible union, and not to us, who profess him to be one from two.

And then about activities: we find a distinct opinion when we have recourse to the quotations of the God-clad Fathers. For Basil, great and wise in divine matters, wrote, in the Treatise of refutations against Eunomius, that he who acts is one thing, and activity is another, and another that which was enacted, and these things are quite removed from each other. For he who acts is he who is impelled towards doing something, but the activity (is) like an active movement and impetus of the will which is directed on and indicates doing something, and is set in motion at once. In the case of activity, that which wills (it) remains complete and momentarily impelled to action, but (activity) is not a hypostasis, but the things which are enacted, which are brought to completion as a result of this and exist, (are hypostases). For when evil Eunomius had said that the Son was made, and was not an off-spring of the Father, holy Basil says to him ensnared in intellectual nets by perverted opinions and human arguments: If, according to your word, the Son is an effect, what do you understand an effect to be? That which is completed from activity. Then he is third from the Father and not second, if the Father is understood as he who acts, and activity is an active movement, and that which is enacted is what is completed by movement. But he says as follows—for we ought to quote the words of the Doctor verbally: BASIL: "If the Son (*Lebon p. 82*) is an activity, and not an off-spring, he is neither the agent, nor the product, for an activity is something other than these. But he is also without hypostasis, for no activity is hypostatic. But if he is that which is enacted, he is third from the Father, and not without an intermediary. For he who acted is first, and then activity, and then that which was enacted."[22]

Therefore what has thus been clarified and made known is that he who acted is one thing, and activity is another, and another (still) that which was acted upon, or effected. And activity is something in the middle, that is, an active movement, between him who acted and

that which was acted upon, even if in the case of God, his wishing is the accomplishment of an action, and it is not easy to find that which is in the middle, when everything exists in a moment, and as in the blink of an eye, as Paul says.[23] We will apply (this) reasoning to what was set down earlier.

And first, let us test this on the example of a man like us. Thus, some of the things which are done by a man like us are intellectual, and some are sensible and bodily. For example, to reckon up and think about something that should be done, and to fulfil and plan in thought, and to fix and determine intention, is a thing which is done intellectually, such as arranging how it is fitting to prepare a city or a house or a ship. But to build a house or to construct a ship, is sensible and bodily. And the man who acts (in both cases) is one, consisting of soul and body, and the activity is one, for the active movement is one, which is the impetus of volition, but the things which are done are diverse, for one is intellectual but the other is sensible and bodily. One can see the same in the case of Emmanuel. (*Lebon p. 83*) For there is one who acts, that is the Word of God incarnate; and there is one active movement which is activity, but the things which are done are diverse, that is (the things) accomplished by activity. For example, bodily to walk on the earth and to make a journey is something human, but to raise up and order to run those who are lame in the feet, and unable to use their soles, but who are prostrate and crawl like reptiles, is most proper to God. But there is one Word which was incarnate, and one activity of his, which is an active movement, which performed the one and the other. And it is not the case that, because these things which were done were of different kinds, we say that consequently there were two natures which were effecting those things, for as we have said, a single God the Word incarnate performed both of them. And just as no-one divides the Word from the flesh, so also it is impossible to divide or separate these activities. For we also recognise a variety of utterances: for some are proper to God, while others are human, but one Word incarnate spoke both the former and the latter. For there are utterances which make known at the same time the divine character of Emmanuel and the humanity as well, as "One Lord Jesus Christ, through whom are all things",[24] and "From whom is Christ, in the flesh, who is God blessed for ever, above all things".[25] And no-one, unless he is mad, dares to divide or distinguish into two these statements, which establish the same (Christ) as indivisible, being both from Israel in the flesh, and God blessed for ever. And again the same one is anointed because he was incarnate, for the act of being

anointed belongs to the incarnation, and through the same (one) everything came into existence. (*Lebon p. 84*)

But what our Saviour said about the death of Lazarus is like those utterances as well, in that it shows at the same time the divine character and humanity: "Lazarus our friend is asleep, but I go that I may arouse him".[26] For it belongs to God that he should say that he would rouse him as if he were asleep, him who for four days had been reckoned among the dead, and had wasted away, and had putrified in the body, and in truth to change death into sleep, because of the hope of the resurrection; but it was human to say "I go and shall awake him". For he was able as God, even while he was far off, to do that. But he mingled the two, establishing that he is indivisibly one and the same Son and Word, who on our behalf unchangeably became man, speaking as befits God and humanly. Thus too it is often possible to see in his actions what belongs to the character of God and (what is) human mingled together. For how will anyone divide walking upon the water? For to run upon the sea is foreign to the human nature, but it is not proper to the divine nature to use bodily feet. Therefore that action is of the incarnate Word, to whom belongs at the same time divine character and humanity indivisibly.

It is possible to see that those things which are contained in the Tome of Leo go clearly against these things, and I quote them: LEO: "For each one of the forms does what belongs to it; the Word doing what belongs to the Word, and the body fulfilling those things which belong to the body, and the one of them is radiant with wonders, but the other falls under insults".[27] For if each form or nature does those things which are its own, those (*Lebon p. 85*) things are of a bastard partnership and of a relationship of friendship, such as a master's taking on himself the things which are performed by a servant, or vice versa, a servant's being glorified with the outstanding possessions of a master, while those things which are not properties of human nature are ascribed to him out of a loving friendship. For he is a man clad with God, who in this way makes use of a power which is not his own, and is impelled by one who acts, like an inanimate instrument, perhaps a saw or an axe, which is used by a craftsman.

But Jesus is not like that, away with you! For he is seen using his own power as God inhominate, and he confirms this with utterances worthy of God. And to the sea he says, "Be quiet, be restrained"[28], and to Peter when he called out "Order me to come to you on the water", he orders "Come",[29] and to the leper "I am willing: be

clean".[30] And he lays down the law with the authority of God and says "But I say to you, do not be angry",[31] and nowhere does he say "The Lord says this", "In the name of the Lord I do such and such things". These things (are so) even though, because it was suitable to the economy, and because of the contentiousness and the difficulty of the coming of the Jews towards God, and (because of) the imperfection otherwise of those who were hearing, in many places he says that he has received a commandment from the Father,[32] and that he speaks those things which he heard from him.[33] But yet, showing (his) royal and unenslaved condition and equality of honour towards the Father, he said that the Father too works likewise,[34] and that the Father is in him, and he is in the Father,[35] because .... ⟨3 folios missing⟩

⟨Therefore he who divides Emmanuel, and defines him in two natures (*Lebon* p. 86) after the inexpressible union, along with the natures divides the activities and properties as well⟩[36] and establishes two natures which act and without diminishment undergo those things which are their own. But he who confesses one nature incarnate of God the Word, and teaches an unconfused union, does not deny awareness of the difference and particularity which lies in natural quality of the natures from which there is the one Christ. But it is foolish and uninstructed to say that Emmanuel was composed from two properties[37] or two activities. For because "to think" is a property of a rational mind, but "blackness" or "whiteness" for example (is a property) of a body, do we say because of this that a man is composed from "thinking" and from "whiteness" or from "blackness"? But no reasonable person says this: but he says that man exists from the natures of body and soul, to which (natures) those (properties) which were mentioned adhere and (from which) they are seen not to exist in isolation. But apart from this, how is it not absurd to speak of two properties or two activities? For there are many properties and not just two, of each nature. For example, of his humanity there is perceptibility, and visibility, and mortality, and being subject to hunger and to thirst and to other things like it. And there are many properties of the divine nature: invisibility, intangibility, being before the ages, (*Lebon p. 87*) being unlimited. The things which are done are similarly many and various, and all these are as many as the human and divine actions that a man can recount.

Thus he who divides Emmanuel in a duality of natures after the inexpressible union, divides with him, as we have said many times, the activities and properties as well. For it is customary often to call the things which are done "activity" and sometimes to call even him

who acts "activity" because activity is, properly speaking, as we have shown in the things said above, itself an active movement. Hence Julius the Theologian too, who was Bishop of Rome, in the Treatise designated "Against those who contend against the divine incarnation of the Word on the pretext of the ὁμοούσιον",[38,39] says this: (JULIUS): "But there is one nature, one hypostasis, one activity, one person, entirely God, entirely man, the same".[40] For because there is one who acts, both his activity and the active motion are one. But as we have said, the things which are done are many and diverse, but we who recognise one nature of God the Word incarnate say that these belong to one and the same, even if some are proper to God and some more human, just as we also believe the utterances proper to God and human were said by one and the same (person). (*Lebon p. 88*)

But those who divide (Emmanuel) by speaking of two natures after the union, divide with them also those things which, as properties, each one of the natures naturally attracts.

But let it not escape your notice that holy Julius, when he confesses one nature incarnate of God the Word, confesses that he also recognises the properties of the natures from which the one Christ is, and the difference between them, while rejecting division. For he wrote this in the same Treatise: (JULIUS): "For the body, and God whose is the body, are one and the same, without the flesh having been changed to what is not bodily, but possessing both what is its own, which is from us by the birth from the Virgin, and that which is above us, by the mixture or union of God the Word".[41] And again, in the Treatise designated "About the union of the body with the divinity of God the Word", he says as follows: (JULIUS): "But it is confessed that in him the created (being) is in union with the uncreated, and the uncreated in combination[42] with the created, while one nature is established from the two parts".[43] AND AFTER OTHER THINGS, "Hence necessarily, it is called both corporeal in everything and divine in everything. And he who is unable in these diverse things which are united to recognise what belongs to each of them, falls away into contradictions which do not agree, but he who both recognises the properties and preserves the union, neither defrauds the natures,[44] nor is forgetful of the union."[45] You see how he said he acknowledges the properties of the natures, and preserves the union, one nature existing from the two parts.

But regarding that thing which your Chastity said, that because (*Lebon p. 89*) the way of our Saviour's birth in the flesh was different from ours—for (he was born) from the Virgin and the Holy Spirit—

it was right that not even the properties of humanity should be seen as regards him, it is advantageous that we should introduce for you the words of wise Basil, which are written in the Treatise which we have mentioned, against Eunomius. For when that man had said that because the Father does not exist by birth, but the Son by birth, and the Spirit by procession, the ousia should also be divided, along with the difference of being of each hypostasis, that man learned in the Spirit and wise, in disposing of the objection says as follows: (BASIL): "If those things, which have the existence of what they are in different ways, have different ousia as well, not even men are alike[46] in ousia. For Adam, who was fashioned from the earth, had one existence, but Eve another, from his side, and Abel another, from copulation, and another had he who was from Mary, for he was only from a virgin."[47] Therefore, if they have the same ousia, both he who was fashioned from the earth, and she who was cut out from the rib, and he who came forth from the conjunction of a man and a woman, and he who was born in the flesh from a virgin, how does it not follow to think the properties of the ousia also appear in the same way on each one of them? But in this instance, because the Word of God had been hypostatically united to flesh which was rationally ensouled, from Mary who bore God, the Word was not allotting to his (own) flesh to suffer everything which belonged to it. But we say they "belonged to it" not so that we may distinguish the Word, for those things which we say the flesh suffers, (*Lebon p. 90*) are the sufferings of the incarnate Word, while his divinity does not lose impassibility. For to whom we say the flesh belongs, to this same (person) we reckon the sufferings of the flesh belong completely. For he does not, because the conception and birth from the Virgin is a wonder, therefore renounce in everything the human laws of nature. For Gregory the Theologian also says this in the Letter to Cledonius: (GREGORY): "If a man says that (Christ) flowed in the Virgin as through a pipe, but not that in her he was formed at the same time in a human and a divine way—in a divine way (because) without a man, and in a human way because in the law of conception—he is like an atheist".[48] And holy Cyril, in the Treatise of question and answer *That Christ is One* says: (CYRIL): "Nor would he have been a curse, when he suffered the cross on our behalf, unless he had become flesh, that is, he became flesh and was inhominate, and underwent a birth like us for our sake, humanly, that (birth) I say, which (took place) through the holy Virgin".[49]

Therefore when you hear that the conception of Emmanuel took place in a divine way and at the same time in a human way, how do

you completely remove him from human properties, which the incarnate Word receives willingly? For unless we say the flesh was capable of receiving the things which belonged to it, with the exception of sin—for this is not a part of the ousia, but a sickness which, as I have said, occurs as a result of inattention—he was able neither to suffer the cross on our behalf nor to endure death. But it is well known that he was undergoing these things in that of which it was the nature to suffer. And he who was incarnate is also he who suffered (*Lebon p. 91*) in the flesh, while he remained, in that he is God, impassible. And if we separate him from our statement that he suffered, we separate him as well, at an earlier point, from the flesh in which he willingly underwent suffering. For because of this the ark was prepared from wood which would not rot, and outside and inside it was smeared over with gold, because gold as a type represented (the) divinity, and the wood (the humanity), so that we see one Christ prefigured from the two of them.[50] And in the same way as the wood does not rot, neither does it sustain corruption from worm or maybe from moth, but it allows the cutting of iron and the burning of fire; so too the humanity which the Word of God united hypostatically to himself did not endure the corruption from sin, which corrupts like (the corruption) from moth and worm. For it was not able to be downtrodden as far as sinning is concerned, but it was capable of receiving the cutting of iron and other torments, since the incarnate Word allowed that it should suffer this when he wished. In this it is said that he was scourged, and pierced by the nails, and died in the flesh, and underwent burial, even though by the resurrection he was seen to be above these things, and he was not left in Sheol, nor did his flesh see corruption.

But that the teachings of the God-clad Fathers agree with these things, hear again the quotation, which is inspired by God, of Cyril, who says as follows in the Treatise of Address to the God-fearing emperor Theodosius: "Is it not then already known—for it is not unknown to anyone at all—that the Only-Begotten became like us, that is, fully man, in order that he might set free our earthly body from intrusive corruption, imparting his own life to it, in the economy through the union. (*Lebon p. 92*)

But he made the human soul his own that he might show it superior to sin, and he imparted to it the firmness and unchangeableness of his own nature, as dye in a fleece. For I think words about these things which far surpass what is not to be seen require examples; for we see with difficulty the divine and mind-transcending mysteries in a mirror and in riddles.[51] But as I think, the matter was not 'not to

be seen', for it supplies in it a consideration which is probable, or rather, valid. For just as (the flesh), because it became the flesh of the Word who gives life to all, was above the grasp of death and corruption, in the same way, I think, (the soul) because it became the soul of him who knew not how to sin, possessed an established and unchanging position in all good things, and became incomparably more powerful than the sin which once opposed us. For Christ (was) the first man on earth who 'did no sin, nor was deceit found in his mouth'."[52,53] AND AGAIN AFTER A LITTLE, "But it is marvellous and there is no-one at all to whom it is not stupifying, that a body, which is corruptible by nature, should revive; for it belonged to the incorruptible Word. And again the soul, having obtained a combination like this [with him][54] and union, descended into Sheol using the power and authority appropriate to God, and appeared to the spirits there."[55] And again he seals up the things said in the Treatise by adding this: AND AGAIN: "(There is) one Lord Jesus Christ, and through him the Father created everything. Therefore he is both Creator as God, and Life-giver as life, and he is composed so as to become one in the middle from human properties and from those which are above man.[56] For he is mediator between God and men, according to the scriptures: for he is God by nature (*Lebon p. 93*) and not without flesh; while truly man, and not mere (man) like us, but he is he whom he was, even though he became flesh. For it is written 'Jesus Christ, yesterday and today, the same for ever'."[57] And that (which is written) in the prophet Isaiah, "And we saw him, that he had neither form nor beauty, but his appearance was not honourable but inferior to men"[58] makes known the greatness of the contempt and insult which came upon him when he was tested. And he was beaten upon his cheeks blows which were utterly shameful, and he did not turn away his face from the disgrace of spitting, but he endured the cross and disregarded the shame, as the Apostle said. For he brought no rejection of the flesh or change or transformation of the human ousia: for it belonged to Christ in this too that he should overcome more than men. And he did not open his mouth, but he came to slaughter without an utterance like a lamb. And he endured everything humbly and with supreme long-suffering:— all this while he was God by nature and knowing no sin, even if he was, the same, man in truth. Greatest of all, (the fact) that his glory also effects the size of the disgrace, means that no man from among men who suffered shall ever be compared to him.

Your Chastity therefore being aware of these things and guided by the teachings of these former teachers of the mysteries in the Church,

you should not limp or be dim sighted, but should confess Emmanuel from two natures, divinity and humanity, and not deny difference and particularity with respect to natural quality of the natures from which the one (Christ) is brought together to an indivisible union. And you should think it iniquitous to divide Christ into a duality (*Lebon p. 94*) of natures after the union, and consequently their activities and properties. For in a duality everything is cut at the same time, and reduced to a diversity which is divided and cut in everything, whether you speak of activities or properties. For when we denounce the division (resulting from) a duality of natures after the union, we do not, as you have thought, instead introduce, as evil men advocate, the phrase "two united natures". But we say what is indisputably the case, namely that duality is cutting and division. For "If the union is true, they are not two in any way, but one Christ is understood from two",[59] as holy Cyril said when he was writing in reply to evil Theodoret's complaints against the Chapters. And he sent the same thing to Succensus, thus: (CYRIL): "So that the two should henceforth be no longer two, but through the two one living thing has been completed".[60]

But let no-one ignorantly think that natural quality is ascribed only to the body, as for example the quality of being solid, or of taste, or of density, or of weight, or of thickness or transparency. For, because of the poverty of human intellects, we are obliged to make use of words having a corporeal signification about divine things as well, and they cannot be spoken of otherwise. Holy Cyril acknowledged this, in the first book of the Commentary on John's Gospel, when he says as follows: (CYRIL): "Therefore as far as approaches subtlety of mind (*Lebon p. 95*) and the acuteness of movement in it, let us look at the varied beauty of the divine nature, but expressing these things about it rather in a human way and in our vocabulary, for the tongue is incapable of extending to the measure of truth".[61] Because of this, the same man in the second book of the same Commentary, interpreting the non-corporeal divinity of the Father and the Son, says as follows: (CYRIL): "The offspring are thought of as being a certain natural quality so to speak, of their begetters, showing what the begetter is in ousia, and displaying the natural quality[62] of their source".[63]

We have, therefore, sent these things as we have understood them. And we rejoice with you at (your) growth and increase towards divine knowledge. Because of this we aptly say to you the word of the Apostle: "Meditate on these things, remain in these things, that your growth may be obvious to everyone".[64] But avoid writing doc-

trinal teachings and do not easily approach this, for such things belong, as you know, to those who are much instructed and have meditated diligently on the Scripture inspired by God, and have grown rich on the toils of the things of the same Spirit, the tested former teachers of mysteries in the holy Church, and not to those recently instructed in the knowledge of the divine teachings. But if somewhere you are compelled to make a pronouncement—as men frequently (affirm that) they will repent, and pursue the orthodox faith, and make profession—do you only lay down the creed of the 318 Fathers, and anathema on those who oppose (it), both on individuals and on teachings, just as previously in our vicinity too those who have repented have done. (*Lebon p. 96*) For it is proper and prudent that we follow them in these words, and proceed in everything in the footsteps of those who journeyed before, and be fearful and stand in awe, lest even unwillingly we put a foot anywhere and in anything untrod and difficult. For the (words), spoken in counsel in the Book of Proverbs, "We should carry knowledge[65] on our lips",[66] as I think, lead in this direction.

But our Lord Jesus Christ, God and Saviour, with whom are treasuries of wisdom and knowledge, as the Apostle has said,[67] grant that you may abound in every word and in all knowledge, and that you may gain the reward of a man zealous in faith and works, both in the present age and in that to come.

The First Letter of the Patriarch Lord Severus to Sergius the Grammarian has ended.

Notes

1. Is. xxi.12.
2. Prov. x.17.
3. Reading ܘܐܬܕܡܪܬ for ܘܐܬܕܡܪ.
4. Prov. xi.2.
5. Lev. x.10–11.
6. Prov. xvi.1 (Hexaplaric ms. only).
7. The root here is ܡܙܓ. Please see Appendix C on "mixture words".
8. PG 77.241B (=ACO I, 1, 6a, p. 159.18–160.2).
9. Cyril, Pusey edn. Vol. 5, p. 499.17–500.4. Syriac only.
10. *Ibid.*, p. 500.6–501.4. Syriac only.
11. cf. I Jn. i.1–3.
12. That is, the Logos.
13. The contrast in Cyril is ἑτέρα μὲν .... ἕτερος δὲ.
14. PG 76.329D (=Pusey edn. Vol. 6, p. 286.3–8). *Apol. pro XII Cap. contra Orient.*
15. PG 76.85A–B (=Pusey edn. Vol. 6, p. 113.7–16).
16. PG 76.105A–B (=Pusey edn. Vol. 6, p. 128.25–129.2).

17. On p. 118.3 the Syriac ܒܡܢܬܐ translates the Greek ἀνὰ μέρος. It is possible that ܒܡ̈ܢܘܬܐ is also intended to represent that Greek phrase, and could be translated "apart". Without this conjecture, we may make better sense by translating, "in (separate) parts".

18. Reading ܡܬܦܣܩܢܐ for ܡܬܦܪܩܢܐ. (= εἰς ἕνωσιν ἀδιάτμητον).

19. PG 75.1289C (= Pusey edn. Vol. 7, p. 364.2–5).

20. PG 76.137B–C (= Pusey edn. Vol. 6, p. 153.18–154.3).

21. cf. p. 118.3. Internal cross-references are to page and line of Lebon's edition of the Syriac text of the *Letters*.

22. PG 29.689C. *Adv. Eun. Lib. IV.*

23. cf. 1 Cor. xv.52.

24. 1 Cor. viii.6.

25. Rom. ix.5.

26. Jn. xi.11.

27. PL 54.767A–B.

28. Mk. iv.39.

29. Mt. xiv.28–29.

30. Mk. i.41; Lk. v.13.

31. cf. Mt. v.22.

32. Jn. x.18.

33. cf. Jn. viii.26.

34. cf. Jn. v.19.

35. Jn. xiv.10.

36. This section is quoted at *Lebon p. 184*, below, from which the words included here in diamond brackets are taken.

37. cf. above, EM p. 72.10.

38. ܕܒܪ ܟܝܢܐ = τοῦ ὁμοουσίου.

39. Lietzmann, H.: *Apollinaris von Laodicea*, (Tübingen, 1904), p. 194. Note on line 15: Title—ἰουλίου ἀρχιεπισκόπου ῥώμης πρὸς τοὺς κατὰ τῆς θείας τοῦ Λόγου σαρκώσεως ἀγωνιζομένους προφάσει τοῦ ὁμοουσίου.

40. *Ibid.*, p. 199.16–17.

41. *Ibid.*, p. 199.23–27.

42. Syriac ܒܡܙܝܓܘܬܐ ܕܐܚܕܐ. Greek ἐν συγκράσει.

43. Lietzmann, *op. cit.*, p. 187, lines 5–8.

44. Greek τὴν φύσιν.

45. Lietzmann, *op. cit.*, pp. 192–3, lines 14–17 and 1–2.

46. As Lebon notes, the Syriac translator here seems to have read ὁμοιούσιοι with Ps. Basil, while Severus, as is clear from what follows, wrote ὁμοούσιοι.

47. PG 29.681A–B. *Adv. Eun. Lib. IV.*

48. PG 37.177C.

49. PG 75.1264B (= Pusey edn. Vol. 7, p. 342.6–10).

50. Severus undoubtedly borrows this parallel from Cyril (cf. *Scholia*, Pusey edn. Vol. 6, Ch. 11, pp. 518–521). That the ark was overlaid with gold outside indicates that the Word was united to the holy flesh. That the ark was overlaid with gold inside indicates that the Word also made his own the reasonable soul that was within the body.

51. cf. 1 Cor. xiii.12.

52. Is. 1.9.

53. PG 76.1161C–D (= Pusey edn. Vol. 7, p. 61.14–62.14).

54. Reading ܕܠܘܬܗ (= H. syr. 22) for ܕܠܘܬܗ̇, and translating ܡܐܬܝܬܐ as "combination".

55. PG 76.1165A. (= Pusey edn. Vol. 7, p. 68.2–8).

56. This passage, quoted here first by Severus, is especially difficult for Sergius. cf. below, p. 102.8; p. 121.2 ff; p. 161.6 ff.

57. PG 76.1193B–C (= Pusey edn. Vol. 7, p. 134.10–18). *De Recta Fide ad Theod.*

58. cf. Is. liii.2–3.

59. PG 76.445B (= Pusey edn. Vol. 6., p. 484.1–2).

60. PG 77.245B ὥστε τὰς δύο, μηκέτι μὲν εἶναι δύο, δι' ἀμφοῖν δὲ τὸ ἓν ἀποτελεῖσθαι ζῶον. (= ACO I, 1, 6a, p. 162.8–9). *Ep. XLVI, Ad Succ. Ep. II.*

61. PG 73.132B (= Pusey edn. Vol. 3, p. 114.23–27).

62. Syriac: ܡܥܒܕܢܘܬܐ. Notwithstanding the marginal note on p. 109 below, the Greek is τὴν κατὰ φύσιν ἐνέργειαν.

63. PG 73.281B, lines 25–9. (= Pusey edn. Vol. 3, p. 255.15–18).

64. 1 Tim. iv.15.

65. Note in margin: Knowledge of (the one who) knows himself.

66. Prov. xvi.23.

67. Col. ii.3.

Letter II of Sergius

The Second Letter of Sergius the Grammarian to the Patriarch Lord Severus.

Sergius, humble Grammarian, to our holy and blessed Lord, to the Father of Fathers and ecumenical Doctor, to the Patriarch.

"Who am I, your servant, that you have looked on a dead dog like me?"[1] For (these) words are more fitting to me than to Mephibosheth. For though the estates of his father's house and a servant for labour were permitted for the mark of honour of that man, (David) did not heal his lameness with this. But more than he, I was enriched, who have escaped from all this poverty of ignorance and my own lameness has been made straight, and these things at a time which is poor as regards the things of (*Lebon p. 97*) God, when the word of the Lord is rare, and when vision is not distinct.[2] And how shall I express what happened to me in the midst of reading in front of a porch? In front of the holy writings I saw the writings of the wise Bishop Antoninus and my name was inscribed. And when I lifted up the seals with calmness, I opened the chapters of the letter and at once I was happily confident, for I feasted well on the sight. And afterwards as I advanced little by little, I cast (my) eyes on chapters of the other writings, and saw something great and divine. When little by little I had altered what I was seeing, I retraced my tracks, and I believed that I was hearing cither music, (which played) "This is the door of the Lord by which the just enter in".[3] And I said many times, "It is not my writing and the letter is not to me". And again I departed outside. And why should I require many words? Youth loves to be rash from ignorance of the beautiful.[4] But being rash again, I compelled (my) eyes to go with me on this road, and I have knocked again, and little by little have entered inside. And who did I become after these things? I need tranquillity[5] that I can speak: but I shall tell this which I have remembered with difficulty; because I had ceased to think of such divine matters; and I was leaping about somewhere out of (my) mind, in the frequent visions which the Fathers were putting out along with most divine words, even though I again thought of the smallness of (my) reasoning.

And when along with these things I meditated also on the visions

of Daniel, I believed that I saw the horn which had eyes and a mouth, which spoke great things.[6] But gradually I became used to marvellous things, and when many times, so to speak, I was called from the midst of the sleep of negligence, (*Lebon p. 98*) I persuaded my tongue to say "Speak Lord, for your servant had heard".[7] And at once he removed ignorance from me, and I was taught rightly to know the wisdom of the Father, the cause of all, and to understand mystical words, and the dark word and symbols.[8] And when I went up to the darkness of these divine things, I heard the trumpet with all ears and I saw henceforward "the true light which enlightens every man who comes into the world".[9] And when I was fully initiated in these great matters, I went out from the letter, which my right hand had introduced into my mind, not like the judge Ehud who killed Eglon.[10] And after these things for those encamped on this side and on that I suddenly became a mighty armed man. But how double war was kindled against us, wait upon the word, Father of Fathers: I shall tell (it).

Some of those who were infected with the lack of knowledge with which I was infected before, many times made crass accusations as they summoned some holy writing of yours to judgement and urged forward many things against proprieties. Some others were coming from Chalcedon somewhere, and were making excerpts from passages of your (writings), and were attempting to cast us out here, while they were publishing these proprieties. And you instruct me to proceed in the middle, and to interrupt the onset of the two of them with words, and were saying that I should call witnesses. And when I received your writing, I read the laws to them. And quite speechless, as they were overcome by the exactness of these divine (doctrines), these (points) of dispute went home to them at once, unless they were perverse in argument.

But I, who pass from war after war, and with difficulty have (*Lebon p. 99*) sacrificed peaceful things to God, and was acquainted with the war-trumpet, suffered a human passion: we observe that those who have been freed from a constant sickness of the eyes have an insatiableness for light, and this has frequently led back to sickness. For the rich diet of your words, Father, made the earlier sickness to wither, but caused a second (illness) of ignorance to spring forth in me. For when I diligently read the dazzling light of wise Cyril in your holy writings, I was obliged to close my eyes, and the salt tear of ignorance flowed.

At all events, you say, O Theologian, that (Cyril) made this contradictory statement: "Not confusing with each other and mixing

the natures".[11] Now, I acknowledge that once the divine union is mentioned, confusion is set aside, (but here) the union is not thought of in a faulty way when the natures are unmixed in a divine and inexpressible mingling and in a hypostasis.[12] How (then) shall I proclaim one nature incarnate of the Word, and accuse of folly those who acknowledge two natures for Christ? And how shall I find fault with that Theological Wisdom[13] which states that the natures are mixed in a composition which is beyond description, which it calls *συμφυΐα*[14] through which I learn that the natures are not (merely) placed beside each other, but are utterly mingled to (become) one image and one hypostasis, so that the composition being thus accurately understood, the ousia of the divine Trinity, which is only concerned with three persons, is not increased? And we shall keep the definition of the Fathers safe, teaching one nature of God the Word incarnate, and not expounding this royal doctrine wrongly like the opposition. For they say they speak of one nature of the Word, but in the word "incarnate" there is seen a mark of the other (nature): (*Lebon p. 100*) not that the Word has joined this to itself hypostatically, and thus there is naturally one from two, but that, so they babble, an accidental union[15] has taken place, (the word) "incarnate" being a token of a nature standing in its own right. The righteous word which truly acknowledges one nature incarnate of the Word refutes these things.

But it is time to return to what was set down earlier. For I am aware of someone who objects and says: "Listen carefully to the consequences: the Son is understood as one in this way as well". But I remember that Nestorius also says this. Thus, I learn that the combination of two or more simples into one belongs to the principle[16] of composition, in which what is complete is also a (constituent) part, and (yet) afterwards the (constituent) parts are not from then on adjudged according to the principle of duality, since once and for all one ousia and quality has come into being.[17] Therefore unless the natures, from which Christ is, were mixed inconfusedly, how shall I say that those things which thus remained unmixed with each other were hypostatically united? How shall I retain the principle of composition, when the natures are retained just as they were? For it is impossible for me to conceive of a union of things mutually unmixed, as they say, and necessarily thereby Christ would have to be thought of (lit. we should have to think of) as two natures.

It seems right, therefore, that I should repeat the discussion about properties which I learned from your holy lines: "For although the Word is something and keeps that thing, he also became something

else, obviously not involving a lessening of divinity, but through the supreme union of inhomination he had at the same time these properties and those which he (already) had, and he shows that he was become one incarnate nature".[18] But holy Father, how I am to understand that the natures are not mixed is a great (obstacle) to me. (*Lebon p. 101*) For after this I am unable to go up to centurions or chiliarchs, but to you Moses, who was worthy to speak these more divine things face to face, and who explains the greater things. For my mind is wearied by labour and is unable to ascend to such a height and all the more when learned men from Chalcedon were stirring up battle from common notions on the one side, and on the other side were excommunicating these Fathers and telling us on all sides (of) the two natures. But when divine grace descends upon my humble tongue, it often drives out the first kind (of difficulty).

But how shall I pass over to this second (type of difficulty), since the laws of the Fathers are read to me and I do not know at (any) one time how to keep silent, lest "the natures" of those who are pursuing should take me? But when I add thought upon thought and make my mind to pass to desire for the fear of God, I seem like one who slips and like those athletes who are exhausted. How not to fall in everything, but to overcome, I shall learn from you, Doctor and Witness of right belief.[19] And with this I shall avoid the second ignorance also for it is time that I say this too.

I remember that in my lines there is (the formula that Christ) is "from two natures", and all the propriety of the inhomination of the Word is a mystery. But I also received the point gladly and approved the fatherly correction that it was thought foolish to say "a gathering of properties",[20] just as no-one will rashly say that a man is constituted from "being rational" and "blackness", although the two words are not being thought equal in every respect. For "being rational" completes an ousia that it should be one: thus (a man is) a rational mortal living thing, and if someone should remove (*Lebon p. 102*) that "being rational", he destroys the subject in every respect. But blackness (is) not in the hypostasis but is a sign of that which is laid down (and) when it fades to whiteness it leaves the ousia (just) as it is naturally.

Therefore as I keep silent wise Cyril again urges on (my) thoughts, who speaks best by means of your priestly tongue, but is not yet understood by me, who am of small account. But I read the law to you as well: "He is composed so as to become one in the middle, of human properties, and those which are above man".[21] The Father seems to say that the incarnate Word was one in every respect, I

mean both nature and propriety, when he mingled the natures along with the proprieties. But (I say) this as a suggestion rather than a decree, for in what opinion should I be headstrong? Again, Masters, I pray that in this knowledge too I may be made perfect by you.

But where else do I fail in (your) letter? I shall make a defence against your fatherly rebuke with testimonia of the truth that I did not suddenly venture to discuss theology but approached the subject with much trepidation of mind and voice and I repeat the old saying 10,000 times "I am of a meagre voice and a slow tongue".[22] For we would teach by means of the written (word) every land and island, so to speak, even if some sort of lament should be necessary, and we will "go to Macedonia"[23] in word, (we) who recall the boldness of teaching of the Fathers. In those cases where it is required that I bring a mystery in writtten form I have drawn on your words in every respect and I am confident in a situation like this. But I shall accept your spiritual bridle with my whole tongue and will not bite it like an uncontrolled colt and make [a path][24] outside the proper sense. But you keep guard too, for you are a lamp (*Lebon p. 103*) of Israel like David[25] or a watchman like Ezekiel,[26] and do not lie hid under a measure,[27] but when you have ascended upon the candlestick of the Church shine again on us who are in the house of Christ, in order that "good will"[28] may touch us as we stretch out (our) mind again to you.

These things belong to the high priest of God. For my part, I (shall receive), so I believe, the reward of my labour, which from contempt I am ashamed that I should even call "labours", (which) will free the mind from every fleshly opinion. But through your divine prayers may I see here the peace of the Church with you true pastors, and may I go yonder with pure confidence that I shall be with you on the right hand side.

The Second Letter of Sergius the Grammarian to the Patriarch Lord Severus is ended.

Notes

1. 2 Kms. ix.8.
2. cf. 1 Kms. iii.1.
3. Ps. cxvii.20. There may be a word-play on ܬܪܥܐ "chapter" and "door".
4. Lebon suggests ὑπὸ ἀπειροκαλίας (from ignorance of the beautiful; want of taste) as underlying ܡܢ ܠܐ ܡܣܟܠܘܬ ܠܫܘܦܪܬܐ
5. ܣܦܝܩܘܬܐ: nothingness; a void; leisure; freedom. The underlying Greek may possibly be ἡσυχία.
6. cf. Dan. vii.11.

7. 1 Kms. iii.9. LXX ἀκούει.

8. ܪܗܒܐ.

9. cf. Jn. i.9.

10. cf. Judg. iii.21.

11. See p. 77 (Lebon) above, (Severus' *First Letter*). PG 76.85B. The Syriac translator attributes the participles to Cyril himself. On p. 77 ܡܙܓ is used to translate συγχέων, here ܒܠܒܠ is used.

12. The passage is difficult. Lebon suggests reading ܪܫܐܝܬ for ܕܫܐܝܬ: ". . . . the union is not *primarily* thought of when the natures are unmixed . . .", but this is probably less satisfactory.

13. So Sergius calls Gregory Nazianzen.

14. cf. PG 37.181C, line 7: τῷ λογῷ τῆς συμφυΐας. The Syriac is: ܫܘܬܦܘܬܐ ܕܐܟܝܢܐ. *Ep. CI, Ad Cled. Ep. I.*

15. ܚܕܝܘܬܐ ܕܠܘܬ ܣܝܡܐ The Greek is possibly ἕνωσις κατὰ θέσιν.

16. ܡܠܬܐ.

17. cf. below, p. 150.19–24.

18. Because of the gap in the ms. the place of this in the earlier letter of Severus is not known.

19. ܕܚܠܬ ܐܠܗܐ = εὐσέβεια.

20. cf. p. 86, line 8.

21. PG 76.1193B. This passage was quoted above by Severus, cf. p. 92.28 (= Pusey edn. Vol. 7, p. 134.13–14). *De Recta Fide ad Theod.*

22. Ex. iv.10.

23. cf. 1 Tim. i.3; Acts xvi.9.

24. Read ܪܗܘܓܐ for ܕܗܘܓܐ (misprint).

25. cf. 2 Kms. xxi.17 and 4 Kms. viii.19.

26. Ezek. iii.17; xxxiii.7.

27. cf. Mt. v.15.

28. cf. Lk. ii.14.

Letter II of Severus

Again the Second Letter of the Patriarch Severus to Sergius the Grammarian.

I now approve of your desire to learn, because when you received a letter which in it brought the words of scripture which is inspired by God, and (the words) of the revered teachers of mysteries in the holy Church who defined exactly the word of truth, you knew from them that it is right for those who are not beginners (in) confessing the faith to acknowledge and to profess the particularity according to natural quality of the natures from which there is the one and only Christ, (natures) I mean of divinity and of humanity: one person, one hypostasis, one nature belonging to the Word, meaning incarnate, and because you have chosen to set out again for discussion that which was difficult for your mind, and (because) you were not ashamed with the bashfulness which brings sin, and you were not afraid with the suspicion which brings (*Lebon p. 104*) destruction, but because you knew again to ask concerning the faith which is believed in because of the salvation of the soul, so that what belongs to truth might shine more brightly.

For it is very pleasant and welcome to me as well when I speak to a man who has a wisdom that investigates and not agreement only that does not test out and try—provided (of course) the range of the investigation does not transgress the measure. But even profane philosophy teaches that the measure is best in everything and the law of the fear of God confirms (it) when it forewarns (and) says "Do not remove the ancient limits which your fathers laid down".[1] As long as we retain these limits, it is good that we thrash out that which you have offered, or is in doubt. For holy scripture again teaches that iron sharpens iron,[2] (and) as one might say, when thoughts are sharpened, they are made more subtle and more acute.

Therefore when wise Cyril says in the Second Volume against the blasphemies of Nestorius, "When the mystery of Christ is brought into the middle for us, the principle of the union on the one hand recognises difference, but on the other hand rejects division, while neither confusing nor mixing the natures with each other",[3] you say that you cannot otherwise understand the undivided union, unless

some mixing and indescribable mingling of the natures is professed, and if this is not granted to you, you call the union "juxtaposition", and mock it.

Therefore what shall we say about this, unless we quote again the words of the Fathers and following scriptures we say to you: "Apply your ear to the words of the wise, and hear my words, and set your heart that you may know that they are beautiful. And if you cast those things into your heart, they will make you rejoice at the same time (*Lebon p. 105*) in your lips, that your hope may be upon the Lord and he may make known his path for you."[4] For why, when the Doctor did not present his doctrine (only) this far, (namely), "not confusing or mixing the natures amongst each other",[5] but wisely added, "But with the Word of God becoming a partaker in flesh and blood, one Son is understood and named in this way as well,"[6] do you not learn from (this) addition the inexpressible nature of the union? For we learn the fact that God the Word became a participator in blood and flesh like us from the Apostle who wrote: "Therefore because the children participated in blood and flesh, he also in the same way participated in the same things".[7]

And so if the divine Apostle brought our construction, I mean that which is from soul and body (and) is inexpressible, as an example (for) the understanding of Emmanuel which is particularly inexpressible, and (which construction of ours) is neither a mixture nor a juxtaposition, why should we apply these things[8] which do not fit to the mystery? Is the soul of a man changed that it should become flesh, or vice versa, the flesh that it should become soul? For this is the peculiarity of mixture. Or is the *συμφυΐα*[9] and union of rational soul with its body to be interpreted in terms of bodies which cleave to each other or are stuck? In no way at all. For we confidently say that it is a natural coming together, for it transcends our comprehension to specify how the human mind is composed with its own body. And hear Cyril the Theologian in his *Scholia* clearly teaching this to us: (CYRIL): "The fact of union is accomplished in many ways. For (example), when men are divided in affection and opinion and are thinking at variance with each other, they are said to be united through reconciliation of affection as they remove (their) differences (*Lebon p. 106*) out of the centre. (Again) for (example), we say that those things which cleave to each other or come together in different ways, whether by juxtaposition (*παράθεσις*)[10] or mingling (*μίξις*)[11] or mixture (*κρᾶσις*),[12] are united. Therefore when we say that the Word of God was united to our nature, the mode of union is recognised to be above human compre-

hension for it is not like one of those (ways) which were mentioned, but is completely inexpressible and not known by any man who lives, but to God who alone knows everything. And it is not at all astonishing that we are worsted in this way by such concepts, (since) when we enquire about how it is as regards our own situation we confess that comprehension is beyond the understanding that is in us. Now in what way do we believe that the soul of a man is united to his body? Who is there who is able to say? But if we (who) are accustomed to think and speak with difficulty (even) of small things, attain, if it is right, to imagine things so subtle and beyond understanding, we say that it is proper to think—yet the expression is inferior to the truth in every respect—that of such sort is the union of Emmanuel as one would think that the soul of a man has with its own body".[13]

Therefore how can you charge this inexpressible and truly divine union which the Word of God has miraculously accomplished, and this by condescending to us, with being that (union) taught by Nestorius which is a conjunction by relationship,[14] and believe that we are obliged to speak of two natures unless we confess, as you say, that at one time Christ had one ousia or quality? But this is nothing other than a real confusion[15] of ousia: therefore what you otherwise delude your hearers with is a persistent deception, (namely) your saying that you agree with us in confessing difference and particularity in accordance with (*Lebon p. 107*) natural quality of the natures from which Emmanuel is. For you think it is impossible to say that he is one unless he changes into one ousia, even when he is made up from two things of a different kind, and you propound for us that extraordinary (saying), and say: SERGIUS THE GRAMMARIAN: "Therefore unless the natures from which Christ is were inconfusedly mixed, how shall I say that these things which have thus remained unmixed were united hypostatically with each other? How will I retain the term "composition" when the natures are retained unmixed as you have said?"[16] For what is that at one time, according to your own words, "mixture without confusion"? For when you ask "How?" and in no other way are restrained from uncertainty, wise Cyril again supplies an answer, that not a mixture of natures but a composition took place, and once it took place the composition persisted, from which was completed one nature and hypostasis of the incarnate Word.

For in the Second Letter to Succensus he wrote as follows: (CYRIL): "For it is not the case that "one" is truly predicated only of things which are simple in nature, but (it may) also (be predicated)

of those which have come together in composition, an example being the situation of man, (composed) from soul and body. For these (elements) which are of different type like this and are not consubstantial[17] with each other, completed one nature of man when they were united, even if the difference in nature of those things which have come together to union exists in discussion of the composition. Therefore those who say that, if the Word incarnate is one nature it follows in everything (and) in every respect that there will be confusion and mixture, as if the nature of (the) man were decreased and stolen away, speak needlessly, for it is not decreased, nor as they say, (*Lebon p. 108*) stolen away. For it suffices for the complete demonstration of the fact that (the Word) became man to say that he was incarnate. For if this had been kept quiet by us, there would be some place for their slander, but because it is added necessarily in what way is there lessening or stealing away?"[18] And in the Treatise of question and answer in which (he shows) that Christ is one, proceeding in the same considerations and exact measures of teaching, he says as follows: (CYRIL): "It is not the case that in everything and from every respect only what is simple and of one type is called 'one', but also those compounded from two or from many things of different types. And that that is the case seems right to those wise in these matters."[19] And in his Treatise concerning the Holy Trinity which he addressed to a certain Hermias he wrote as follows: (CYRIL): "For he who is the undying beauty of God the Father and (his) likeness and aspect, God the Word who is of him and in him, abased himself to emptiness, not that he was compelled to this by anyone, but in the will of the Father, in his own will he became man, and without damage in any way he preserved the glory of his nature unchanged in himself, but took up manhood according to the economy. And he is understood one Son from two, a divine and human nature, which have run and come together to one, inexpressibly and inexplicably composed to union, and in such a way that cannot be understood."[20]

Since therefore, as you have heard many times, composition possesses the (quality) of being above reason and inexpressible, why do you resort to mixture and damaging confusion, and openly attribute inexpressibility to that? For if the divine union of inhomination and incarnation, and those two (natures) from which there is one Christ indivisibly, suffered the same thing as bodies which are mixed, (*Lebon p. 109*) or (if) one of them departed from its own natural quality[21] and ceased being that which it was, I do not see what is then remarkable and inexpressible.

But great Athanasius, whom if one were to call "The law of Orthodoxy", as did Gregory the Theologian, it would not swerve from what is proper, in his Treatise concerning faith calls the incarnation "composition", while showing it is truly inexpressible by forbidding unmeasured investigation. For he wrote as follows: (ATHANASIUS): "From (their questions) 'How?' and 'In what way?' and 'What follows?' even they have arrived at unfaithfulness. And they have prepared a dwelling-place instead of an incarnation, and instead of union and composition, a human activity, and instead of one hypostasis of our Lord Jesus Christ, two hypostases and persons, and in place of the Holy Trinity, unfittingly and unlawfully, they have thought of a quaternity. Unfittingly (indeed) in that they join a man with God, and number a servant with the Lord, and place a created person together with uncreated persons; and unlawfully, in that they make one hypostasis two, introducing to the Trinity a fourth hypostasis, which is foreign in everything, and of a different rank, and the last and least of all rational spirits."[22]

How alike, then, to these are the (doctrines) of Nestorius? For those who held that God the Word assumed our composition and participated like us in blood and flesh do not say, like Nestorius, that first of all an infant was formed in the womb, and thus through the love of friendship and through kindness (the Word) dwelt (in him) in (*Lebon p. 110*) a brotherly way,[23] and gave (him) the title and rank of Son, and the equality of an equal name. And see how wise Cyril quotes Diodore saying this: (DIODORE): "While the flesh was of Mary (and) when it was not yet taken up, it was from the earth and was in no way different from other flesh. For as Levi was tithed in the loins, but when he was born he assumed the rank, so also our Lord, while he was in the womb of the Virgin and of that ousia, did not have the rank of Sonship. But when he was formed and became the temple to God the Word, which receives the Only-Begotten, he assumed the rank of the name, and participated also in the rank itself."[24] And against these things, confuting him, (Cyril) learned and wise in the Spirit says: (CYRIL): "O excellent Sir, I say that you spew forth for us words which are unschooled and much infected with absurdity. For the holy body was from Mary, but, then, in the first beginnings of the becoming firm or constitution in the womb, it was holy as the body of Christ, and one sees no time in which it did not belong to him but rather was in common, as you said, and in equality with other flesh."[25]

And so how are we not cast outside of the truth, when we treat a conjunction by relationship in honour and an (in) dwelling and an

equality of the name of sonship as equal to hypostatic union, and speaking against (the words) of the holy and theological Fathers, we call the incarnation an inhabiting, and composition a human activity which takes place for a man clothed with God, who is impelled and enriched (with) divine partnership from the inspiration of the Spirit? For in the case of a conjunction by relationship, the independently existing infant has its own person (*Lebon p. 111*) and hypostasis, and similarly, the Word which dwelt in him is seen in his own hypostasis and person, and a union by relationship of the two persons takes place, which is only yoked by equality of name and by the honour of sonship. But in the case of hypostatic union and natural composition which is proper to God as well, because the flesh endowed with a reasonable soul had existence in very union with the Word, (namely, the flesh) which was assumed from the Holy Spirit and from Mary the Mother of God and perpetual Virgin, and it did not exist independently before the union with the Word, (therefore) the Word himself is believed immutably and without change to have become a child, while he remained that which he was and did not change or convert that which he took up, and he humbled himself to gradual growth, and exit, and full conception. And thus he was gloriously born from the holy Virgin, who remained a virgin even after the birth and was reckoned among mothers without lapsing from the boast of virginity. For now, how will anyone dare to say that he is two natures or two hypostases, he who was gloriously completed one Christ from two? For we will see no time, after (the time) when the Word "rested" on the Virgin according to the word of the Gospel,[26] in which that body endowed with a rational soul, which was united to him, did not belong to him.

Because of this Athanasius, (who is) wise in these divine matters, said that there is one nature incarnate of the Word, so that by means of this utterance which is utterly secure we may acknowledge the indisseverability of the union. For the Word himself, who had existence before the ages and is forever together with the Father, and is seen in his own hypostasis and is simple in ousia, became composite in the economy, and (that) word "incarnate" ensures that it is understood that the flesh endowed with a reasonable soul existed in relationship to the Word himself, and was not independently completed in its own hypostasis. (*Lebon p. 112*) For in the Treatise of Address to the God-fearing emperor Theodosius, Cyril, wise in all things, says as follows: (CYRIL): "Therefore being impelled towards the truth from every direction, (and) being particularly careful to tread in the footsteps which seem right to the divine scriptures,

and following the opinions of the Fathers, we believe that he who is from the root of Jesse, he who is from the seed of David, he who is from woman according to the flesh, he who is under the law with us as man, and above us, above the law as God, he who for our sake and with us (was) among the dead, he who above us on his own account is Lifegiver and Life, is in truth Son of God. And we do not make the manhood stripped[27] of divinity, nor do we divest the Word of humanity after the inexpressible and inexplicable union, but we confess one and the same Son, one thing from two objects, who was seen inexpressibly from two, meaning in a union of the supreme kind and not in a change of nature."[28] And above, in the same Treatise, he says again in a similar way: (CYRIL): "For he who is with him who begot him from eternity and (is) Son from before all ages, because he descended to the nature of man—not that he lapsed from being God, but rather he took up manhood—is rightly understood to have become also from the seed of David and had a birth (as) a child in his manhood. But what was assumed is not foreign to him, but his own in very truth: it is reckoned therefore as one[29] with him, just as one sees the composition of a man, for it is intertwined from things which are unlike in nature, I mean, soul and body; but thus one man is understood from two."[30,31] (*Lebon p. 113*)

But because you brandish up and down the word "mixture", (on the grounds) that it is spoken by Gregory the Theologian, know that he used the word as well when he wanted to establish the supreme union, being completely unafraid of the danger of confusion[32] or mingling[33] which usually takes place with moist and fluid bodies. None of this happens to the nature of divinity so long as God remains, and he will remain for ever, nor will he involve himself that he should suffer change. And on this hear as well the instructive voice of holy Cyril, in the First Volume against the blasphemies of Nestorius, answering as follows: (CYRIL): "For some of the holy Fathers as well have used the word 'mixture', but because you say you are afraid lest it be thought that some confusion has taken place, as in the case of liquids which are mixed with each other, I set you free from (this) fear. For (the Fathers) did not think in this way: how could they? But they use the word when they are at pains to indicate the supreme union of those things which have come together. Now we say they were united in an inseparable union, and the Word from God has his own flesh unchangeably. And we find that even the Scripture inspired by God does not use the word very judiciously, but places it rather as is useful and simply.[34] Thus Paul the Theologian wrote about some people, 'But the word of the report did not

profit those who were not mixed in faith with those who heard.'[35] For were these about whom the saying is (written) about to be mixed with each other in the same way as wine with water, and will they suffer some sort of confusion of hypostases with each other? Or (*Lebon p. 114*) will they rather be united in mind, as is written in the Acts of the holy Apostles, that among the people of those who believed, there was one heart and one mind.[36] But I think the latter is true, not the former. Therefore be without fears concerning this, for the mind of the saints is certainly prudent."[37]

But Gregory the Theologian in the Sermon on the Feast of the Epiphany, wanting to establish the sublimity of the union which, as you have now heard, is supernatural, said: (GREGORY): "God went forth with the assuming: one out of two which were opposite, flesh and spirit, of which the one deified and the other was deified. O new mingling![38] O wonderful mixture![39] He who is, became, and the Creator is created, and that which is incomprehensible is comprehended by means of (the) mind as an intermediate, which is in the middle (between) divinity and the grossness of flesh."[40] But in the First Treatise on the Son, showing that he recognises the union of God the Word to flesh endowed with a soul and intelligence (as) composition and not mixture, he wrote as follows, quarrelling with the Arians who were attributing words which were humiliating and to do with the economy to the existence of the Word which was before the ages, and not applying them to it when it was emptied and incarnated and enduring humility for our sake: (GREGORY): "In short, attribute those things which are more exalted to the divinity and the nature which is superior to sufferings and the body; and those things which are more lowly to the composite (one), to him who was emptied for your sake and incarnate—and it is not worse to say, he was made man as well—and was afterwards exalted, so that you, letting go of what is fleshly and lowly[41] in doctrine, may learn to be more exalted and to mount up with the divinity, and not continue in these visible things, but ascend with these intellectual things, and may recognise what is the principle[42] of nature and what is the law[42] of the economy. He who now is disdained by you was once (*Lebon p. 115*) above you: he who now is a man, was (once) not composite. Therefore what he was he remained, but what he was not he assumed."[43]

See (now) that we have clearly learnt that (Gregory) recognised the incarnation (as) composition, and not (as) mixture and confusion, even if it should happen that he used the term "mixture" for the establishment of the supreme union. For if we are going to stick

to the exaggerated use of words and not search out the sound meaning which shines out plainly from all his treatises, we would say, by not following carefully and intelligently, that because he said "The one deified and the other was deified" the flesh was deified and was changed into the ousia of divinity. And again, because he said, "It is not worse to say that he also became man", we should go on to think that God the Word fell to the ousia of humanity and one and the same person undergoes opposite effects from the two sides, since the followers of Nestorius as well, bringing up the words of this Father theologian, and thinking that they can beg from them a defence of their wickedness, pervert what is written in this way in the Sermon on Epiphany, or Nativity: (GREGORY): "He was sent out, but as man: for he was double, because he was also tired, and hungered, and thirsted, and was afraid, and wept according to the law[44] of the body."[45]

But since we know that (Gregory) does not, like these unclean men, say that the Son is double in natures and in hypostases, we reject the stain on the honour of this holy Father. For he recognises God inhominate, one from two. Nestorius does not confess this, but shuns this (formula) "from two", which establishes composition and completes one hypostasis and nature of the Word incarnate. For in (*Lebon p. 116*) the Sermon on the Epiphany he says: (GREGORY): "God went out with the assuming, one from two which were opposite, of which the one deified, and the other was deified".[46] But this "was deified" is understood and is said because the flesh shone out with the glory proper to God, as wise Cyril says,[47] and not because it had fallen into the nature of divinity. For Gregory the Theologian himself rejects this inaccurate understanding, when he said as follows in the Letter to Cledonius: (GREGORY): "If someone should say that the flesh is now laid down, while the divinity is stripped of the body, and not that it both is with the assuming and is also coming, may he not see the glory of the advent. For where is the body now, unless it is with him who assumed (it)? For it was not placed in the sun, as is the folly of the Manichaeans, that it should be honoured through disgrace or be poured out and dissolved in the air, like the nature of speech and the pouring out of a scent and the impermanent course of lightning. But where is that which was touched after the resurrection, or which is to be seen by those who pierced (him)? For divinity on its own is not visible. But he will come with the body, as I said,[48] in such a way as[49] he was seen by the disciples on the mountain, or appeared with the divine element overcoming the fleshly."[50] For his face was radiant like the sun on the

mountain, as we hear the Gospel, and his garments were white like light.[51] But these things do not indicate a change of ousia, far from it, but the brilliance and the multitude of the glory which is proper to God. For how was he going to be seen by those who pierced (him), if the flesh which was pierced is changed from being visible to being invisible?

And Cyril the Theologian in the First Letter to (*Lebon p. 117*) Succensus wrote as follows: (CYRIL): "It is equally nonsensical to say that the body was changed into the nature of divinity, and that the Word was changed into the nature of flesh. For just as the latter is impossible, for (the Word) cannot be transformed and is immutable, so also is the former. For none of the things which are comprehensible, (that is, none) of the creatures, is able to be changed to the ousia or the nature of divinity, and flesh belongs to the created order. Therefore we say that the body of Christ is divine because it is the body of God, and is brilliant with inexpressible glory, incorruptible, holy (and) life-giving. But that it was changed into the nature of divinity, no-one of the holy Fathers thought or said, nor do we affirm this."[52]

But the Fathers called (Christ) double because the study of Christ is twofold, and some things are written about him in a human way, and some things as is proper to divinity. And this wise Cyril, who proceeds exactly in everything, referred to holy Athanasius in the Letter to the Monks, quoting instructively as follows: FROM ATHANASIUS: "Therefore the aim and character of divine scripture, as we have frequently said, is this, that the teaching in it about our Saviour is twofold, that he was God for ever, and is Son and Word and the brilliance and the wisdom of the Father; and at the end he became man for our sake when he assumed flesh from the Virgin Mary who bore God."[53, 54] And (Cyril) himself writes as follows, making a defence against the complaint from Theodoret against the Fourth Chapter: (CYRIL): "But I say it would be far better and (*Lebon p. 118*) far more learned to attribute the human words not to another person, which is understood independently and apart[55] (as) Son, (namely) to the form of the servant as those men are accustomed to say, but to attribute them rather to the measure of his humanity; for it was right that being God and man at the same time, he should proceed by means of both words".[56]

You see that the form of the words is twofold, but Christ himself is not double in natures or hypostases, but is one from two. Hence, (Cyril) in the Second Volume against the blasphemies of Nestorius, completely forbids mention of "double", wanting to block all access

to those who divide (Christ), thus: (CYRIL): "It is not the case that because the Word from God the Father assumed flesh and went out a man like us, he is for this reason called double. For he is one and not without flesh, he who in his own nature is without flesh and body.[57] For just as if someone killed a man like us, he is not (then) justly accused of having committed wrong on two men, but only on one, even if perhaps (the man) should be understood (to consist) of soul and body, which were united with each other (and) which are not the same in nature, but different. The same thing should be understood in the case of Christ, for he is not double, but one sole Lord and Son, the Word who is from God and the Father, but not without flesh."[58] In the same way, in the Third Letter against Nestorius he says this: (CYRIL): "For the one and sole Christ is not double, even if he is understood (as brought together) from two different elements, having come to inseverable union, just as man is also understood from soul and body and is not then double, but one from two."[59] (*Lebon p. 119*)

Do you not perceive that we should use holy Cyril (as) a builder and establisher of divine teaching, if we are going to resist the Nestorian faction accurately with the words of the holy Fathers? For though I was able to cite many and various things which were written by Gregory the Theologian, and (which) were very seriously mutilated by those who divide the one Christ, I desisted, since I was unwilling to trouble your understanding, for doubtless you had renounced mixture and were wanting a defence against these things, which is not easy to those who are untrained, but to those who have taken into account all these things which were said by the Doctor, they appear accurate and clear of any blame and reprehension. Or did not also Peter, chosen first of the Apostles, write this about the compact and profound letters of Paul, thus: "There are in them things which are hard to understand, which unlearned and unstable men pervert, as also the rest of scripture, to their own destruction"?[60]

For it is possible to see as well those who have drunk from the cup of the error of Eutyches corrupting that saying of holy Gregory, which he wrote in the Sermon on Epiphany: (GREGORY): "That which was without flesh becomes incarnate, the Word becomes thick".[61] For they think, being beside themselves, that the Word has become thick like water when it condenses to ice, and as they mistakenly strive for the confirmation of this (idea), they quote as well that which is said in this way, in the Sermon on New Sunday[62]: (GREGORY): "And he becomes poor in becoming solid (as) flesh,[63] in

order that we might be enriched by his poverty".[64] But they are quite evidently proved to be in the wrong, inflicted with utter madness, and chopping off little words like mice, and taking an attitude towards scripture in the Jewish way, even though (*Lebon p. 120*) the Doctor wrote in this way in the First Treatise on the Son: AGAIN FROM GREGORY: "At the beginning he was without cause: for what is the cause of God? But at the end he became for a reason, and that was that you, scoffer, might be saved, you who disparage the divinity because it assumed your grossness".[65] Hence, therefore, it is recognised in advance that (when) he says that the Word became thick with our crassness, that means that he united an *οὐσία*, not a *φαντασία*, to himself hypostatically and in truth. For he also said about this: (GREGORY): "The Word grows thick; that which was invisible becomes visible; that which was untouchable is handled; that which was without time takes a beginning".[66]

And I could cite very many words which those who quarrel with orthodoxy have used as weapons against us, having excerpted in various ways the sound teaching of the holy Fathers, and they are proved to be in the wrong and are shamefully worsted by the complete context of what has been said by these men. For they have even composed a book of up to 250 so-called testimonies (taken) from excerpts of the proven doctor Cyril, and introduced him as the advocate of the error of the two natures. And while God stretched out his hand in the capital, we too have published a book against the error, to which the title is *Philalethes*, as a weapon against them, having set out these words of Cyril, and (now) everyone will know what is the true meaning, and what is sacrilege and what an instance of a lie. It is not surprising then if some people have held my poor words worthy of mutilation too! Therefore let these things not disturb you in the slightest: but it is time to say, like Qohelet, about this too: "There is nothing new or fresh under the sun",[67] but there is a similar vanity in their anxieties and they are inflicted with a related lack of reason. (*Lebon p. 121*)

But because you also try to obtain your former opinion from this quotation of holy Cyril which he speaks about Emmanuel, "He is composed (so as to become) one in the middle, of human properties, and those which are above man",[68] and, explaining (it) in I do not know what way, you say "The Father seems to say that the Word incarnate made to cleave natures along with properties, and is one in every respect, I mean both nature and particularity", (then) I am quite astonished. For, while (Cyril) (uses) a plural word, and discriminates (between properties) by difference, and says, "Of human

properties and of those which are above man", you mingle[69] everything to one particularity, as you have expressed it above, (namely) that at one time there took place one ousia or quality. For what are the properties which are above man? Certainly, divine in some way. And the human? It is already recognised that they are all the properties of flesh which is ensouled with a rational and intelligent soul. But the properties are of natural quality: for example, of divinity—the inability to be touched, and the inability to be seen; and of humanity—the ability to fall under sight, and the ability (to fall) under touch. But because the Word, which is invisible in ousia, was united in hypostasis to visible flesh, which has an intelligent soul, it is written that he was seen and touched, as we have said many times. For difference of natural quality stands firm and unchangeable, but the principle of the union allows that those things which in nature are properties of the flesh should be called properties of the Word because of the economy, and in the same way made the properties in ousia of the Word to be called properties of the flesh. (*Lebon p. 122*)

What then; should we tinker with the definition which is thus distinct and again present the message of true religion[70] (in terms of) confusion and blending?[71] And how, (when) the Doctor said, "Composed (so as to become) one in the middle", do you say in contradiction, "At one time, one ousia or quality has taken place", and again, "The Word incarnate is one in every respect, (I mean) both nature and particularity"? For if the Word incarnate became of one ousia and of one quality, as you have said, and of one particularity, he would be reduced, according to your definition, from being composite to something which would be simple, and wise (Cyril) made a mistake in that he still goes on calling him "composite", when he is like this.[72] But how do you say "one particularity", and not remember our saying that the Tome of Leo says: "Each one of the natures retains its particularity without diminishment",[73] so that we should think and say that these (natures and properties) adhere (to each other) in a division? For where (on the one hand) Christ is divided in a duality of natures after the union, each one of the natures proceeds without diminishment in those (properties) which are its own. But on the other hand, where the one nature of God the Word incarnate is professed—because he is Emmanuel, according to the word of holy Cyril—to be gloriously composed (so as to become) some one thing from two, it allowed the flesh—as is proper for the economy—sometimes also to suffer what belongs to it.[74] But this "sometimes" makes clear in every respect that it used as well properties which were above man, when he wished this. And also because

of this he used to walk over the crests of the waves, and he entered when the doors were closed and stood in the house with the apostles; and he allowed (them) to touch (him), and he did not deny handling of (his) body. For thus also, when he ascended bodily to heaven, the angels pointed as with a finger to the disciples, saying, "Men of Galilee, why do you stand looking (*Lebon p. 123*) into heaven? This Jesus who has been taken up from you to heaven is coming thus in the way that you have seen him go to heaven".[75] Therefore how will anyone with a Godfearing mind, and (who) cleaves to the teachings of the Apostles believe that the body which is subject to being seen, and so was seen and is expected to be seen, was changed to the divine ousia?

Therefore, because you ask us these things as a pupil and say that you have not assented to this within yourself,[76] but you ask if the Word incarnate is one in every respect, (I mean) both nature and particularity, as it was expressed by you above, "at one time there took place one ousia and quality", we give you advice, Beloved, in a brotherly and loving way, (and) we quote that scriptural passage, "Spring away from evil like this; do not delay, make your way far from it, for it does not follow the ways of life, but its paths are slippery and unknown".[77] For holy Cyril said in the Treatise against the Synousiasts: (CYRIL): "For if they say that the flesh of the Word was changed to the nature of divinity, it is fully necessary that it should be understood that he has renounced in every way his wish that he should become man. And see how Paul, who is wise in everything, says, 'For there is one God, and one mediator between God and men, the man Jesus Christ, who gave himself a substitutionary ransom on our behalf'.[78] For he is mediator as God and man at the same time, the same (person), who reconciles us to God and the Father through himself and in himself."[79] AND AGAIN AFTER A LITTLE: "And how will anyone dispute that, unless his still being and being thought like us is not suitable for him, it follows that he should say, 'When he comes, will the Son of Man find faith on the earth?',[80] and not rather, 'When the Word of God comes naked and without flesh, will he find faith in himself (*Lebon p. 124*) like this, among those on earth?' But because he openly and clearly calls himself Son of Man even at the time of the advent from heaven, it is evident that he has not changed the flesh into something else, but has it the more gloriously, incorruptible, without stain and adorned with unapproachable light. For he descends from heaven not in the former state of weakness—how could that be?—but in the glory of his Father with the holy angels."[81]

⌜But I am particularly astonished at how sometimes you call the

incarnation a composition, and (then) again you say that "at one time there took place one ousia or quality". Did the union therefore begin with composition, but when composition ceased, was it reduced to one ousia, in order that, as you say, the holy Trinity should be kept a Trinity and not receive a superfluous person?⌝[82] But you have heard both the divinely inspired scripture and the God-clad teachers of holy mysteries say that the Word ascended to heaven endowed with a body, (the Word) who had previously descended from there without a body when he undertook to enter emptiness, and that he is composite and composed in a glorious way. For they taught us in various ways, with those terms which are now being used. For if we were to say like Nestorius, that a man complete in his own hypostasis adheres to the Word in honour and only benevolently, (then) they would be right to fear a quaternity. For that unclean man says somewhere: (NESTORIUS): "Let us confess God in (a) man, and let us worship the man who is worshipped along with God Almighty by means of a divine conjunction".[83] But because those who are reared on true religion confess and proclaim one hypostasis from two, the Trinity remains a Trinity, even if the Word was incarnate and inhominate, and is one in hypostasis even while incarnate; he who before was simple, but now (*Lebon p. 125*) is gloriously and inexpressibly composed to flesh endowed with a soul and with a mind, and is not divided into two, and remains without confusion: the same one consubstantial[84] both to God the Father and to us.

But you again equip (yourself) as with something which is mighty and inescapable and you introduce the term, which pleases you, of *συμφυΐα*, (because) Gregory the Theologian professes *συμφυΐα* of the natures in the case of the divine inhomination and you think that this brings to one ousia those things which are different in natural quality—divinity and manhood—from which neither confusedly nor defectively there is one Christ.

Recognise, then, that the truth is not like this. For in the case of the inhomination the Theologian called *συμφυΐα* what wise Cyril calls "a natural coming to be one",[85] and hypostatic union—which we say the soul of a man like us has with its own flesh—(and) which completes together one hypostasis from two. But (Gregory) used the term in the Treatise on Baptism as well about the one ousia and divinity which is seen in the holy Trinity, when he wrote as follows: (GREGORY): "The infinite *συμφυΐα* of three infinite things".[86] But above he called the equality of nature[87] of three hypostases "*συμφυΐα*", which cannot be understood in the same way in the case

of inhomination. For in (the case of) the Trinity, each hypostasis exists independently, and denotes its own person, but (there is) one and the same ousia of the nature according to which it is understood generically, and this he calls *συμφυΐα*. But no-one understands *συμφυΐα* in this way in the case of the inhomination, (*Lebon p. 126*) namely, that the hypostases would be separated to two, but that the two of them would have one ousia, or it would again be found that the Trinity is a quaternity, and from (this) formulation of an equality of nature[88] of the flesh in relation to the Word, nothing is gained. For the unity in the case of inhomination is from the composition of things of different type, and not consubstantial[89] with each other. But in the case of the divinity which is apparent in the Trinity, the union (is) not from composition—for each of the three hypostases is not composed with another—but is simple and not composite. But community of ousia and identity of divinity produces unity and lack of difference in everything, and an absence of division and separation, except for the distinction in hypostases.

Therefore there is one meaning of "*συμφυΐα*" in the case of (Trinitarian) theology, and another in the case of the economy and inhomination, and they are diametrically[90] opposed to each other. For Gregory the Theologian himself said as follows, writing in the First Letter to Cledonius: (GREGORY): "But I say *ἄλλο καὶ ἄλλο* in distinction to how it is in the case of the Trinity: for there it is *ἄλλος καὶ ἄλλος* lest we should confuse the hypostases; but not *ἄλλο καὶ ἄλλο* for the three of them are one and the same in divinity",[91] and in the case of the incarnation, he said the opposite before: FROM HIM AGAIN: "But these things from which our Saviour is are *ἄλλο καὶ ἄλλο* unless the invisible is to be the same as the visible, and the without (*Lebon p. 127*) time as that which is under time. But the Son is not *ἄλλος καὶ ἄλλος*: away with you".[92]

But the next thing that we shall learn is that in the case of the incarnation he calls the composition "*συμφυΐα*" and not "equality of nature".[93] For (Gregory) called *συμφυΐα* the coming together of our soul with the body, which is taken even by the Apostle for an example of the divine inhomination, in the Treatise on the funeral of Caesarius his brother, writing as follows: FROM THE SAME MAN: "But after a short time (the soul) will take up its kindred flesh, in which together it philosophised about the (life) beyond, from the earth to which she[94] had yielded and entrusted it, in what way God knows, who bound together and loosed these things, when alongside the flesh she takes possession of the glory from heaven, and just as she shared in its hardships, because of the *συμφυΐα* also

will she bestow her own pleasures".[95] Therefore shall we because of the term *συμφυΐα* foolishly think that the body with the soul of a man is completed to one ousia? And who with intelligence would venture to say this?

But we find the same Doctor also calling our composition "mixture" in the Treatise on love of the poor, thus: (GREGORY): "(Our) mixture is like this, and because of this it seems to me that when we are lifted up because of the image, we will be withdrawn because of the dust".[96] But he already applies the term "deification"[97] to us, and he wrote as follows in his Sermon on Epiphany about the glory which will be given us: FROM THE SAME MAN: "(There is) a living creature (which is) guided here, and journeys to another place, and (at) the fulfilment of the mystery, it is deified by (its) inclination to (God)".[98]

Therefore just as in the study of a man like us, (the terms of) *συμφυΐα*, and mixture and deification (*Lebon p. 128*) do not indicate that there is a change in him of ousia or identity, so also they do not in the case of inhomination for God the Word.

But take note of this, lest because of the term *συμφυΐα* you become too blind as regards the establishment of your former opinion, (that) it is also used of harmony and agreement[99] of the soul, and of the habitual leading of the ascetic life. For wise Basil said as follows, writing to Gregory the Theologian: (BASIL): "What is the *συμφυΐα* and unanimity of mind of the brothers who are deified and exalted by you? What is the emulation of the best and the incentive, that we are kept in the written precepts and rules?"[100]

But it is time to lead out a little stream from the waters of Athanasius, who is glorious in everything, against those who believe that the flesh has come to the same ousia as God the Word, so that the Trinity, as they think, should remain a Trinity, and with it to drown the cunning (argument). For he wrote as follows in the Letter to Epictetus: (ATHANASIUS): "Let those who even thought that it was possible that there would be a quaternity in place of the Trinity, if it should be said that there is a body from Mary, very much be put to shame. For (they say) if we say that the body is consubstantial with[101] the Word, the Trinity remains a Trinity since the Word introduces nothing foreign to it. But it we say there is a human body from Mary, there would necesarily be a quaternity in place of the Trinity because of the addition of the body, since the body is foreign in ousia and the Word is in it. But when they say these things like this, they do not understand how they contradict themselves. For, even if they do not admit the body which is from Mary (*Lebon*

p. 129) but (affirm) it is consubstantial[102] with the Word, they will be shown to affirm a quaternity according to their own doctrine nonetheless, whatsoever they pretend lest they should be thought so to think. For just as the Son, according to the Fathers, while he is consubstantial[102] with the Father, is not the Father, but the Son is said to be consubstantial[102] with the Father; so also, the body (being)[103] consubstantial[102] with the Word, is not the Word, but is other than the Word. But since it is other, according to their own argument, their Trinity will be a quaternity. For the true Trinity, which is truly completed and indivisible, does not accept an addition, but that which was found by them (will). How can they still be Christians, when they understand God to be other than he is?"[104]

Therefore, let us not bring the flesh to equality of nature[105] with the Word, on the pretext of these (words) of the Fathers, who have applied the term "mixture" without danger to the supreme union. For even if we should say that it took (its) origin from Mary, but afterwards changed to the divine ousia, we would end up in the same depth of wickedness (as) those who believed that not even at the beginning did the Word unite that (flesh) to himself from the ousia of the Virgin. For we find even holy Cyril, who thus explains to us that the term "mixture" was spoken of by the Fathers, used the term at the same time, without, as a result of this, raising up the flesh to the divine ousia and confusing the difference in ousia of those things which have run together inexpressibly to union, and have completed for us one Christ from two.

For in the Letter to the Monks, of which we have just made mention, he proceeded in this way, taking our composition for (*Lebon p. 130*) the provision of an example of the union in the incarnation or inhomination: (CYRIL): "But the mystery concerning him is somehow like our own birth. For the mothers of those who are on earth, waiting upon nature for child-birth, have in the womb flesh which gradually congeals and through some inexpressible actions of God comes and is completed to human birth.[106] But God placed the spirit in the living creature, in a way which he knows, for 'He creates the spirit of man in him',[107] according to the words of the prophet. But the principle of the flesh is one thing, and similarly (the principle) of the soul is another. But even though they were mothers only of bodies from the earth, because thus they brought forth the complete living creature, that is, I mean, from soul and body, they are not said to have brought forth a part. And no-one says, to give an example, Elizabeth bore the flesh, but consequently did not also bear the soul. For she bore the Baptist ensouled, and as one man from

two, from soul, I mean, and body. Let us accept that something like this took place in the birth of Emmanuel. For he was born, as I have said, from the ousia of God and the Father, his only-begotten Word. But because he assumed flesh, and made it his own, and was also called Son of Man and became like us, it does not seem shocking to me that we should say—rather we are compelled to confess—that he was born in the flesh by means of a woman, just as also the soul of a man is born with its flesh, and is counted as one with it, although in nature it is understood to be other than it, and is according to its own principle. And if someone should wish to say that some mother is 'flesh-bearer' and consequently not 'soul-bearer' as well, he talks far too much. For, as I have said, she bore the living creature, (*Lebon p. 31*) skilfully composed from things which are unlike. And from two, yet there is one man, while each one of them remains what it is, but they have run together to a natural union, and, as it were, mix with each other that thing which each one of them has as its own."[108]

How do you understand, in the cases of the structure of a man like us, how (Cyril) says a living creature is composed from things which are unlike each other, and not consubstantial[109] with each other, but the two of them have run together to natural union, and as it were mixed with each other that thing which each one of them (had) as its own naturally in ousia? Because of this, when there is a mortal body the whole living creature is called mortal, and when there is a rational soul, the whole living creature is called rational, as we said when we were writing before as well. It is the same therefore in the case of Emmanuel too: in some places all of him is called man, when our Saviour says, "Why do you seek to kill me, the man who told you the truth?"[110] and in others it is written that all of him descended from heaven.[111] And Julius the Theologian also said as follows in the Treatise of the title[112] "Concerning the union of the body to the divinity of the Word": (JULIUS): "Thus also, he is consubstantial[113] with God in invisible spirit, the flesh being included in this description, because it is united to him who is consubstantial[113] with God. And again, he is consubstantial[113] with men, the divinity also being included with the body because it was united to him who is consubstantial[113] with us, while the nature of the body is not changed in the union with (the Word who is) consubstantial[113] with God, or by sharing the title of being 'consubstantial',[113] just as the nature of the divinity is not changed either in sharing the human body (*Lebon p. 132*) and in the title of 'flesh consubstantial[114] with us'."[115] And in the Book of Treasures, wise Cyril says as follows

when he used the term "mixture": (CYRIL): "For the body did not become that of some other man but his own, and because of this it is reckoned as his own. For there is one Christ, from humanity and from God the Word as it were mixed, not as a result of change into what was not (before), but as a result of assuming the temple from the Virgin."[116]

But do not suppose that what you said the opposition cites is new. For what they say is old and foolish and laughable in a variety of ways, for instance, their claim that, when we say "One nature of God the Word" and add "incarnate", we are introducing the other nature.[117] They have become many times over foul by the denial of the flesh[118] and the confession of the Word as simple after the union.[119] But it is well known that the word "incarnate" indicates composition, and one hypostasis from two, and removes distinction of the hypostases and natures. For we have already quoted that in *That Christ is One*, holy Cyril said as follows: "It is not the case that in everything and from every respect only what is simple and of one species is called 'one', but those things as well which are composed from two or more and of different species. For so those who are skilled in these matters think is right."[120]

Thus those who divide Emmanuel to overthrow this wise Doctor have attempted something that is the daughter of stupidity itself, and the sister of contradiction.[121] For in the Eighth Chapter or Anathema he said as follows: (CYRIL): "If someone should venture to say that the man who was assumed should be worshipped along with God the Word, (*Lebon p. 133*) and should be co-glorified or together should be called God, as if (they were) one with another, and does not rather honour Emmanuel with one worship and offer one hymn of praise, in that the Word became flesh, let him be anathema".[122] But Andrew of Samosata, (one) of the chief authorities in that time, finding fault with the Chapter, said against holy Cyril: (ANDREW): "But you will be caught, fallen into the same (errors). For you have written in one of your Treatises, that the Son sat with[123] the Father, along with his flesh. How can you then find fault with someone who says that the man and God the Word are worshipped together, seeing that '*σύν*' and '*μετά*'[124] have the same import and meaning."[125] And Cyril makes a defence against this and shows (Andrew) to have erred with the ultimate error, equating a duality of hypostases with one hypostasis and person and nature from composition. And he wrote as follows: (CYRIL): "For the opposition says, 'Truly even you will be caught somewhere, for you have written in a letter that the Son sits with the Father, along with

his flesh, and how after that will you find fault with someone who says that it is right that God the Word and the man should be worshipped together, and together called God? For it is the same thing to say 'σύν' and 'μετά'.' Let us therefore rebuke those who do not know the meaning of what was said, and who do not look at the nature of the facts. For on the one hand, when the discussion is making an examination about one person, or nature, or hypostasis, and those things from which it is, or is naturally composed, then the term 'σύν' or 'μετά' ensures for the thing signified the fact of its being one through composition, and it does not define it dividedly into two. And on the other hand, when hypostases are previously divided into two, and (are so divided) that each one of them should be independently and individually known, (when) 'σύν' or perhaps 'μετά' is applied, (*Lebon p. 134*) then we say that (the term) has given a sign (that) (they) are two or more still, and not one through composition. For example, if I should say, perhaps, that the soul of a man and his body are honoured together if some honour should come from someone to one man, who is from two, or if someone should say the soul is one living thing along with its body, he would in no wise be defining the one (man) as two men, but rather is seen not to be ignorant of those things from which he is, or is naturally composed. But when he says that Peter and John are together called men, or that along with Peter also John went up to the temple, it is not consequently the case that there 'σύν' or 'μετά' gives a sign of one man. For Peter is not composed with John, nor do the two of them complete the constitution of one man. Therefore why do they doctor the truth, in an unlearned way dividing the one to two Christs?"[126]

Therefore since there is a great and immeasurable difference, and, if we speak scripturally,[127] (as great a difference) as the east is removed from the west, between natural composition or hypostatic union, and a conjunction of honour, which binds two hypostases by an equality of name, how should we be obliged by the followers of Nestorius to take refuge in one ousia (resulting) from a confusion of ousiai, in order that we might turn aside from a [duplication][128] of natures, as you are saying. It is not so: it is not! Let no-one make you err by the persuasion of words, as the Apostle says.[129]

I pleasantly asked your Chastity: when one ousia and quality has come into being at one time, as you say, how do you then say there (still) remained a difference in ousia of the natures from which Christ is? For if there should be one quality and ousia, then (the marks) of the difference have taken to flight. For at any rate you say—because your intention is to hint at (lit. hints at) (*Lebon p. 135*) what has been

said on this point all over the place—the lesser was changed to the more exalted, and the whole of Emmanuel is divinity in ousia, (and) how then will he be seen at the time of the second and glorious coming by those who pierced (him)? For when the visible ousia has once changed to the invisible, he is reduced to what does not fall under sight, and the divine scriptures deceive, which established that he is to be seen by those who pierced (him). But in this matter, it is time that I give a few words, and I come not, as the Apostle said, to visions and revelations of the Lord,[130] (but) to the words of the wisdom spoken by God, and I shall say, like (Paul): "I have become a fool: you drove me (to it)".[131]

For I said as follows in what was written to you before: "But to say that Emmanuel was composed from two properties or from two activities[132] is foolish and unlearned. For, because 'to understand' is a property of a rational mind, but 'blackness' or perhaps 'whiteness' (is a property) of a body, do we say because of this that a man is composed from 'understanding' and from 'whiteness' or 'blackness'? But no-one of intelligence says this: but he says that man exists from the natures of body and soul, to which (natures) those (properties) which were mentioned adhere and are visible and do not exist in isolation."[133] But when you read these things, you quoted the passage, saying that [we said][134] "from 'being rational' and from 'blackness'".[135] But "to understand" and "being rational" are not the same.[136] For "being rational", which is a reasonable mind, exists in a hypostasis, but "to understand" (is) a movement and activity of a rational mind. Therefore, when we have said "from 'understanding'", how do you answer "from 'being rational'", (*Lebon p. 136*) and in this have perverted the truth? But after this you thought that we were speaking about blackness which is smeared on a tablet, and takes place, and again does not take place, and in this way you have said that a quality is that which leaves an ousia just as it is naturally, when it fades to whiteness. But we were speaking about the blackness which is seen in a human body (and) which is an inseparable accident, as for example that [137] of the Ethiopian, which it was right for us to learn from the words of Jeremiah does not naturally happen to change. For he says, as if about something which is impossible, "If the Ethiopian should change his skin, and the leopard his spots".[138] But be sure that we are not seeking accurately to define what a propriety is according to the definitions of pagan philosophy. For those things are set at naught and are outside our court. For who does not know that the faculty of laughter is the propriety of "man", and neighing of "horse"? But we have one care, namely

that we should establish and demonstrate plainly that where a composition and natural coming together of ousiai or natures is constituted, as in the case of the constitution of a man like us, it is superfluous and quite senseless to say that the living creature is composed from those things which appear in the ousiai.

But you are also learning and very clearly, from these things which are said, that the definitions and laws of pagan philosophy do not help you at all in the case of this which was previously set down. For the wise men in these matters say that the propriety of the human mind is to learn, to err, to remember; but the propriety of the human body is to be composed with organs in such a way so as to serve the activity of a rational mind, and as holy Basil said, to be created upright, and apart from the other living creatures, to be provided with a direction of gaze towards heaven.[139] For just as (*Lebon p. 137*) a man experienced in the craft of music does not otherwise fashion the preparation of a reed (-pipe), which is equipped to receive the blowing of a tune of this sort or of a properly controlled breath, except in such a way that it is (fashioned) appropriately to the tune which is blown, so that he will not have to change the instrument, which is equipped to serve the motion of the player; so too the Creator moulded the human body in such a way that it would be fitting and be appropriate for the dwelling-place and staying of a rational soul, so that it should not have any difference whatsoever from the bodies of the other living creatures which do not serve the interests of rational souls. Therefore, because to learn, to err, and to remember is the propriety of a human soul, and to be moulded in such a way (the propriety) of a human body, shall we say that a man is composed from learning and remembering (and) from a fashioning of the body in such a way? We would be mocked, and quite rightly, since it is right to say that a composite living creature is composed from ousiai or natures, and we would be saying (that) the composition (came) from the properties existing in them. And this is the case in the instance of a man like us.

But note that in the case of the divine nature it is impossible for us to speak precisely (of) propriety, for God is not receptive of these, but we are obliged to say something of this thus only in a metaphorical way. Because of this, Evagrius, being very capable in these matters, says in one of his Chapters: (EVAGRIUS): "If either genus or species or difference or property or accident or what is composed from these is affirmed for every enquiry, we find that none of these which were mentioned (*Lebon p. 138*) (applies) in the case of the holy Trinity. Let us worship in silence what is inexpressible."[140] And he

says these things rightly, because God is understood to be above ousia or nature. For in the Treatise entitled "εἰς τὸν κατάπλουν"[141] to those (who came) from Egypt, Gregory the Theologian says as follows: (GREGORY): "I recognise two supreme differences in the things which exist, which are Lordship and servitude. It is not what, amongst us, either tyranny has ordained, or [poverty][142] has separated out, but what nature defines, if it should seem good to someone so to call it. For what is first is also above nature."[143] Holy Cyril as well, in the First Book of the Commentary on the Gospel of John said as follows: (CYRIL): "But God will again be above this, in that he is above ousia, and there is nothing in creation which is supremely comparable to him so that a picture might be taken of the Holy Trinity, which (picture) has no difference, [as to exactness] of doctrines".[144] For we also do not know what God is in ousia or nature.

Henceforth, in the case of (Trinitarian) theology, and in the case of the economy of the inhomination of the only-begotten God the Word, we do not use terms in a precise way, but, as a result of the poverty of the terms at our disposal, we make the demonstrations of the things which are understood. Because of this, when we make terms about the inhomination, we say that it is the propriety of the humanity to hunger, or to thirst, or to be weary, but we do not say this in any precise way, for this is not the propriety only of man, but also of the other living creatures, which by nature breathe the air, and live lives subject to the senses and are nourished. Because a propriety, expressed precisely, is that thing which (*Lebon p. 139*) belongs to something alone, and without sharing with another. But because to hunger and to thirst or to be tired are not properties of the bodiless God, because of this, in a comparison in relation to him, we call these "properties of humanity". But, even if they are in nature properties of (humanity), they are also properties of God the Word, because of the economy. And he is said to have hungered, and thirsted, and to have been weary from a journey, because he was united hypostatically to a body whose nature it was to suffer these things. And he who divides them, and assigns these separately to the humanity, and estranges them from the only-begotten God—although he is in no way diminished according to the principle of his own impassibility—unties the economy and estranges him who is in the likeness of God, and who did not think it robbery that he should be equal with God, from voluntary emptying and humiliation for love of man, which he accepted that he should undergo for our sake. On which Cyril, (who is) wise in everything, in the Treatise of question and answer, *That Christ is One*, said these things: (CYRIL):

"Therefore along with the principles of the incarnation, there enter as well those things which because of it, according to the economy, came upon him who endured voluntary emptying, for example, to be hungry and to be weary. For just as he could not be weary, seeing he is all-powerful, and it could not be said that he was hungry, (seeing) he is the nourishment and life of all, unless he made his own a body which would naturally hunger and be weary, so too he could not be counted among sinners; for thus we say he became sin. And he would not have become a curse, when he underwent the cross for our sake, unless he had become flesh, that is, was incarnate and inhominate."[145] (*Lebon p. 140*)

But while these things are explained by us in this way as we understand (them), it is also necessary that I should add this, lest someone should run to the types of the law, and thence should fail because of ignorance and besmear the hypostatic union with an inadequate meaning. For our Lord is prefigured there in many ways, now as in a golden ark, now as in manna kept in a pot, now as in the composition of incense, now as in fine linen and jacinth, and in things like this, (and) in garments from there, and in sacrifices of calves and of rams, and of meal and in confections. For these things were foresigns of the shadows of the legal scripture, which were making partial and obscure suggestions of the truth and were quite deficient and inferior in exactness.

Holy Cyril also wrote in this way about the "averter of evil" in the Letter to Acacius: (CYRIL): "But (examples) are inferior to what is true, and sometimes (only) give partial illustrations of the things which are signified. But we say the law was a shadow and a type, and (is like) a picture which is placed as an illustration for those looking at the realities. But shadows are the first delineations of the skill of those who paint on boards."[146] But he taught these things in the Second Volume against the blasphemies of Nestorius, and rebuking the madness of that man, he says:[147] (CYRIL): "Tell me again: how do you describe inseparable conjunction? As union—namely, of course, the hypostatic (union) which we teach, struggling on behalf of the doctrines of truth,—or (as) that (conjunction) which is estimated in terms of juxtaposition,[148] and which is (*Lebon p. 141*) understood as being the proximity of something to something else? For the scripture inspired by God thus accepts the expression, and says to the consecrated Moses as he composed the description of the former tabernacle: 'And you shall make fifty rings of gold, and you shall fasten the curtains[149] one with another with the rings'.[150] For there were five of them and each one of them has something special

of its own, so that it would be different, apart from the others, (and) it was fastened with rings. But we do not say that there was a union like this in the case of Christ. For it is not the case that, just as one thing cleaves to another, or as in the manner of mental agreement, or in the way of proximity of bodies, so also he is (joined). For, as I have said many times already, the Word from God made his own the body taken up from the holy Virgin, and we assert that he was in truth (thus) united, and not to flesh that has no soul."[151]

But because I have heard that some men have read the letter which I sent to you earlier, who, from ignorance and a presumptuous lack of culture, do not much agree with the words of holy Cyril, may they know that they have set themselves outside the holy conflicts which (are waged) against the council which was at Chalcedon. For Dioscorus, a witness of Christ, who alone did not bend the knee to Baal at (that) assembly of vanity, wrote thus to Domnus who formerly presided (over the church) in Antioch, about those who presumed to compose evil treatises against certain compositions of wise Cyril: DIOSCORUS: "They are therefore composing writings for which they should be blamed, which do not agree with, but are opposed to the holy scriptures, and to the (writings) of our blessed brother the Bishop Cyril, who is praised in everything. For this in truth demonstrates that they are blameworthy (*Lebon p. 142*) and are not in agreement with the holy treatises. For our wise and prosperous Father was an ecumenical Doctor, and he, if anyone, wrote correctly and without blame. For he was not only a skilled workman with words, for nature gave him this glory along with the others, as it were from the cradle, but also, as he was enriched with a gift from above, he made known as much as he was able the mystery of the inhomination of the only-begotten Son of God. And there is no-one of his writings which does not exceed all admiration, whether you mention a book, or a letter, or a commentary made off the cuff, or a public homily, or the chapters or anathemas: all are proven and accurate, and have a beautifully polished sense, and agree with the divine words, so that aptly we may say about them, 'Who is wise, that he knows these things? And intelligent, that he understands these things? For the ways of the Lord are straight, and the righteous walk in them, but the wicked will lose strength in them.'"[152]

Therefore, how are they not condemned to shame, those who boast that they are zealous in opposition to the Council of Chalcedon, but because of inexperience[153] are not able to put on the armour[153] of the (battle-) rank, which is the teaching of holy Cyril? But you chaste brother, remain in this (armour),[154] and lay low the

enemy, and the Lord will fight on your behalf,[155] for the battle belongs to the Lord. And may no-one venture to revile the ranks of the living God,[156] as someone who proceeds outside the laws of the battle ranks, and turns aside to the right or to the left, while seeing him guarding himself from all sides against the arrows of the enemy.[157]

But it is good that your Holy Wisdom should know that for a long time we have been praying that you may receive the rewards of your toils, both in this (*Lebon p. 143*) world, and in that to come. And it is not our custom in a fleshly way to fawn upon those about whom we pray, but we honour the ordinance of the gospel and the example which our Lord handed down, saying to his disciples, "Truly I tell you, there is no-one who forsaking houses or brothers or sisters or father or mother or wife or sons or fields for my sake and for the sake of the gospel will not receive an hundred times now at this time houses and brothers and sisters and mothers and sons and fields with persecution, and in the world to come, everlasting life".[158] We in no way say that when our Lord said these things, he promised in a fleshly way, or otherwise provocatively, or led the disciples to the point where they would crave these things and be scornful of what is good in truth and is never given up, but as he said in another place, "Seek the kingdom of God and his righteousness, and all these things will be added to you",[159] in the same way here, wanting to confirm the importance of the promises, he says, as a way of addition, that these things are given an hundred times in the present time.

But I rejoice along with you at your fuller understanding, and that you have wholly come to belong to the future hope. And I say, exulting at the same time, what was said by God to those of the Israelites who said to Moses, "Everything which the Lord God has said to you, we shall obey and do",[160] (namely), "I have heard the words of this people, everything which they have said to you. They have said rightly all (that they have spoken). Who will grant that they will have a heart like this, so that they will fear me, and keep my commandments all their days, so that it will go well for them?" Come then in the same opinion, and apply yourself to progress, (*Lebon p. 144*) "forgetting what is behind, and reaching out to what is ahead".[161] And leap clear from that foolish doctrine, which brings to one ousia the (elements) from which there is without confusion the one Lord and God and our Saviour Jesus Christ; and tell it you have recovered, and especially so, if you are about to "write to Macedonia"[162] about the faith. For when you said that you confess at the same time particularity, and difference as regards natural

quality, and not that which individually and in every way distinguishes the natures from which there is the one and undivided Christ, and you also proceeded to confuse everything into one ousia and quality and particularity, both I am found extracting from your confession, as scripture says, a sheaf inadequate to make flour,[163] and you (are found) collecting your wages in a purse full of holes,[164] of which the prophet Hosea teaches[165] the former, and Haggai the latter.

But these things were added only jokingly because of love, lest the message have an undiluted[166] astringent, but that it should be gently mixed with pleasure and some sweetness. For we would be thought to do wrong, if we removed you, even by this, from the mixture. But the apostolic word bids and commands saying: "All the time let your talk in grace be seasoned with salt".[167] But may it apply to us, as we share in the apostolic salt, and since we adhere to their doctrine, let us scorn these superfluous things of debate. But let us ratify (our) reasonings with faith, so that thus we may acquire wisdom from there. For the prophetic word says, "Unless we believe, we shall not understand".[168]

The Second Letter of the Patriarch Severus to Sergius the Grammarian is ended.

Notes

1. Prov. xxii.28.
2. Prov. xxvii.17.
3. PG 76.85A–B. Also cf. above, p. 77.23–26, and p. 99.12–13 (= Pusey edn. Vol. 6, p. 113.11–14).
4. Prov. xxii.17–19.
5. PG 76.85B (= Pusey edn. Vol. 6, p. 113.14). *Adv. Nest. Lib. II.*
6. PG 76.85B (= Pusey edn. Vol. 6, p. 113.14–16).
7. Heb. ii.14.
8. i.e. concepts of mixture and juxtaposition.
9. ܥܘܡܩܘܬܐ ܕܐܣܟܡܐ cf. Syriac text p. 99, line 22, above.
10. ܡܫܘܚܬܐ ܕܪܘܒ.
11. ܚܘܠܛܢܐ.
12. ܡܘܙܓܐ.
13. PG 75.1376C–1377A (= Pusey edn. Vol. 6, p. 510.8–512.6).
14. ܝܚܝܕܝܘܬܐ ܐܢܫܝܘܬܐ.
15 ܚܘܒܒܐ.
16. cf. p. 100 above.
17. ܫܘܝܢ ܒܟܝܢܐ ܕܐܘܣܝܐ = ὁμοούσια. (Harvard syr. 22 = ܫܘܝ ܟܝܢܐ).
18. PG 77.241B–C (= ACO I, 1, 6a, p. 160.2–13).
19. PG 75.1285C (= Pusey edn. Vol. 7, p. 360.9–12).

20. PG 75.692D–693A.
21. Note in margin: Where there is ܐܝܟܢܝܘܬܐ it is ποιότης (in Greek).
22. Lietzmann, *op. cit.*, p. 296.3–15. *Quod unus sit Christus.*
23. H. syr. 22 = ܐܘܣܟܐܝܬ: "in a relational way".
24. PG 76.1449D–1450A. Latin only. The text is preserved in Syriac: cf. Severus, *Philalethes*, CSCO 133 (Syr. 68), p. 140.2–12.
25. PG 76.1450A. Latin only. For the Syriac, cf. *Philalethes*, *op. cit.*, p. 140.14–21.
26. Lk. i.35.
27. The Syriac is ܚܣܝܪܬ ܡܢ ܐܠܗܘܬܐ. Greek: οὔτε ψιλοῦντες θεότητος.
28. PG 76.1200B–C (= Pusey edn. Vol. 7, p. 149.14–150.9).
29. ܐܝܟܚܕ. Greek: ὡς ἕν.
30. Note in margin: The interpreter put "from two" (ܡܢ ܬܪ̈ܝܢ) here in place of συναμφότερον.
31. PG 76.1169C–D. (cf. Pusey edn. Vol. 7, p. 81.12–82.1).
32. ܚܘܒܫܐ.
33. ܚܘܠܛܢܐ.
34. i.e. for convenience.
35. cf. Heb. iv.2.
36. Acts iv.32.
37. PG 76.33B–C (= Pusey edn. Vol. 6, p. 72.21–73.12).
38. ܚܘܠܛܢܐ = μίξις.
39. ܡܘܙܓܐ = κρᾶσις.
40. PG 36.325B–C.
41. The Greek is χαμερπές.
42. The Greek for both is λόγος.
43. PG 36.97B–100A.
44. νόμῳ.
45. PG 36.328C.
46. PG 36.325B–C.
47. cf. Cyril, *Scholia*, ch. 9 (Pusey edn., Vol. 6), p. 516.1–14.
48. ὡς ἐμὸς λόγος.
49. τοιοῦτος δὲ οἷος.
50. PG 37.181A–B.
51. Mt. xvii.2.
52. PG 77.236C–D (= ACO I, 1, 6a, p. 156.11–18).
53. τῆς θεοτόκου.
54. PG 26.385A and PG 77.13C–D (= ACO I, 1, 1a, p. 12.5–8).
55. ܕܝܠܢܐܝܬ ܘܡܢܬܢܝܬܐ ܠܒܪܐ = Greek: ἰδικῶς καὶ ἀνὰ μέρος Υἱῷ . . . .
56. PG 76.416A (= Pusey edn. Vol. 6, p. 428.24–430.3).
57. The Greek in Migne reads αἵματος.
58. PG 76.84D–85A (= Pusey edn. Vol. 6, p. 112.26–113.7).
59. PG 77.116A (= Pusey edn. Vol. 6, p. 26.26–28.2).
60. 2 Pet. iii.16.
61. PG 36.313B.
62. i.e. Sunday after Easter, Low Sunday (καινὴ κυριακή).
63. καὶ πτωχεύει τῷ σὰρξ παγῆναι.
64. PG 36.612B.
65. PG 36.100A.
66. PG 36.313B. *Or. XXXVIII*, *In Theophania.*
67. cf. Eccles. i.9.
68. PG 76.1193B, line 13. Also cf. above, p. 92.28 and p. 102.8. (= Pusey edn. Vol. 7, p. 134.13–14). *De Recta Fide ad Theod.*
69. ܫܠܦ.
70. ܕܚܠܬ ܐܠܗܐ = Greek: εὐσέβεια.
71. ܠܒܘܠܒܠܐ ܘܠܚܘܒܫܐ Elsewhere I translate both roots as "confuse".
72. i.e. he is as you, Sergius, assert.

73. PL 54.765A.

74. cf. PG 76.1413C. (= *Ad Reginas de Recta Fide Oratio Altera*, Pusey edn. Vol. 7, p. 328.4–5).

75. Acts i.11.

76. cf. p. 102.12 ff. above.

77. cf. Prov. ix.18A; v.8, 6.

78. cf. 1 Tim. ii.5–6.

79. PG 76.1431B (Latin only). The passage is preserved in Syriac. cf. *Philalethes*, *op. cit.*, p. 49.3–11.

80. Lk. xviii.8.

81. PG 76.1431C–1432A (Latin only). The passage is preserved in Syriac: cf. *Philalethes*, *op. cit.*, p. 50.6–19.

82. Preserved in Greek in Leontius of Jerusalem. PG 86.1848A–B. *Contra Monophysitas.*

83. Friedrich Loofs, *Nestoriana* (Halle, 1905), p. 249.2–4. ܢܩܝܦܘܬܐ translates the Greek συνάφεια.

84. ܒܪ ܟܝܢܐ.

85. Lebon suggests this is σύμβασις φυσική.

86. PG 36.417B.

87. ܫܘܬܦܘܬ ܟܝܢܐ.

88. ܫܘܬܦܘܬ ܟܝܢܐ.

89. ܩܕܡ ܟܝܢܐ.

90. Note in margin: A diameter is where there are two things which confront each other in a primary sense, as is the case of the position at full-moon, when the moon is in the eastern side of the sky and the sun in the western.

91. PG 37.180A–B.

92. PG 37.180A.

93. ܫܘܬܦܘܬ ܟܝܢܐ.

94. i.e. the soul.

95. PG 35.781C–784A.

96. PG 35.865C.

97. ϑεοποίησις.

98. PG 36.324A.

99. ܫܘܝܐ ܕܪܥܝܢܐ. Dr S. P. Brock has suggested ὁμόπνοια as the underlying Greek.

100. Severus' reference is wrong. It is Gregory Nazianzen, *Ep. VI To Basil*, PG 37.29C. I owe this reference to Dr Lionel Wickham and Bishop Kallistos of Diokleia.

101. ܒܪ ܟܝܢܐ = ὁμοούσιον.

102. ܒܪ ܟܝܢܐ = ὁμοούσιον/ος.

103. *sc.* according to them.

104. PG 26.1064B–1065A.

105. ܫܘܬܦܘܬ ܟܝܢܐ.

106. The Greek is: εἰς εἶδος τὸ ἀνϑρώπινον.

107. Zech. xii.1.

108. PG 77.21B–D (= ACO I, 1, 1a, p. 15.12–33).

109. ܩܕܡ ܟܝ̈ܢܐ.

110. cf. Jn. viii.40.

111. cf. Jn. vi.38.

112. Lietzmann, *op. cit.*, p. 185.

113. ܒܪ ܟܝܢܐ = ὁμοούσιος/ον/ου.

114. ܒܪܟܝܢܢ = τῆς ἡμῖν ὁμοουσίου σαρκός.

115. Lietzmann, *op. cit.*, p. 188, lines 9–18.

116. PG 75.333A.

117. cf. p. 99.30, above.

118. i.e. leaving out σεσαρκωμένη.

119. i.e. again without the addition σεσαρκωμένη.

120. PG 75.1285C (= Pusey edn. Vol. 7, p. 360.9–12).

121. Lebon comments here: Sensus harum vocum haud clarus.
122. PG 77.121A–B (=Pusey edn. Vol. 6, p. 36.20–26).
123. συνήδρευσεν. Syriac: ܝܬܒ ܐܟܚܕܐ.
124. ܐܟܚܕܐ/σύν/ together, and ܥܡ/μετά/with.
125. cf. PG 76.352C (=Pusey edn. Vol. 6, p. 322.11–16). *Apol. pro XII Cap. Contra Orient.*
126. PG 76.352C–353A. (=Pusey edn. Vol. 6, p. 322.11–324.15). *Apol. pro XII Cap. Contra Orient.*
127. Ps. cii.12.
128. Reading ܫܠܝܘܬܐ (=H. syr. 22) for ܫܦܝܘܬܐ.
129. Col. ii.4.
130. cf. 2 Cor. xii.1.
131. 2. Cor. xii.11.
132. H. syr. 22 reads ܦܘܪ̈ܫܢܐ for ܡܦܪ̈ܫܢܘܬܐ. This reading would seem to be supported by Sergius, p. 155.4, above.
133. cf. above, p. 86. cf. also, p. 72.23 and p. 101.24.
134. Reading ܐܡܪܬܘܢ (=H. syr. 22) for ܐܡܪܬܘܢ.
135. cf. p. 101 above of Lebon's edition.
136. τὸ λογίζεσθαι and τὸ λογικόν. cf. Lebon, CSCO 120 (Syr. 65), p. 102, note 5.
137. *sc.* blackness.
138. Jer. xiii. 23.
139. *Homilia in illud, Attende tibi ipsi.* PG 31.216C.
140. This is from the *Gnosticus* of Evagrius, §143 (ed. Frankenberg, p. 550). For the Greek, see Socrates, *H. E.* III, 7 (PG 67.396B). The use of this text by Severus is mentioned by J. Muyldermans, *Evagriana Syriaca* (Louvain 1952), p. 170, note 138. I owe this reference to Bishop Kallistos of Diokleia.
141. PG 36.241, note 51.
142. Reading ܡܣܟܢܘܬܐ (=H. syr. 22=πενία) for ܡܣܟܢܘܬܐ.
143. PG 36.248D.
144. PG 73.85A. This is taking Lebon's suggested emendation, reading ܐܝܟ ܠܚܬܝܬܘܬܐ for ܚܬܝܬܘܬܐ, which follows the Greek ὡς εἰς δογμάτων ἀκρίβειαν. (=Pusey edn. Vol. 3, p. 72.5–9).
145. PG 75.1264B. (=Pusey edn. Vol. 7, p. 341.28–342.8).
146. PG 77.217B–C.
147. Note in margin: Take note.
148. The Greek is τὴν κατὰ παράθεσιν.
149. Note in margin: In place of "curtains" (τὰς αὐλαίας) which is here, it says "court" (αὐλήν) in the Greek. (PG 76.84C reads αὐλαίας).
150. Ex. xxvi.6.
151. PG 76.84B–C (=Pusey edn. Vol. 6, p. 111.30–112.16).
152. Hos. xiv.10. For Dioscorus' Letter, see "Akten der Ephesinischen Synode vom Jahre 449", ed. J. Flemming, *Abh. der Kgl. Ges. der Wiss. zu Göttingen*, Phil.-hist, Kl., n.s. 15, Berlin 1917, p. 137 (of translation). I owe this reference to Dr Lionel Wickham.
153. cf. 1 Kms. xvii.39.
154. cf. 2 Tim, iii.14.
155. cf. Ex. xiv. 14.
156. cf. 1 Kms. xvii. 36.
157. The sense of this passage is far from clear.
158. Mk. x.29–30.
159. Mt. vi.33.
160. Deut. v.27.
161. cf. Phil. iii.13.
162. cf. 1 Tim. i.3, and p. 102 above.
163. cf. Hos. viii.7.
164. cf. Hag. i.6.

165. This is taking ܥܒܕ ܦܝܠܘܣܘܦܘܬܐ to represent just the verb φιλοσοφέω. cf. p. 127 above, and PG 35.781C.

166. The Syriac is ܦܝܠܣܘܦܐܝܬ.

167. Col. iv.6.

168. cf. Is. vii.9.

Letter III of Sergius

The Third Letter of Sergius the Grammarian to holy Severus the Patriarch. (*Lebon p. 145*)

Only late have I become aware of my ignorance. And at first I did not attend to my artifice, which I did not know: for "honour lies still where there is no danger", as one of our number said. But I was not steadfast in relation to the divine laws, nor did I hear the cither[1] when he prayed: "Lord, place a watchman on my mouth, and a door, a keeper on my lips".[2] Then I pushed aside the doctrines of the wise, and made a mock of these various texts: "Who will give a guardian upon my mouth, and a seal of shrewdness upon my lips lest I should fall as a result of them, and my tongue should fight with me?"[3], and "A slip from the floor is better than one from the tongue",[4] (and) "The folly of one who is silent was searched for, and it was not found".[5] Therefore I have learned this sin, (I) who am a man with a babbling tongue. You did not agree that with evil I would cure evil, and I have received a sentence of double ignorance. But I am grateful to those who give rebuke, and I acknowledge thankfulness to God that I am corrected, again with a frank mind, among those who counsel wisely, for "The haters of correction die in disgrace",[6] and "The ear which hears the correction of life shall dwell in the midst of the wise",[7] and "He who keeps corrections loves his own soul",[8] and "He who kept correction will be glorified".[9] My soul was admonished by all these good (words); (and) thus I have borne your holy and divine letter.

But at once from the beginning, I was cut off in (mid) speech—for I shall repeat the whole disputation—when I heard that iron sharpens iron. You commanded that I should look a little within myself, and I induced my gaze within, and saw my reasoning (was made) of clay, and very frail. And afterwards I turned quickly to the parable, for I will not forsake (*Lebon p. 146*) the wise, "How can the (clay) pot associate with the (iron) kettle? It will knock and itself be broken".[10] Then with difficulty I recollected that I should act wisely, and I was descending to the remaining words. Then, but then, the beginning of the whole marvel happened to me: (my) eyes cringed back from the light, and were completely unable henceforth to en-

lighten (my) mind. (My) understanding was dizzy, (my mind) which was in danger of (lapsing into) the sleep of despondency. But what, what opinion have I reaped from (my) lack of learning? I shall be accused of the teaching of the changers of ousiai. Therefore I shall make a defence about what my opinion is concerning them, taking God as a witness of the statement, (to show that) those men are reckoned foolish by me, and followers of the madness of Eutyches.

First they trample underfoot the mysteries of the divine birth (that was) for our sake. For when the flesh has been dissolved into divinity, it is no great thing that the virginity should be preserved, when the Spirit only passed through her. Therefore let us come to Father Cyril (that we may enquire) about this true saying. For she gave birth to the Word from God the Father according to the flesh, when he became flesh. For the marvel is seen in this, that while the laws of birth are preserved, God is born in a fleshly way, while (at the same time) nature is overcome, for virginity is not done away with, even though bodily birth took place. But how have these (accusations) of an impure doctrine befallen me, when I confess composition (just) like the Fathers? For if a man takes completely pure gold, and another (takes) debased (gold), (and) when he purifies it, unites it (to the other), in this way this (constitutes) an addition of ousia and not a composition. But who would be so bold as (to say) like a young man, that in the case of the perfect Trinity, there is an addition of divinity, taking what did not exist before, but came into existence at the end? (Such an attempt would belong) either to the audacity (*Lebon p. 147*) of Nestorius, which strives in the pagan way to deify, or to the empty-mindedness of Arius, which drunkenly (moves) the creature into divinity. All things which belong to the Word are settled and superior to all change. For in the beginning was the Word, and (he was) with God and was God, and became flesh.[11]

But just as he was embodied, and has not endangered the ousia of divinity and is even now true God as well, so too he has preserved his own true flesh. Thus the prophets did not deceive about the advent, saying that God comes visibly. Thus we do not err in the direction of illusion because we have become among the perceivers of the Word, and touched him with (our) hands.[12] For if we should blaspheme (saying) that, like a cloud and every vapour which went up into the air from the earth, and is dissipated by the rays of the sun, this happened also to the body of our Lord by the mingling with divinity, (then) God was not seen, was not touched, did not hunger, did not thirst, was not weary, and undertook none of these things which are

ours, nor was he fastened to the cross, and I am quite unentitled to say that he died, he who no longer was embodied with a mortal body. Nor would Thomas carefully seek out and look for the mark of the nails: for to what side would he place (his) hand? The doors would be closed, and Jesus would be seen in the middle: and we would not be astonished. And if he says, "Touch me and see, for a spirit does not have flesh and bones, as you see I have",[13] will we shut our ears to the truth? But who is astonished when a spirit hastens to heaven? For God is spirit,[14] and we know his wisdom is an ethereal spirit, passing through every intelligible spirit, pure (and) most ethereal.[15] As far as these first principles go, we are not mad in them, blessed Father of Fathers—and we do not learn these from your accurate voice! (*Lebon p. 148*)

But I believe that there is one nature of the Word incarnate after the inexpressible union, and I do not vitiate the incarnation in any way. You find fault with me, on the grounds that I change the body of the Word. But I acknowledge along with that (body) the soul as well, in that I fully attend to and accept that he says, "He who eats my flesh and drinks my blood has life for ever".[16] I also attend to these words: "I have power to lay down my soul and take it up again",[17] and there was no confusion of the humanity. Let us grant to God that he was truly incarnate, so that he should be able even to suffer on our behalf, so that death might be despoiled in that God died. Let us believe that he rose in a fleshly way from the dead, lest we renounce[18] the resurrection of our own flesh. This Jesus, in the same way in which he was seen by the disciples going up to heaven, will come at the second advent, and he will sit upon the throne of his glory, while the holy angels stand by him: thus he will separate out the goats and the sheep, to the right and to the left. For the [judge][19] endured to be embodied on our behalf—he who accepted the form of a servant, and in shape was found as a man[20]—and that he should display related parts: for which are the right hands and which the left, to an uncontained spirit? But in accordance with your teaching, the quotation, "They shall look on him whom they pierced",[21] (shows) that the Word still keeps in the body the marks of the sufferings (undergone) for love of man.

Therefore I name the whole Jesus God, but incarnate. I acknowledge Israel went down to Egypt with seventy-five souls,[22] but not with (souls) only, but I understand (with souls) which were embodied. And I give heed truly to these words: "There is one mediator of God and men: the man Jesus Christ",[23] but I do not lapse into a debased[24] opinion in this. For I acknowledge (*Lebon p. 149*) "the

man attested by God for us",[25] wholly perfect God, who was perfectly made man, and the prophet calling out in a divine way, "I shall pour out from my Spirit onto all flesh".[26] Nor do I uselessly understand only the body, but I accept the whole constitution of men, even when a part customarily indicates a whole: as sometimes I call the world *τὸ πᾶν* even though I have learned that the heaven is called this.

This true doctrine has run into my mind with pure wonder, in relation to all the words of the holy Fathers, and I run, and lawfully and religiously I keep within bounds. Therefore let Gregory the Theologian say confidently (now) mixture (*κρᾶσις*) (now) mingling (*μίξις*), now composition (*σύνθεσις*):[27] for through equality of name, I recognise one fact, which was made known to me from many names. For I understand the supreme union of God to flesh endowed with a soul, and without confusion maiming the meaning, for (the flesh) has not changed to that which is eternal. And let him also say these words which are worthy of wonder: "Of them, the one deified, but the other was deified".[28] These teach neither a change nor a confusion. For even if iron is said by us to be hot, it is not thought that it was changed into fire itself. For once united to fire, it still even thus remains iron. For if the fire that we know rejects the ousia of matter, it is destroyed, since it does not naturally persist in another way than by being mingled with some ousia of matter. And in the case of that (quotation): "The Word became thick, and congealed",[29] I utterly reject (the idea) that I should be lame in my understanding (of it). For since I enquired about (those) words, I have explained (them) according to your pious opinion, (in saying that the Word) received our thickness of body. And (*Lebon p. 150*) as far as I was able, (I) who am propped up now with a feeble mind, I resisted before the Assembly those who again seize doctrines contrary to this from the Father.[30] And that, "He became double",[31] I have resolved according to your examples. And I have unravelled those sayings which are published by them, "It is (to be) understood (as referring to) his Father, and not to him who is seen"; "(What) is understood, is not of him".[32] Therefore we are not overthrown by those putting forward these (opinions), and ones like these, because God directs (us). But how is it astonishing that these men borrow the (sayings) of the holy Fathers in the cause of what is evil, when they even oppose the divine scriptures, and imagined that from there they would strengthen their wickedness?

But now it is time that I make a defence of (some) statements which are criticised, and assist with a staff those things which are

lying sadly low. And it is a difficult business, that I should impart life to those things which are thus dead, but anointed by your holy prayers, I shall make an attack upon the conflict, giving first a definition of composition. For as I deal with the mystery, I have not yet used (defined) terms, although I have spoken in this way. But I have learned that the principle of composition is like this: (namely) the coming together from two or more simples, which have come to some one thing, in which also what is complete (in itself) is a part, (and) afterwards the parts are not investigated with regard to the principle of duality, since once and for all there has come into being one ousia or quality.[33] (Please) understand me about this too, that what was said as regards ousiai, (namely) that some are simple, and some are composite, (should be said) in the same way as regards the signs of ousiai, that we know some simple and some composite. But because I also confess composition in the case of the divine inhomination, I shall introduce (it), so that we may debate about it as well. (*Lebon p. 151*) And you, Doctor (and) Father, bear patiently the words of my poor understanding, for I do not contradict (what you have said)—far be it that I should act so madly—but since I wish to escape from a false opinion, I confidently venture to undertake such a contest.

The words *φύσις* and *οὐσία* mean the same as far as we are concerned, the one being derived from *πεφυκέναι* and the other from *εἶναι* and you, O Theologian, agree with me (on this). For you have said somewhere in (your) letter, "Where composition and natural coming-together of ousiai or of natures is constituted".[34] Therefore, if we teach "from two natures, one nature of the Word incarnate", how do we sin against the mystery, if, by means of words with the same meaning, we fulfil the same doctrine, (in saying) that from two ousiai there is one ousia of the Word incarnate? But this "incarnate" I have omitted, in as much as it is frequently declared, but I do not dissolve the composition because of this. And I turn (my) mind to mere surmise, and I urge you, O Father, to endure for a little my presumption with regard to the precision of the philosophers; even if they are outside our fold, we shall greatly clarify the explanation. Among these philosophers, Aristotle, who is called *ὁ νοῦς* said these words somewhere, as he provides an illustration of ousia: ARISTOTLE: "But ousia is, if we will speak with an example, such as man, horse."[35] But it is not the case that he does not acknowledge the composition of the living creature because of this. For everything which is simple is understood, rather than falling under the senses. Therefore how do I defraud the truth, when I call the incarnate Word

"ousia", and understand this (ousia) (to be) incarnate? (*Lebon p. 152*) Thus it is right for me to explain as well the matters concerning quality, saying that the quality of the ousia of the Word who shared with me in flesh and blood,[36] also shared in the corporeal signification. Since these things are said by a mind which desires to speak the truth, they will not be called to account. For it is right that we should judge words in relation as well to the persons who make the sayings, and we ought to examine a few of the many (statements).

But now we will take up again that statement with regard to making a defence. We know that the things which belong to a genus also extend to species.[37] And we say that a living creature is an ousia endowed with a soul and sensation. And we know that a man and a horse and a bull are (instances of) this (ousia) along with some different propriety which belongs to each one of them. Therefore using the same name we call simples and composites and all these things which are mentioned "living creatures", and in this, the generic name of the ousia is applied by means of the hypostases which are particular ousiai, as it seems right to Father Basil as well.[38] Therefore, if we call the simple Son, even though he became composite for our sake, one hypostasis, and we are completely sure that he is endowed with a body, why may we not also take the name of the highest genus, and call the Son "ousia", while defining that this was incarnate? For even Father Cyril, as you yourself quote him, asserts that "one" is predicated not only of simples, but also extends to composites. For he says as follows: CYRIL: "For 'one' is not said in truth, only as regards things (which are) simple in nature, but also as regards those which are brought together in composition, as is the case with man".[39]

I am saying these things because of rebukes. But henceforth I come to the second rebuke. (*Lebon p. 153*) I was considered, O Father, to be a fraud, because sometimes I marvel at properties, and sometimes I eschew them. And in myself I appeared (as) a many-footed man,[40] because I take on a variety of colours. But I, in truth, on the contrary, will be neither of these things: it is not the case that I have spoken with (my) neighbour, while evil (is) in (my) heart. For I studiously shun the curse which by day and by night is sung on the cither. But I, from (my) first words, was of the same mind, and in every respect have believed that the invisible and intangible God the Word, along with the flesh also accepted the properties of the flesh, and became visible and tangible on our behalf. These are not (the properties) of simple divinity, but of (divinity) embodied, (which) because of the economy, also endured these (properties) of ours. But

because the saying seemed to some to have been said in too clumsy a way, I earnestly desired to be made acute by you. And this happened to me through God and your word, that condescended to such an extent, that it should descend upon me, who am particularly of small account. And thenceforward in every respect I had a formula which could not be contradicted, as it will be kept orthodox in every way. But it is good for me again to have regard for (some) one of the experts, and from that (source) send for a word of instruction. I have enlightened it like the dawn, and declared it afar. I have affirmed the "teaching as prophecy, and bequeathed it for other generations".[41] But confidently I add, "I have not toiled for myself alone, but for all those who are seeking it".[42]

But what is this third thing which as it were stares at me, and violently seizes on my heart? For I was believed to have understood that the lower was changed into the higher.[43] But this is completely renounced by those who still confess composition. (*Lebon p. 154*) For if I had attempted by boiling water through the continued application of fire, to change the wet ousia to air, that which is said would have been thought to have been in my mind. But now I shall give my opinion on this point as far as I am able. On all accounts, according to exact terms, body is considered that which is without soul; while we acknowledge flesh only (as) that which is alive. We learn that that[44] which is present to all things which breathe, both to us and to composed living creatures, is mixed from four elements. Therefore, (there is) on the one hand flesh and blood to the rational and irrational (alike). But on the other hand, the quality of soul is thought to introduce a change, and this indicates something rather significant, but it is not the case that the nature of the flesh of men is changed. Likewise, I acknowledge on the one hand that the ensouled flesh which is united to the Word—for I fear after this to say "mixed"!—is human and of our nature, but on the other hand, in so far as it is composed to (be one with) God, it exists (with) those special (properties) in comparison to our flesh. For it did not accept sin (as a result) of transgression; it was not obliged to hunger and thirst and sleep, but to be occupied with the Word to which it was united, which willed to suffer these things for the sake of the confirmation of the inhomination.

Therefore, this is not to change (an) ousia, but accurately to wonder at the mystery, that when the Word was composed in union to dense flesh, he made it more glorious than anything. For he is born without a seed, and a virgin is (his) mother. And he is fed, not needing it, but desiring it. But he is without all sin, and walks among

the Jews without being seen. And the nature of wet things serves (his) feet like the dry land. And when death drew near, he removed it on the third day. And the air provided a crossing when he ascended. But that which is beyond all speech (is this): he sits in heaven God incarnate at the right hand of majesty. For he established us along with him, and made us sit (*Lebon p. 155*) along with him with his Father. Thus he is coming at the second advent.

And a fourth saying has become a risk to me, so that (I am) again called to judgement, on the grounds that I have set aside ousiai, and interweave composition from signs. But I do not acknowledge that I suffered (from) this ignorance. For a quality does not exist without an ousia, nor should we recognise ousiai without signs. Therefore when I said that two ousiai were composed, along with them I was also uniting the signs.[45] But accurate speech determines that we should speak of God as being above ousia. But when God, the cause of all, says to Moses, and (Moses) wrote this word in place of a name, "He who is, sent me",[46] I make so bold—but I have taken my cue from him—to call God "ousia" as well: for God is, and is above those things which are. Therefore let us call him "ousia", and "above ousia". But you have defined, and very clearly, that the propriety of God (is) grace:[47] "Why do you call me good? No-one is good, except one, God".[48] For if a propriety is that thing which belongs to someone and to him alone—(and) now according to the quotation above it belongs to God alone to be good—(then) clearly something of this sort is a definition of a propriety. Nevertheless it is necessary that we reverence these great matters in silence. For God is in truth above ousia and propriety.

I have ventured (to say) these things to you, O Father of Fathers, and I have run far from my rank: not because I did not know myself at all, but because I was afraid that I might be trapped in (your) written accusations. And I prostrate myself at your holy feet, that you enact a law on those who have your second letter, (*Lebon p. 156*) that they read my defence as well, lest as time takes up these words of yours—for it keeps everything securely—it will tell posterity that I stumbled with an opinion like this, and this be thought to be the common rebuke of all the churches of God which have used the spark of my feeble tongue because of the remoteness of bishops in the east. But certainly some people, wanting to find fault, (will) think the matter is presumption. But I define ignorance as the death of the soul, and since I very much want to be alive, I fear to fail (in) this. But for those who in astonishment deride my search, I shall read again the wise law: "If you will invoke wisdom, and will give up your

voice to knowledge, and if you will search for it like silver, and glean for it like treasure, then you will know the fear of the Lord, and you will find the knowledge of God".[49]

But because a pair of the prophets are running after me, (along) with your holy writings, I should run with the pair. And first I will say to you from great Haggai, "You have sown much and [brought in][50] little".[51] For you have cast some divine seed upon earth that has a not very open heart, (namely) my mind. But cultivating this with great care, you urge on even rocky places, that you may take fruit even from (otherwise) fruitless (plants). And then I will also say the words of Hosea to you: "You are chastising and healing us: you are striking and curing us".[52]

These things are in reference to your divine letter, which teaches in truth, which finds fault in a peaceful way, which heals with grace. (*Lebon p. 157*) And I ask God that long life be given to you, and that we, the orthodox Church, may again keep the feast with your lawful presence, as (we do) now in the text for your utterance, but then adorned in the true colours of your advent, we will write these (words of the) psalms in (our) understanding, "You have had pleasure, O Lord, in your land; you have turned away the captivity of Jacob; you have forgiven the sin of your people; you have covered all their sins".[53]

The Third Letter of Sergius the Grammarian to the holy Patriarch Severus is ended.

Notes

1. *sc.* David.
2. Ps. cxl.3.
3. Sir. xxii.27.
4. Sir. xx.18.
5. cf. Ps. ix.36.
6. Prov. xv.10.
7. Prov. xv.31 according to the Vulgate and some minuscules.
8. Prov. xv.32.
9. Prov. xiii.18.
10. Sir. xiii.2.
11. cf. Jn. i.1 and 14.
12. cf. 1 Jn. i.1.
13. Lk. xxiv.39.
14. Jn. iv.24.
15. cf. Wisdom vii.22–23.
16. Jn. vi.54.
17. Jn. x.18.
18. The Syriac is ܢܒܕܪ. Lebon suggests that this is an attempt to translate *ἀποκηρύσσειν*.

19. Reading ܕܢܟܝܐ for ܕܡܝܟܐ.
20. cf. Phil. ii.7.
21. Jn. xix.37.
22. Deut. x.22.
23. 1 Tim. ii.5.
24. Lebon notes: ψιλός: Id est: ad sententiam iuxta quam Christus est ψιλὸς ἄνθρωπος.
25. cf. Acts ii.22.
26. Joel iii.1.
27. For σύνθεσις as the Greek noun underlying ܪܘܟܒܐ, cf. p. 109.14 (Greek in Lietzmann, *op. cit.*), and p. 134.1 (Greek in Migne).
28. PG 36.325C. *Or. XXXVIII.*
29. cf. PG 36.313B and 612B. *Or. XXXVIII and XLIV.*
30. *sc.* Gregory Nazianzen.
31. cf. PG 36.113A, 328C. *Or. XXX and XXXVIII.*
32. Lebon comments here: Sensus huius sententiae neque clarus neque certus mihi videtur.
33. cf. above, p. 100.11–16.
34. p. 136, lines 18 and 19.
35. Aristotle, *Categories*, 4.1b.27.
36. cf. Heb. ii.14.
37. Plural.
38. cf. Basil, *Ep. XXXVIII, Gregorio fratri de discrimine essentiae et hypostasis*, PG 32.326 ff.
39. PG 77.241B (=ACO I, 1, 6a, p. 160.2–4). *Ep. XLVI, Ad Succ. Ep. II.*
40. Dr Lionel Wickham has pointed out to me that behind "many-footed" there may lie πολύπους, the octopus, which is well known for changing its colours.
41. cf. Sir. xxiv.32–3.
42. cf. Sir. xxiv.34.
43. cf. pp. 134–135 above.
44. *sc.* flesh.
45. cf. p. 72.10, 17–20 in Sergius' *First Letter*.
46. Ex. iii.14.
47. ܛܝܒܘܬܐ. Lebon notes: Read ܛܒܘܬܐ (goodness) or ܛܒܬܐ which suits what follows.
48. Mk. x.18.
49. cf. Prov. ii.3–5.
50. Reading ܣܟܠܬܗܘܢ for ܣܠܟܬܗܘܢ (misprint).
51. Hag. i.6.
52. Hos. vi.1.
53. Ps. lxxxiv.2–3.

Letter III of Severus

The Third Letter of the same Patriarch Severus to the Grammarian.

When I read this third letter of your Chastity, which was given me very late, I wanted to keep silent, and to let alone those things which are written by me and by you. For it is not in my authority—as you said (it was)[1]—that I should give permission that these things of yours be read, these things which are written with your authority and free will. For such a thing would be easy, and it might possibly bring me prestige and would show everyone very clearly to which sayings I had given answers. For after the second letter, it seemed superfluous to study the same things with idle talk in another way, and again to remind him who renounces reminding, and is indignant. For some wise man says, "There is reproof which is inappropriate".[2]

But because this is not appropriate for me, and it is not, as one of the prophets said, the portion of Jacob,[3] that we should prosper on the failings of brothers and derive prestige from there, (*Lebon p. 158*) but rather (it is appropriate) that we should think and say what Paul said to the Corinthians, "But we pray God that you do nothing evil, not that we may appear proven, but that you may do good even if we should appear in a poor light".[4] Because of this I have thought it right—and this while I am in this manner of flight, and secret and toilsome sojourning—with due love again to [remind][5] you in a brotherly way. For what my intention was otherwise (namely) either to maintain strict silence, or to point you out with scorn, is not only foreign to true religion but also to good manners, and is particularly hateful to God, for the sacred writing says somewhere, "He who winks his eyes with deceit gathers griefs for men, but he who reproves openly makes peace".[6]

Therefore your Chastity is reminded in every respect, that at the beginning, when you wrote to the holy Bishop Antoninus, you said about yourself that (but) lately you had gazed upon divine matters, and that you were a child in religious doctrines, and you had thought that it was in no way right that we should confess the particularity of the natures from which the one Christ was completed inexpressibly and above reason. And I, being far separated and

asked to answer your question, quoted from the words of wise Cyril, that in everything and in all respects it was right that we confess the particularities of the natures from which Emmanuel is, that is (particularities) that (lie) in natural quality, and not such that the natures should be cut off independently and separated from each other. For whoever does not confess this, arrives at the opinion of those who confuse ousiai. For (Cyril) says as follows in those things which he wrote to Diodore: CYRIL: "Therefore let us acknowledge that the body which was born at Bethlehem, even if it is not the same (*Lebon p. 159*)—I mean in natural quality—with the Word which is from the Father, yet it became his, and not of some other son beside him. But one Son and Christ and Lord is understood even when the Word was incarnate".[7] AND AGAIN AFTER OTHER THINGS: "Because we also say that in terms of particularity, flesh is in every respect of another nature from the Word which sprang from God and the Father, nevertheless, it became his by an inseverable union, so that even the Word who appeared from the ousia of God and the Father was called the seed of Abraham in the flesh, for the economy calls him this, and it does not at all injure his being that which he is. For although he is God by nature, he also truly became man, and is Son of God and the Father, not counterfeit and not of a lying name".[8] AND AGAIN AFTER A LITTLE: "But it is not the case that it is anywhere (and) in any respect unnoticed that you attempt to put to confusion those who have an orthodox doctrine, (that is) those who teach an unconfused union, and you are not ashamed as you stand in opposition, and stir everything up and down, showing the flesh (is) of another nature, (of another nature) I mean, as it were in respect to the Word from God, and if someone should confess this with you, shunning the ignorance of the confusers of natures, you at once divide the one (Christ) into two".[9]

Notice that in these things which were quoted, the Doctor clearly showed that not to confess otherness of the natures which have come together to union, and particularity, and difference as far as natural quality is concerned, does not fall outside the iniquity and foolishness of those who confuse ousiai, but comes under the rebuke which belongs to them. And as it were from the other side again, (*Lebon p. 160*) those who divide Emmanuel make this natural difference a pretext for division.

Tell me then, did I make you a confuser of ousiai when I reminded your Chastity of these things? Or have I written the charge of heresy against you, (I) who showed you the path of the Fathers, when you confessed that you were inexperienced in divine doctrines and need-

ing someone to direct (you) to accuracy? Not at all! For the very appearance of the discourse and the truth openly proclaim this. But when you wrote again the second letter, and rolled around the same things in it again, and say that hypostatic union is to be considered a juxtaposition[10] in accordance with the empty words of Nestorius, unless we confess that the natures were mixed, one ousia or even quality having taken place at one time, and you have made clear this opinion by means of words which you have added, I have abbreviated what you wrote, but the gist is as follows: "Therefore if the natures from which Christ is, were not mixed inconfusedly, how shall I say that those (natures) which thus have remained unmixed were united hypostatically with each other? How do I keep the definition of composition, when the natures are preserved unmixed, just as they were?" And again I was obliged to answer you kindly in accordance with my ability, and to show clearly that hypostatic union is a natural coming together in natural union, and inexpressibly and inestimably completed one hypostasis and nature of the Word incarnate, which shuns juxtaposition,[10] and similarly mingling and confusion and mixture, in (just) the same way that a man like us exists from a rational soul and from body, and from things of different sort and not consubstantial[11] with each other, there is one nature and composite hypostasis, and it is not the case that it began from composition, but after the union (*Lebon p. 161*) it ceased being composite. For you had wanted to say this, you who were affirming that from mixture unmixed, and from confusion unconfused, at one time one ousia and quality took place. Later on you added (a section) as well about holy Cyril, and said "The Father seems to say that the Word incarnate attached natures along with properties, and is one everywhere, I mean (one) nature and particularity".[12] And you said that in your own case you did not adhere to this, and you asked if I too was of this verdict.

Therefore how, when I have decreed and shown by means of many *testimonia* that it is not right for us to say that Emmanuel is of one ousia and quality and one particularity, are you again contending about these ill-sounding expressions and have set up a defence of these ill-sounding expressions, passing by all those things which were written by you in the second letter? By means of these things the whole purpose (of the argument) was directed to this, that unless we understand the natures to be mixed not even the Trinity remains a trinity, but becomes a quaternity, (that is) unless we confess that the Word incarnate has become one ousia and quality.[13] Since you wanted to establish this as well, you introduced (the term) "συμφυΐα"

(both) so that it might be of advantage to you as regards the same questions of mixture, and to demonstrate that those things from which Christ is are one ousia and quality. And again you learned from us, as we reminded you in a brotherly way, that the term "συμφυΐα" is not indicative of (just) one meaning, but when it is applied to the holy Trinity, it establishes the equality of ousia of three hypostases; but when it is applied in relation to (*Lebon p. 162*) the divine incarnation, it makes known the natural coming together of things of different ousia, and not of the same type with each other, from which was completed one nature and hypostasis, that is of the incarnate Word.[14]

Therefore you have turned these reminders into complaints in a way I do not understand, and you have made me an accuser instead of a teacher. And you have repeated words which were written to you by us in opposition to those who hold the opinion of a confusion of ousiai, and as if you were contending against a fictitious accusation, you have [made out][15] that you do not think thus as the folly of the confusers of ousiai wishes. And hence you have at once jumped up, and as you have said,[16] have anointed yourself[17] with my prayers, and it has seemed good to you that you should become an advocate of expressions which introduce the confusion of ousiai, by means of these things which you have said—(namely) that the coming together from two natures became at one time one ousia and quality. And you have done the same thing as a young man, who finds fault with a harlot, and uncovers her impudence, who is of the people[18] and a hawker, and the clamour of her beauty from ornaments, and as the Proverb says,[19] dissipation and its licentiousness, and afterwards when evening has come, he was beneath her roof and lodged with her.

But let us consider of what sort are (these words) of (your defence): how valiant and astonishing! You say that you have said "one ousia" instead of saying "one nature", and you have omitted this (word) "incarnate" in as much as it is very often confessed. But you said "one quality" as well, on the grounds that the quality of the ousia of the Word has had a share in bodily activity.[20] Now, are these things tolerable? Are these (beliefs) proper to Christians and to those who look for the judgement and the resurrection, and hear the Word of God calling (*Lebon p. 163*) out in the Gospel: "You will be justified by your words, and by your words you will be found guilty".[21] Do these things not provide the opposition with a suitable cause for laughter against us? Do we not deservedly say in lament that (song) of David the singer of holy things: "We were a reproach

to our neighbours; an object of derision and a laughing stock to those round about us".[22]

For to dismiss the whole intention of those things which were written by you, which we previously set out above, and to attend to this part only which has been said, in isolation from all these words which were said before and those which were set down after, to such an extent obliges us to say, and to cut off a multitude of inadequate and useless nonsense, from which the simplicity of the truth turns away its face, (the simplicity of the truth) of those who handed on as a sacred anchor to the holy Churches, as against those who divide into two the one Christ, (namely) that it is proper for us to say "one nature incarnate of God the Word", that is of great Athanasius and wise Cyril: "Where therefore have you read in their compositions that they have called Emmanuel one ousia and quality, or one ousia incarnate of the Word?"[23] You are unable to say! For since they knew that the error of confusing the natures is contrary on the other side to those who divide the Christ, they used polished and exact terms. However, it is quite clear that one can easily find in the God-clothed Fathers—for I speak to you from my teachers, since I do not use any expression in this matter belonging to the pagan experts—the term "ousia" used instead of "one nature" and "hypostasis", in the way that holy John, who attained to the high priestly throne of Constantinople, says about the only-begotten Son of God and the Father, in the Fourth Treatise of the Commentary (*Lebon p. 164*) on the Gospel of John: (JOHN): "But this Word is a hypostatic ousia which proceeded from the Father impassibly".[24] And Basil, who is wise in these divine matters, in the First Treatise against Eunomius, says about him: (BASIL): "But since he is one in existence and one simple ousia, not composite, he names himself differently at different times, and in thoughts he makes to fit the titles which are different from each other".[25]

But none of the orthodox Doctors, I mean those who have expounded (doctrine) in the churches, ventured to call the Word one ousia or sign when it was composed with flesh of the same nature as ours, which had a rational and intelligent soul. Therefore do you alone, tell me, walk this untrodden path, and travel through the torrent and thistles? Was there a need for these truly circuitous explanations? But these things in no way bring credit to you. For even if we believed you[26] and were silent, no-one would read these things which are written by you, and say that they are such that you have written a defence. So now it is (high) time for me to say to you that thing of Homer, and very aptly, since while writing you made mention of your skill: "ἀλλ' οὐ πείσονται Τρῶες καὶ Δαρδανίωνες".[27]

Because of this, with a loving intention, we exhort your Love, that you bid farewell to crafty words like these, and that you reverence simplicity of faith, and do not rush easily to speech about doctrines, but reckon that it is right to cleave to the Fathers in everything, if at any time you should fall into the necessity of writing or speaking like this. For it is not a slight thing that (*Lebon p. 165*) we should stumble in these matters, or say something which is not properly threshed out, or that we should not everywhere guard ourselves beforehand as far as is understood from marauders and the grasps of the opposition. For if we are going to search for those things which are not said warily, it is time for us to say that the holy Trinity also is one hypostasis, because we find Eustathius of blessed memory, who was Bishop of Antioch, in the Commentary on the ninety-second psalm, said in these words (that) the Father and the Son are one hypostasis: (EUSTATHIUS): "The two do wonderful things at the same time invisibly, but the divine Scriptures very often attribute the majesty of their work to one, since they introduce a duality from unity, but teach a unity from duality, in which there is one hypostasis of divinity".[28]

But who does not know that *οὐσία* is derived from *εἶναι* but *φύσις* from *πεφυκέναι* and again *ὑπόστασις* from *ὑφεστηκέναι* and *ὕπαρξις* is derived from *ὑπάρχειν*? And in this meaning these terms are not at all different from each other. For thus the Luminary of the Church, Athanasius himself, made known, when he wrote to the Bishops in Africa: (ATHANASIUS): "From these things, it is right, brothers, that we should notice that those who were at Nicea breathe (the words) of the scriptures, since God himself says in Exodus '*Ἐγώ εἰμι ὁ ὤν*'[29] and by means of Jeremiah, 'Who stood [in his hypostasis][30] and saw his Word?'[31], and after a few things, 'And if they had stood in my hypostasis, and if they had heard my words'.[32] But if[33] hypostasis is ousia, and has no other meaning than that which is, (*Lebon p. 166*) which Jeremiah calls '*ὕπαρξις*' saying, 'Neither have they heard the voice of his being'.[34] For *ὕπαρξις* is *ὑπόστασις* and *οὐσία*: for it is[35] and exists.[36] For since Paul too understood this, he wrote to the Hebrews, 'He is the radiance of (his) glory, and the likeness of (his) hypostasis'.[37] But since these men, who seem to know the scriptures, and call themselves wise, are unwilling to say 'hypostasis' in relation to God—for they wrote this at Ariminum and in their own other assemblies—how was their deposition not just, since they say, even they, like the fool in (his) heart, 'There is no God'?[38]"[39]

Therefore (just) as we learn from the quotation of the Doctor that

there is interchange of these terms of εἶναι and ὑφεστηκέναι, in the same way we are instructed by those (Doctors) to recognise the difference of ousia and hypostasis, and we hear holy Basil writing to Amphilochius and saying as follows: (BASIL): "Ousia and hypostasis have this difference, which the common has in comparison with the particular".[40] And because of this, when the Fathers deal with theology, and explain a term concerning the inhomination, they use these terms which are rightly distinguished, so that there might be not even one thing not uncovered in these considerations when they are set out. Thus when wise Cyril writes in the Second Volume against the blasphemies of Nestorius, he says: (CYRIL): "For one nature is now understood after the union, that which is incarnate, belonging to the Word".[41] And when he writes the Third Letter to the same man, he says: (CYRIL): "Therefore it is right that we attribute all the words in the Gospel to one person, and to one hypostasis, that (hypostasis) of the Word incarnate".[42] For he knew that the term "nature" is also frequently applied for the signification of kind, as when (*Lebon p. 167*) Basil said in the Treatise on Faith: (BASIL): "There the Father and the Son and the Holy Spirit, one nature uncreated".[43] And Gregory the Theologian, in the Treatise on Pentecost: (GREGORY): "O Sirs, confess the Trinity of one divinity, (or) if you wish, of one nature".[44] And holy Cyril too, in the Fourth Volume against the blasphemies of Nestorius said: (CYRIL): "For one nature is understood of the divinity in the holy and consubstantial[45] Trinity".[46]

But you, setting aside the teachings of these men, produce Aristotle, as if from somewhere impenetrable, praising him, and saying, "Aristotle, who is called ὁ νοῦς",[47] and you think (him) worth your announcing (him) for us with thunder from hides, as somewhere Salmoneus[48] is said to have done in the fable. For know, know clearly, that Gregory the Theologian, who was accurately instructed in the opinions of the philosophers, and was able to become an expositor of them, and does not, like us, say such and such from hearsay, passes sentence of condemnation on the opinion of Aristotle which introduces the soul of man (as) mortal—even if those who play at being Aristotelians and stretch out a great beard, and while they praise (him) with words, attempt with a proud mind to conceal his iniquitous opinion, interpreting in what way they like the term "ἐντελέχεια", for this is what he calls the soul of man. For that Doctor of true religion, whom we have mentioned, wrote in this way in the Treatise against the Eunomians, [GREGORY]:[49] ("Attack ....) Aristotle's petty Providence, and (his) system, and discourses about

the mortal[50] soul, and the humanism of (his) opinions".[51] (*Lebon p. 168*)

But yet it is not our business that we should investigate this, how Aristotle thinks about the soul. "For what concern is it of mine, that I should judge also those outside?",[52] says holy Paul. For I know this clearly, that none of those who consider that the human soul is rational and intelligent and not mortal says this, that it is one ousia and quality along with a mortal and sensible body, or (with) the man who is composed from these. And we say this particularly strenuously in the case of Emmanuel—that no-one of intelligence says that the nature of God the Word and flesh endowed with a soul and with a mind, which was united hypostatically to him, has become of one ousia and quality.

And I am unable to see this either, (namely) how you distinguish qualities from natures, and (then) say that the quality of the Word has shared with the quality of the body.[53] For whom have you seen of the Father Theologians, who ever burst[54] (out with) this particularly foolish statement in the Church? For all of them hold to a union of natures, in which—beyond doubt—those naturally fitted signs are seen inseparably. For because of this, when you ask "What then? The moment we say Emmanuel is from two natures, are we obliged to confess as well (that he is) two proprieties?", I have given sentence in saying that this is superfluous, and by means of many and uncontentious discourses I have demonstrated that which has been said. And you have again called a reminder like this "an accusation", saying: "A fourth expression has become a risk to me, as I am called to judgement on the charge that I have set aside ousiai, and interweave composition out of signs".[55] For when you repeat the same things, and (then) again deny that you are saying (them), (*Lebon p. 169*) as far as I can see, nothing can be found to be said as a cure. For on the one hand you are ashamed of and renounce those reasonings, by means of those (things) which have already been written and proved to be in the wrong and exposed, but on the other hand you fasten onto the terms, and just like your tragedian,[56] you say, "*ἡ γλῶσσ' ὀμώμοχ' ἡ δὲ φρὴν ἀνώμοτος*".[57]

But because you have written, "Let us be indulgent to the accurate (findings) of the philosophers, even if they are not of our fold, (and) particularly to (their) interpretations of terms",[58] know that you have written this outside of the law of the Church. For none of the Doctors of true religion said, "We make pagan philosophy a [leader][59] in our studies of terms and of words", but they say they accept it subsequently, as a handmaid, in so far as it agrees with the

teachings and considerations of truth. And at once, therefore, Amphilochius of reverend memory, when he sent a letter with verses in metre to Seleucus, wrote somewhere in this way: "Like a judge introducing a sentence in agreement with the law, command the study of words which is found among the pagans to serve, as is proper to the freedom of true studies, and to the all-wise study of the scriptures. For it is right that the wisdom of the Spirit which is from above and comes from God should be mistress of the instruction which is below as of a handmaid who is not puffed up in vain, but is wont to serve modestly. For it is right that that which is below should be subject to that which is from God."[60]

But great Basil, on evil Eunomius' making mention of "possession" and "privation",[61] before he rebuked his artifice, made this very thing alone the great pretext of complaint, (namely) that from contemptible philosophy (he) should introduce (*Lebon p. 170*) new terms into the discourse of true religion. For he wrote as follows in the First Treatise of those against (that) adversary: (BASIL): "But it is not difficult to show that he gabbles these things from the wisdom of the world, from which he has lifted up his neck,[62] and in this way has set down innovations in terms. For they belong to Aristotle, as those who have read his work *The Categories* would be able to say—discussions about possessions and privations, saying that privations are secondary to possessions. But it was sufficient for us, to show he was speaking not from the teachings of the Spirit, but from the wisdom of the princes of this world,[63] to quote against him these (words) of the psalm, 'The transgressors of the law have related babble to me, but not as your law, O Lord'.[64] And as we learn that these things which are said are not from the teachings of our Lord Jesus Christ, his voice will be remembered: 'When he lies, he speaks according to his own nature',[65] and in this way we should cut short the greater part of his words, since henceforward we make known to everyone that there is no partnership between us and them: 'For what is the unanimity between Christ and Beliar, or what portion has the believer with the unbeliever?'[66]"[67] For in the Letter to the young men, the Doctor says that first it is right that we should grasp the doctrine of truth in concepts and in terms, but as something extra and subsequently (we should) also use profane philosophy, which completes the ornament and grace of the leaves which bend towards the fruit. And he wrote as follows: (BASIL): "Now if there is some affinity between the (bodies of) teachings, a knowledge of them would be necessary for us; but if not, at all events, (by) placing them side by side, we will learn the difference (between them), (which

is of advantage) not least for the establishment of that which is better. But yet, to what (true) comparison (*Lebon p. 171*) can you hit upon, as you compare each one of the disciplines? But (perhaps), just as it is the peculiar virtue of a plant to sprout fair fruit, but the leaves which hang upon the branches also bring some decoration: so too the first fruit of the mind is truth, yet it does not lack grace,[68] or that it should be decked in profane wisdom, as the leaves provide some sort of covering and a not unpleasant appearance for the fruit".[69]

Therefore even holy Cyril makes use of this example, when he wrote in the Second Letter to Succensus: (CYRIL): "For it is not the case that 'one' is predicated truly only of simples in nature, but (it is predicated) also of those which have come together in composition".[70] But in the Treatise of question and answer, *That Christ is One*, as if adding (it) as something extra he said this: (CYRIL): "For so it seems good even to the pagan experts".[71]

Therefore why, when I have reminded your Chastity with humble intention of these things, and of things like these, are you indignant at the lines?[72] For did you not say that you are not expert in the doctrines of true religion, and, "I am a young child in these (matters)"?[73] For we shall again bring to your remembrance these sayings of yours. But in (your) letter you falsely call me an Ecumenical Doctor. For I am become a fool because you compel me.[74] But is it an insult that the schoolmaster should draw lines over inaccurate words? So then will the youth also be indignant when the professional scribe denounces letters which are not well written?

But now you say that you have been left as a spark in the East, and (are) the voice of the Church:[75] (*Lebon p. 172*) (something) which even if someone else should say of him, a man would blush. But we did not know that this was the case for you as regards yourself, and we wrote letters as to a student, and one needing to be led. And because of this, we wrote confidently, knowing your untried nature in these matters, which excused you and (your) questions seemed to be from a desire for instruction and not from contentiousness. But now, since you struggle on behalf of words said in an unlearned way, you have made inexperience and ignorance a premeditated sin. Because of this, and since I have pity on your soul—I say this with God as my witness—I have proceeded to this third piece of advice, and I advise you to keep distant from words of this sort.

For if we grant, according to your word, that I have the rank of the sun, though I am ashamed as I say this openly, while you again are a spark, it ensures that a spark, which from all respects is an issue

of the sun, should shine out with (beams) which are like the sparkling of the sun. Therefore show (me) when, in the six years I spoke in the Church of the Antiochenes and wrote many letters, at any time I once said Emmanuel is one ousia, and of one signification and of one particularity.

But why do you say that you were wounded by us, and you wish to be healed, as if we were striking (you)? For (all we are doing is) remind you, making use of the teachings of the Fathers, in which there is every doctrine for healing and recovery and ordinance and strength. But you do not realise that you wound yourself, and thrust away the healing voices of the Fathers. Thus, when I said in the second letter that God is above ousia, but we use the term "ousia", using (*Lebon p. 173*) at the same time the poverty which is with us, and I brought to this (point) the evidence of Gregory the Theologian and of holy Cyril,[76] I was again believed to have made an attack upon what is said, and (it seemed right to you) to introduce and say, as something unusual, what is well-trodden[77] for all God-fearers, (namely), "I call God ousia, because I have learned from him who said, 'He who is, sent me'",[78] as if the term "above ousia" introduces that which is without being, and (as if) the Fathers had not heard wise Paul saying: "It is right for him who applies himself to God to believe that he exists".[79] For that which is above ousia in all respects is, in that it is. Therefore it ill became you, plotting undue things, to oppose the words of the Doctors with empty attacks.

But again when I said that no-one ever applies "propriety" with any precision to God, as (he would) to things which are subject to definitions, and I introduced the chapter of Evagrius[80] who wrote: (EVAGRIUS): "If either genus or species or difference or property or accident is affirmed for every enquiry, yet none of the above mentioned can be found (to apply) in the case of the holy Trinity. Let us worship in silence what is inexpressible",[81] you have tried to trip up the saying which we would state scripturally, and have written: "But you have defined, and very clearly, that the propriety of God (is) grace:[82] 'Why do you call me good? No-one is good, except one, God'.[83] For if a propriety is that thing which belongs to someone and to him alone—(and) now according to the quotation above it belongs to God alone to be good—(then) clearly (*Lebon p. 174*) something of this sort is a definition of a propriety".[84] Therefore what are you saying, (my) fine man? Is goodness thus the (official) propriety of God, just as laughter (is supposed to be) of man, and neighing of horse? Well then, state first what God is in ousia, and thus we may recognise what precisely his propriety (is). For it is clear

from the start that an ousia is something other than a propriety, for a propriety appears in relation to ousiai. But it is necessary that you attribute accident as well (to God), and those other things from which definitions are brought together, and (thus) you bring God under the limitation of definitions.

But because you thought that the scriptural testimony which says, "No-one is good, except one, God", confirms this ill thought-out statement for you, take note of the scripture which said, "To the only wise God".[85] Therefore, because a propriety properly is that which belongs to one man, according to your words wisdom is also found clearly to follow the principle of a propriety. Therefore by means of these witless and illogical (exercises) two proprieties have appeared for us (in God). But yet, having relied in this way on cool audacity, you have knocked upon the stern of the boat, as it is said, and you have made peace with us at the end, and have honoured those things which are not your own, and have said, "But yet, it is necessary that we should honour these great matters in silence, for God is above ousia and propriety".[86]

But yet, note that wise Basil, in the Letter to Terentius takes goodness not (as) a property but (as) ousia, writing as follows: (BASIL): ". . . . the term 'οὐσία' is generic, like goodness or divinity or anything else which is thought of".[87] (*Lebon p. 175*) And in the Third Treatise against Eunomius he said: (BASIL): "But if we affirm that the ousia of God (is) light, or life or the good, the totality of his existence is life, and all light and all good. But the life has joined to it τὸ ἀγγένητον. How can that which is simple in ousia not be incomposite?"[88] Because of this the Doctor said not fixedly but hesitantly, that the ousia of God is either divinity or goodness, or light or life, because in truth we do not know what God is in ousia. But to the term "ousia" are referred those things which in this way in common and in equality of honour apply to the three hypostases which are distinct in their own characteristics, of whom the Father is not begotten and is from no-one, the Son is begotten, and the Holy Spirit (is) by procession.

And you were indignant at the lines! But while you rage at the voices of the Fathers, again speaking scripturally, I will not be indignant, but will endure humbly the hopping about of your mind. And do not imagine that you are arguing with someone of your own profession, or one who raises his eyebrows from his robes. And do not imagine it a mighty achievement to become an advocate of words which (as) I have very often said, are unpracticed and full of mistakes, lest the prophetic word be thought to refer to us as well, as

about someone from those who were before, (namely) "He loved shame (more) than his glory".[89] For better is humility, which our Lord approved for us, saying, "He who humbles himself will be exalted".[90]

But if you persist in these things, which I pray will not be the case, with words of this type of which I suppose you are become an advocate, in accordance with the Gospel, I shall shake off (my) garments and the dust of my feet,[91] and say to them what (*Lebon p. 176*) has been said by the wise man who has been quoted many times above: "There is a word which is clothed about with death: may it never be found in the inheritance of Jacob!"[92] But I urge you that you run on your own, and that you write under (your own) authority not only these things which have already been written by you, but also all others which you wish (to write), but let me alone. You would be an advocate of my ignorance before the judgement seat without dissimulation. For since I know these things which are written by you, and they go beyond what is right, if I were to be silent, on all accounts I would pay the punishment for silence, and for many I would be a source of harm, as one who was silent in those matters where it was particularly inappropriate that I should be silent. But on the other hand, it is right that I be reckoned with those who have already died, (I) who strive not to be seen,[93] and am now more than ever put to flight by enemies in (my) tracks, as I hear, and I am unable without fear to publish discourses in opposition, for those who wish to be involved in them. For as God hears, I say that in love for you, I sent both those things which were written before, and now these, while at the same time I prayed and took pains to procure irreproachability for you on all hands. For it is right that we should not only have a mind giving praise but a tongue giving praise as well. For it is not our striving in any old way that is crowned, but our striving lawfully, and not our emulating in some way or other, but our doing so with knowledge. For it belongs to wisdom that we learn with a humble and balanced and unquarrelsome mind. For the same wise man says again, "The wisdom of a poor man will lift up his head, and make him sit in the midst of the great".[94] And the instruction of (the Book) of Proverbs gives command saying, (*Lebon p. 177*) "If you will invoke wisdom, and will give your voice to knowledge, and if you will search for it like silver, and glean for it like treasure, then you will know the fear of the Lord, and you will find the knowledge of God. For the Lord gives wisdom and from his countenance wisdom and knowledge, and he lays down treasures for those who do rightly (for) redemption".[95]

But as for those who want to introduce the Henoticon—which contains a confession of the orthodox faith—at a time when the wickedness at Chalcedon and the Tome of Leo, which blasphemes more than anything, remains dominant, and do not, as is lawful, explicitly anathematise (these things), in the manner which prevailed in the days of Macedonius and Flavian of ill-repute, and by this contrive to lead astray those who are more simple, I have said and I have written everything rightly and wisely. To which (simple ones), the practice, which Dioscorus of reverend memory—the Archbishop of Alexandria, who was our co-worker—established, brings great benefit, when he showed before everyone the purity of the Church, both in doctrine, and in the absence of the joining of communion with heretics, and drew many from those who were separated, and joined (them) (as) limbs to the body.

The Third Letter to Sergius the Grammarian has ended.

Notes

1. cf. pp. 155–156 in the text above.
2. Sir. xx.1.
3. Jer. x.16.
4. 2 Cor. xiii.7.
5. Reading ܐܠܗܘܬܟ for ܠܗܘܬܟ.
6. Prov. x.10.
7. Cyril, *Contra Diodorum Tars. Episc.*, (Pusey edn., Vol. 5), p. 499.17–500.4.
8. Place not found.
9. Cyril, *Contra Diodorum Tars. Episc.*, (Pusey edn., Vol. 5), p. 502.10–17.
10. The Syriac is ܣܝܡܐ ܕܬܘܣܦܬܐ. cf. p. 140, line 29 above, where the Greek underlying ܒܣܝܡܐ ܕܬܘܣܦܬܐ is *κατὰ παράθεσιν*.
11. ܩܕܡ ܚܝܠܐ.
12. cf. above, p. 102.8 ff., and p. 121.2 ff.
13. cf. p. 99 above.
14. cf. pp. 125 and 126 above.
15. The Syriac is ܥܒܕܬ ܥܘܬܕܐ which is very obscure. Possibly the underlying Greek is from *κατασκευάζω*: cf. Lampe, *Patristic Greek Lexicon*, (Oxford, 1961) under *κατασκευάζω*, §7.
16. cf. p. 150 above.
17. Note in margin: Anointed: as an athlete.
18. Note in margin: Who is of the people, because she is a whore before everyone.
19. cf. Prov. vii.11.
20. cf. p. 152 above, lines 3 and 4. Here Severus reads ܡܥܒܕܢܘܬܐ (activity) where Sergius had ܡܫܘܕܥܢܘܬܐ (signification, denotation). One might notice that on p. 135.15 above, Severus read ܡܥܒ̈ܕܢܘܬܐ (activities) where Harvard Syriac 22 reads ܫܘ̈ܕܥܐ (signs; marks; indications).
21. Mt. xii.37.
22. cf. Ps. xliii.14.
23. This is a difficult passage to translate, and what is offered is only one attempt. Here the passage in inverted commas ("Where therefore ....") follows from "obliges us to say," ....

24. PG 59.47C.
25. PG 29.525A.
26. Note in margin: Believed you: ratified you (as) true.
27. *Iliad*, 8.154.
28. Eustathius: *Fragmentum Commentarii in Psalmum Nonagesimum Secundum*, pp. 212–3 in J. B. Pitra, *Analecta Sacra* (Paris, 1883), Vol. 4. Also see M. Spanneut, *Recherches sur les écrits d'Eustathe d'Antioche, avec une éd. nouv. des fragments dogmatiques et exégétiques* (Lille, 1948), pp. 32–33; and No. 38, p. 107 (Latin only).
29. Ex. iii.14.
30. The Syriac reads ܒܩܝܡܗ. Lebon notes: Read ܒܩܘܡܗ. The Greek is *ἐν ὑποστήματι*.
31. Jer. xxiii.18.
32. Jer. xxiii.22.
33. Lebon notes that the Syriac translator read "*εἰ δέ*" in place of "*ἤ δέ*".
34. Jer. ix.9.
35. *ἔστι*.
36. *ὑπάρχει*.
37. Heb. i.3.
38. Ps. xiii.1.
39. PG 26.1036A–C.
40. PG 32.884A. *Ep. CCXXXVI.*
41. PG 76.60D (= Pusey edn. Vol. 6, p. 94.10–11).
42. PG 77.116C (= Pusey edn. Vol. 6, p. 28.21–23).
43. PG 31.465C.
44. PG 36.440B.
45. ܫܘܬ ܟܝܢܐ = *ὁμοουσίῳ* (H. syr. 22 = ܒܪܬ ܟܝܢܐ).
46. PG 76.180D (= Pusey edn. Vol. 6, p. 187.17–18).
47. cf. p. 151 above.
48. Apollodorus, I.9.7. cf. S. P. Brock, *The Syriac Version of the Pseudo-Nonnos Mythological Scholia* (Cambridge, 1971), Scholia to Invective ii.2, pp.132–133.
49. The text reads: ܐܪܝܣܛܛܠܝܣ. Lebon notes: This word belongs to the quotation: emend ܕܐܪܝܣܛܛܠܝܣ [[illegible]].
50. Migne reads: *τοὺς θνητοὺς περὶ ψυχῆς λόγους*. Severus, or the translator, might seem to have read "*θνητοῦ*".
51. PG 36.24B–C.
52. 1 Cor. v.12.
53. cf. above, pp. 152.3 (Sergius) and 162.25 (Severus). One should note how Severus has re-phrased Sergius on both occasions.
54. Note in margin: It is "expounded" [ܦܫܩ] in another manuscript.
55. cf. above, pp. 86.8; 101.24; 135.14; 155.4 ff.
56. Note in margin: (The word) ܐܠܗܐ (is derived) from ܐܠܐ.
57. Euripides, *Hippol.* 612.
58. cf. p. 151, above.
59. Reading ܪܫܐ for ܕܫܐ (misprint).
60. PG 37.1592–1593: lines 240–250.
61. *ἕξις* and *στέρησις*. See below, and Aristotle, *Categories*, ch. 10.
62. So the Syriac translator has rendered the Greek *ὑφ' ἧς ἐκτραχηλισθεὶς*: "by which he has been overthrown". PG 29.532A.
63. cf. 1 Cor. ii.6.
64. Ps. cxviii.85.
65. Jn. viii.44.
66. 2 Cor. vi.15.
67. PG 29.532A–B.
68. Note in the margin: He calls beauty "grace".
69. PG 31.568B.
70. PG 77.241B (= ACO, I, 1, 6a, p. 160.2–3).

71. cf. PG 75.1285C (=Pusey edn. Vol. 7, p. 360.12).
72. Note in margin: He calls the heretical marks "lines".
73. cf. the foot of p. 72 above.
74. cf. 2 Cor. xii.11.
75. cf. p. 156 above.
76. cf. above, p. 138.6 ff, and 12 ff.
77. Note in margin: Trodden: ploughed.
78. cf. above p. 155.13 ff.
79. Heb. xi. 6.
80. cf. above, p. 137.26–138.2.
81. cf. Socrates, *H.E. III*, 7 (PG 67.396B).
82. Note in margin: He seems to call Christ "grace". But Lebon suggests that it should be read ܛܒܘܬܐ: "goodness". cf. above, p. 155.16 ff.
83. Mk. x.18.
84. cf. above, p. 155.16 ff.
85. Rom. xvi.27.
86. cf. above, p. 155.22 ff.
87. PG 32.789B.
88. PG 29.640B.
89. cf. Hos. iv.18.
90. Lk. xiv.11.
91. cf. Mt. x.14.
92. Sir. xxiii.12.
93. i.e. by the authorities.
94. Sir. xi.1.
95. Prov. ii.3–7.

The Apology of Sergius

Of the same Sergius to the Patriarch Severus.

To my master in Christ, (and) to the Fathers (who are) philosophers. Sergius, humble Grammarian. Treatise of apology.

Shem and Japheth (are thought) commendable sons in (their) race, because when (their) father lay naked, they did not endure even the sight, but with noble shame, covered (him) with a garment.[1] But Ham is like a runaway slave: for he laughs, and made sport of the drunkenness of him who begot (him). (*Lebon p. 178*) We, immoderate men, foolishly act worse than this, and are scornful in the unrestrained manner of enemies. For as the Father establishes us in the fair raiment of virtue, and drank all the cluster of discretion, and is watchful in himself, we falsely attribute nakedness and the worst drunkenness to him, still craving for the earthly Israel—(that Israel) which when Moses in an outstanding way managed the governorship, very much reviled that just man. We have emulated that Absalom, who even cast eyes on the kingdom of (his) father. Even the Book of the Law has not held in check the shamelessness of our words, which decrees death on sons who even justly speak against those who begot (them).

But some, doubtless, will reject me as a demagogue, and will tell me that integrity was given up, but later I put on an act in some way for the sake of appeasing (your) person. But calling to witness him who tests the hearts and the kidneys, and the judgement throne, taking up my tract, I will make my apology anew, making integrity first in honour. May I be found guilty in the midst of ten thousand ministering angels, if anything was done in this matter for the sake of the appeasing of (mortal) man: but may I fall short of the hope to come, if I intentionally sin against the truth.

But I think this struggle which I am undertaking is arduous, since two sorts of opponents are rising up against me. For as some of the opponents of the Father misrepresent (his) words to their own confusion, expecting the song to be inharmonious, we will say in opposition to them (borrowing) from our harp, "May the deceitful lips be silent, which speak wickedness against the just man".[2] But in the same way, doubtless some of our own side have gone astray because

of the ambiguity (of the term) "propriety", (*Lebon p. 179*) and revile the Father because of uncertainty. We will instruct these with the wise proverb, "Hear, O sons, the instruction of (your) father", and "Give heed that you may know the meaning".[3] For when the meaning of the ambiguity is sought out, it lays open the contentious way. And I plead that we give heed to those things which are said, setting aside every contentious ambition.

Even the wise pagans confess that God is cause, but they also teach second and third gods. The sons of the Hebrews worship one God, but they make him barren, and separate the Rational from the Rational,[4] and are jealous of the Holy Spirit. Therefore how have we learnt about these matters? God indeed (is) cause, but he is the first and the middle and the last: "Before me there was not, and after me there will not be another".[5] Again, we confess one God, but we know the oneness of the Trinity in mystical theology. The Manichaeans profess the Trinity, and this after some mighty work, which they change beforehand. Sabellius also professes the Trinity, but he does not acknowledge the hypostases of it. But Arius who was mad set his Trinity in heathen ideas, enumerating together and imagining all these ousiai belonging to it. But we, children of the mystery of true instruction, confess the Trinity in the pattern of those things which were said before, but at the first both in distinct hypostases and pointing towards one ousia. Mani and Apollinaris and Eutyches profess one nature of God the Word after the birth from the Virgin; but the first supposed the inhomination to be imaginary, while the second stumbled to imperfect opinions,[6] but mad Eutyches introduces not only a shadow, but a complete change, outside the mystery. But as for us, how do we (judge) concerning the one nature which was composed from divinity and perfect manhood? It is clear that the flesh did not exist before (the union), but comes (into existence for the purpose of) that mystical union. Therefore notice (*Lebon p. 180*) how on the one hand the terms (are) common, but on the other hand these doctrines define what is set down.

Thus even Nestorius, and all those who are fellow-drinkers of Nestorius, profess properties, but not (properties) of the incarnate Word, but of those natures which they understand in Christ, even after the false union which (is accepted) among them. But then Nestorius, finding fault with Father Cyril, writes from exile to Theodoret: (NESTORIUS): "Herein in a secret way, he confuses the properties of the natures".[7] But Theodoret said in a statement of opposition to the Third Anathema: THEODORET: "Therefore how does he ascribe wickedness to those who divide the properties of

the natures of God who was before the ages and of the man who was assumed at the end of days?"[8] AND IN THAT ON THE EIGHTH: "Well then, professing the properties of each one of the natures, we worship our Lord Christ".[9] AND IN THAT ON THE TENTH:[10] "Passions are proper to the passible, for the impassible is higher than passions. Therefore the form of the servant suffered, it being recognised that the form of God is along with it; therefore it was not God who suffered, but the man from us assumed by God".[11] But Leo says with all fury: LEO: "The particularity of each one of the natures is kept. For each one of the natures keeps without loss its own particularity".[12] AND AGAIN: "For each form effects in companionship with the other the particularity which belonged to it: the Word effecting this which is of the Word, but the body completing this which is of the body. For the former of them is radiant with marvels, but the latter fell under insult".[13] But the many-headed wickedness of Chalcedon says: FROM THE SYNOD OF CHALCEDON: (*Lebon p. 181*) "One Lord Jesus Christ is known in two natures, and the difference of the natures is not suppressed anywhere because of the union, but rather the particularity of each one of the natures is kept".[14]

Therefore what did the Father of the Church[15] say as a result of these unholy (statements)? Did he, like those who were quoted before, set up two natures, understanding these in Christ after the union, and attributing (an individuating) particularity to each one of them? Not at all, but speaking in agreement with the Fathers, he attributes these (properties) of our flesh to the Word who was incarnate. Therefore those men say that the Temple of the Word was seen, hungered, thirsted, suffered, rose; but the Father along with Cyril proclaims Emmanuel, or rather along with Isaiah, Emmanuel who the Word was born from a woman, and along with John cries out in a loud voice that (the Word) was seen and touched,[16] and clearly establishes that he hungered and thirsted, and that he was fastened to the cross, and having endured death for three days, he proclaims that he bestows life on men.

But I ask whence do these things (come) to the Word, that he should be seen and touched, that he should suffer in a human way? Surely because he was incarnate? For the particularity of the Word (is) invisibility, untouchableness, being high above every passion; but of an ensouled body, to hunger and to thirst and to suffer. Therefore (even) as he remained the Word—thus preserving to himself the properties of divinity—yet preserving the integrity of the flesh, (so) too he receives these (properties) of our flesh. Therefore

we profess the same God the Word, visible and invisible, for when he was seen by men, he was invisibly with the Father; the same who was born from the Father Almighty, and (was born) God from the virgin mother; in the former case incorporeally from before all ages, (*Lebon p. 182*) (in the latter case) corporeally within the last times; the same impassible and passible: impassible in the ousia of the Father, but passible in human flesh. You see how the definition has preserved for him immutability, (holding) him at the same time God and body. Of him who displays the particularity of a body in a godly manner, we do not say that the natures exist and each one (of) them is seen out of its own properties and activities, but we hold that the Word himself became flesh, and displayed these (properties) of the flesh.

And let no-one think the definition is foolish, introducing particularity and nature (existing) independently: for the principle of things which are composed joins[17] some two or more, but completes one nature of the living creature: it allows the particularity of each one of them to appear, but yet not divided but recognisable together, as we are able to find out in the case of the nature of man. To be cut is a property of a body, but to perceive a blow is of an animated body: but it does not receive cutting in some (one) nature, but show perception in another, but there appears in one and the same composite nature both cutting of the body and perception of the soul. A (man) rejoices, and by means of a laugh makes known the cheerfulness of the soul: and he is grieved, and a tear has announced distress. Thus also in the case of the one composite nature of Christ, we will see the Word is born, but from a virgin mother: it is not the case that in one nature it happened to him that he should be born, but in another he effected what is strange, as Leo raved, saying, "The Word performs that which is of the Word, but the body completes that which is of the body",[18] but (there is) one nature which is born, and in a miracle effected being born; hungered, thirsted, not compelled, but willingly; walked, but the sea was able to be walked on by (his) feet; (*Lebon p. 183*) and at the end he died, not that he had awaited the necessity of death, but when it was right, he dissolved death, for "I have the power to lay down my life and to take it up again",[19] and he taught the truth of (these) words by means of the resurrection.

You see how some natures receive their [properties][20] and activities not cut apart or separately recognised, but the divinity and the humanity of the Word who was incarnate appear together. Let them show me what was done after the incarnation (which) was merely human. And I will not say a tear, for that came divinely, for he was immediately summoning Lazarus whom he pitied, and though he

was putrifying, the dead man became alive and made haste to run. They speak of sweat and perplexity in relation to the Passion? But these things also (happened) divinely, and surpass our reasonings, so that by means of human passions he might lead men [to][21] impassibility. But what will they say about (his) death? Will he await this utterly human thing, which takes possession of the body? We are persuaded: thus God is he who preserved even the properties of divinity, and suffered humanly. For because of this he also became a complete man that he might bear our weakness, and giving (his) back on our behalf to scourging, he conferred honour upon the wound which the ancient [serpent][22] set against our soul.

I have these things, which I learned from the Father. But it is right that we should demonstrate (this) in the very words (of the Father), and should make the confirmation of the definition more firm. For he says as follows in the First Letter: FROM THE PATRIARCH SEVERUS: "Because we say as well that a man like us is a living creature, rational, mortal, and capable of reason and knowledge: and because there is one nature and hypostasis from two, the whole living creature is said to be (*Lebon p. 184*) mortal, and the whole (living creature) is called rational, and we do not say that we do not know in what it is rational, or in what it is mortal—but our knowing this does not divide the composition from which the one living creature is composed. (It is) the same as well in the case of the study of Emmanuel".[23] AND AGAIN: "Therefore if someone should wrongfully divide Emmanuel with a duality of nature after the union, there also occurs a division at the same time, along with the difference of the natures, and the properties are divided in every respect aptly for the natures".[24] AND AGAIN: "But we shun dividing the one Christ into a duality of natures after the union. For when he is divided, the properties of each one of the natures are divided at the same time".[25] AND AGAIN: "And the properties of the humanity will become (the) properties of the divinity of the Word, and again the properties of the Word will be acknowledged (as) the properties of the flesh".[26] AND AGAIN: "Therefore the properties of the Word became (those) of manhood, and again those of manhood, properties of the Word".[27] AND AGAIN: "But we anathematise speaking of 'Two natures after the union', (where) (those natures) will consequently attract their own activities and properties".[28] AND AGAIN: "The natures are not implied independently and in individual existence, for to say this belongs to (the position of) those who mutilate (Christ) with a duality after the inexpressible union, and not to us, who profess him to be one from two".[29] AND

AGAIN: "Therefore he who divides Emmanuel, and defines him in two natures after the inexpressible union, along with the natures divides the activities and properties as well, and establishes two natures which act and without diminishment undergo what is their own".[30] AND AGAIN: "Therefore he who divides Emmanuel to a duality of natures after the inexpressible union, divides with him, as (*Lebon p. 185*) we have often said, the activities and properties as well".[31] AND AGAIN: "For because there is one who acts, his activity is also one and the active motion".[32] AND AGAIN: "But when they divide (Emmanuel) by speaking of two natures after the union, they divide at the same time also those things which each nature attracts naturally as properties".[33] AND AGAIN: "Those things which we would say the flesh suffers, are sufferings of the incarnate Word, although his divinity is not defective, in that he is impassible; for to whom we say the flesh belongs, we hold the sufferings peculiar to the flesh in all respects also belong to him".[34] AND AGAIN: "We will reckon (it is) iniquitous to divide (Christ) into a duality of natures after the union, and consequently the activities and properties, for everything is cut with a duality and is reduced to a split diversity and divided in everything, whether you speak of activities or properties".[35] But in the same way, and from the Second Letter: FROM HIM: "But the principle of the union, because of the economy, allows those things which in nature are properties of the flesh to be called properties of the Word. In the same way, it made those things which in ousia are properties of the Word to be called properties of the flesh".[36] AND AGAIN: "But even if they are in nature properties of humanity, they became, because of the economy also properties of God the Word, and he is said to have hungered and thirsted, and been tired from a journey".[37]

What words more God-fearing than these, or what teaching more in agreement with the Fathers, says that the properties of the body became in all respects (those) of the Word? But those who confess before that (the Word) lacks the properties of the flesh, in every respect renounce even the incarnation. From where do we learn that he was truly incarnate? (*Lebon p. 186*) Surely from the fact that he voluntarily displayed all that belongs to the flesh? Surely it did not belong to the Word before the incarnation that he should hunger and thirst? Surely since these things belong to our nature, they became God's by means of the supreme union of the body? Thus they are no longer made the properties of natures as it were existent in their own principle, but of the only-begotten Son of God, who was composed impassibly to (be one with) a body.

When we write these laws of the Fathers in (our) minds, we will not provoke to anger the Spirit of God, by acting deceitfully against the truth. Will we suffer a sorrow more miserable than all, because while admitting that we err on behalf of the fear of God, we still put up such a fight in the sight of everyone?—When we will have sacrificed beforehand our captain, will we go to the barbarians, that now we may appear easily caught, being widowed[38] of order, from lack of leadership? For justly one after another,[39] the sees of the interior region declare this (man) our leader, among whom he was the first in the east (as) Patriarch to drive out the folly of Chalcedon—and at a time when our affairs had become grievously ill: for first Paul, and then Diodore, is the defiler of the eastern congregations, (and) with these also Theodore; and Nestorius too was from here, and fell sick in Byzantium, and Ibas and Theodoret and Andrew are not from somewhere else either. From us too Cyrus and John sprang up, and Persia, the evil twig, planted similar evil opinions.

Well then, it is right that we should honour him who turned away all the sickness of the whole place. But let us not turn our sword against ourselves. Therefore let us honour the Father with truth, for the Law punishes abusive sons, for "He who speaks evilly to (his) father or (*Lebon p. 187*) mother will surely die".[40] But the Wise Man of the Church accepts sober sons, for "A wise son gives joy to his father".[41]

The Apology of Sergius the Grammarian is finished.

Folio 1^a reads:

This is the book of Michael bar Qt", which he bequeathed to the monastery of the Syrians which is in the desert of Skete of Egypt. May God make his soul to rest in the dwelling places of the righteous and just and write his name in the Book of Life, and make ⟨his deeds⟩[42] a good remembrance, through the prayer of the one who gave birth to God and of all the saints. Amen.

Notes

1. cf. Gen. ix.22–23.
2. Ps. xxx.19.
3. cf. Prov. i.8 and iv.1.
4. H. syr. 22 = ܡܒܘܥܐ (spring, fount).
5. cf. Is. xliii.10.
6. ܡܕ̈ܥܐ could possibly mean "intellects".
7. Loofs, *Nestoriana*, *op. cit.*, p. 198 (*Fragment of a Letter to Theodoret*).
8. PG 76.404.C–D (= Pusey edn. Vol. 6, p. 410.27–29). *Apol. contra Theod.*

9. PG 76.429A (= Pusey edn. Vol. 6, p. 454.11–12). *Apol. contra Theod.*
10. Lebon notes: Read "TWELFTH".
11. cf. PG 76.449B. Sergius omits some of the Greek which is in Migne (= Pusey edn. Vol. 6, p. 490.18–23). *Apol. contra Theod.*
12. PL 54.765A and cf. 763A. *Ep. XXVIII, ad Flavianum* ("*The Tome*").
13. PL 54.767A–B.
14. cf. T. H. Bindley and F. W. Green: *The Oecumenical Documents of the Faith* (London, 1950), p. 193.118–121; ACO II, 1, 2a, p. 129.30–33.
15. *sc.* Severus.
16. cf. 1 Jn. i.1.
17. The Syriac is ܡܣܬܡܟܐ from ܣܡܟ, not from ܫܠܡ.
18. PL 54.767B.
19. cf. Jn. x.18.
20. Reading ܕܫܠܝܬܐ for ܕܫܠܛܬܐ.
21. Reading ܠܠܐ for ܠܐ.
22. Reading ܚܘܒܐ for ܚܘܒܝ.
23. cf. above, p. 76.
24. cf. above, pp. 77–78.
25. cf. above, p. 79.
26. cf. above, p. 79.
27. cf. above, p. 80.
28. cf. above, p. 80.
29. cf. above, pp. 80–81.
30. cf. above, pp. 85–86.
31. cf. above, p. 87.
32. cf. above, p. 87.
33. cf. above, p. 88.
34. cf. above, pp. 89–90.
35. cf. above, pp. 93–94.
36. cf. above, p. 121.
37. cf. above, p. 139.
38. i.e. being left without a Bishop.
39. Reading ܒܬܪ ܒܬܪ for ܒܬܪ.
40. Ex. xxi.16.
41. Prov. x.1.
42. Reading ܠܡܒܪܘܗܝ for ܠܡ⟨...⟩ܗܝ.

Appendix A

Occurrences of ܕܝܠܝܬܐ, ܡܫܘܕܥܢܘܬܐ, ܡܫܘܕܥܢܘܬܐ and ܫܘܕܥܢܐ.

Page	Writer	Word	Greek or Latin	Translation
71.3	Sergius	ܕܝ̈ܠܝܬܐ		proprieties
71.5	Quotation of Antoninus	ܕܝ̈ܠܝܬܐ		proprieties [although possibly Antoninus intends "particularities"]
71.9	Sergius	ܕܝ̈ܠܝܬܐ		proprieties
71.12	Sergius	ܕܝ̈ܠܝܬܐ		proprieties
71.13	Sergius	ܕܝ̈ܠܝܬܐ *read* ܕܝܠܝܬܐ		propriety
71.15	Sergius	ܕܝ̈ܠܝܬܐ		proprieties
71.17	Sergius	ܕܝܠܝܬܐ		propriety
71.22	Sergius	ܕܝܠܝܬܐ		propriety
71.27	Sergius	ܕܝܠܝܬܐ		propriety
71.28	Sergius	ܕܝܠܝܬܐ		propriety
71.29	Sergius	ܕܝ̈ܠܝܬܐ		proprieties
72.2	Sergius	ܕܝ̈ܠܝܬܐ		proprieties
72.10	Sergius	ܕܝܠܝܬܐ		propriety
72.12	Sergius	ܕܝܠܝܬܐ		propriety
72.17	Sergius	ܕܝܠܝܬܐ		propriety
72.19	Sergius	ܕܝܠܝܬܐ		propriety
72.21	Sergius	ܕܝܠܝܬܐ		propriety
72.23	Sergius	ܕܝܠܝܬܐ		propriety

(continued overleaf)

Appendix A (*cont.*)

Page	Writer	Word	Greek or Latin	Translation
73.10	Severus	ܕܝܠܝ̈ܬܐ		particularities
74.11	Severus	ܕܝܠܝܬܐ ܟܝܢܝܬܐ		natural particularity
74.19	Cyril	ܕܝܠܝܬܐ ܗ̇ܝ ܕܒܟܝܢܐ	*ἐν ἰδιότητι τῇ* *κατὰ φύσιν*	particularity that belongs to the nature
74.25	Severus	ܕܝܠܝܬܐ		particularity
74.27	Severus	ܕܝܠܝܬܐ		particularity
75.1	Cyril	ܐܝܟܢܝܘܬܐ ܟܝܢܝܬܐ	[only in Syriac]	natural quality
75.7	Cyril	ܐܝܟ ܡܠܬܐ ܕܕܝܠܝܘܬܐ	[only in Syriac]	with respect to particularity
75.21	Severus	ܕܝܠܝܬܐ		particularity
75.21	Severus	ܐܝܟܢܝܘܬܐ		quality
75.25	Severus	ܕܝܠܝܘܬܐ		particularity
76.26	Severus	ܐܝܟܢܝܘܬܐ		quality
77.6	Severus	ܐܝܟܢܘܬܐ [prob. ܝ dropped out]		quality
77.9	Severus	ܐܝܟܢܝܘܬܐ		quality
77.15	Severus	ܐܝܟܢܝܘܬܐ		quality
78.3	Severus	ܕܝܠܝ̈ܬܐ		properties
78.13	Cyril	ܕܝܠܝ̈ܬܐ	. . . . *τὰ ἑκατέρας ἴδια*	properties
78.16	Severus	ܐܝܟܢܝܘܬܐ		quality
78.19	Severus	ܕܝܠܝܘܬܐ		particularity
78.21	Severus	ܕܝܠܝܬܐ		particularity
78.22	Severus	ܐܝܟܢܝܘܬܐ		quality
79.4	Severus	ܕܝܠܝ̈ܬܐ		properties
79.9	Severus	ܕܝܠܝ̈ܬܐ		properties

79.10	Severus	ܕܝ̈ܠܝܬܐ ×2		properties
79.11	Severus	ܕܝ̈ܠܝܬܐ ×2		properties
79.15	Severus	ܕܝ̈ܠܝܬܐ		properties
80.6	Cyril	ܕܝ̈ܠܝܬܐ	*Γέγονε τοίνυν ἴδια μὲν . . . .*	properties
80.7	Cyril	ܕܝ̈ܠܝܬܐ	*. . . . ἴδια δὲ . . . .*	properties
80.11	Severus	ܕܝ̈ܠܝܬܐ		properties
80.12	Severus	ܕܝ̈ܠܝܬܐ		properties
80.15	Severus	ܕܝ̈ܠܝܬܐ		properties
80.22	Severus	ܕܝ̈ܠܝܬܐ		particularities
80.23	Severus	ܕܝܠܝܬܐ		particularity
80.24	Severus	ܡܫܘܕܥܘܬܐ		quality
85.5	Severus	ܕܝ̈ܠܝܬܐ		properties
86.2	Severus	ܕܝ̈ܠܝܬܐ		properties
86.6	Severus	ܕܝܠܝܘܬܐ		particularity
86.8	Severus	ܕܝ̈ܠܝܬܐ		properties
86.10	Severus	ܕܝܠܝܬܐ		property
86.19	Severus	ܕܝ̈ܠܝܬܐ		properties
86.20	Severus	ܕܝ̈ܠܝܬܐ		properties
86.24	Severus	ܕܝ̈ܠܝܬܐ		properties
87.8	Severus	ܕܝ̈ܠܝܬܐ		properties
88.3	Severus	ܕܝ̈ܠܝܬܐ		properties
88.7	Severus	ܕܝ̈ܠܝܬܐ		properties
88.22	Julius	ܕܝܠܝܬܐ	*τί τὸ ἴδιον ἑκατέρου*	what belongs to . . . .
88.24	Julius	ܕܝ̈ܠܝܬܐ	*τὰ ἴδια*	properties
88.26	Severus	ܕܝ̈ܠܝܬܐ		properties
89.3	Severus	ܕܝ̈ܠܝܬܐ		properties
89.22	Severus	ܕܝ̈ܠܝܬܐ		properties
90.22	Severus	ܕܝ̈ܠܝܬܐ		properties

(*continued overleaf*)

Appendix A (*cont.*)

Page	Writer	Word	Greek or Latin	Translation
90.24	Severus	ܗܠܝܢ ܕܝܠܗ		its properties
92.28	Cyril	ܕܝܠܝܬܐ	ἀνθρωπίνοις τε αὖ καὶ τοῖς ὑπὲρ ἄνθρωπον ἰδιώμασιν	properties
93.26	Severus	ܕܝܠܝܘܬܐ		particularity
93.27	Severus	ܐܝܟܢܝܘܬܐ		quality
94.2	Severus	ܕܝܠܝܬܐ		properties
94.5	Severus	ܕܝܠܝܬܐ		properties
94.18	Severus	ܐܝܟܢܝܘܬܐ		quality
94.20	Severus	ܐܝܟܢܝܘܬܐ		quality
94.22	Severus	ܪܘܫܡܐ		signification, sense
95.7	Cyril	ܐܝܟܢܝܘܬܐ	φυσική τις . . . . ποιότης	(natural) quality
95.10	Cyril	ܐܝܟܢܝܘܬܐ	τὴν κατὰ φύσιν ἐνέργειαν	(natural) quality
98.18	Sergius	ܕܝܠܝܬܐ		proprieties
98.21	Sergius	ܕܝܠܝܬܐ		proprieties
99.31	Sergius	ܪܘܫܡܐ		mark
100.4	Sergius	ܪܘܫܡܝܘܬܐ		mark, token
100.16	Sergius	ܐܝܟܢܝܘܬܐ		quality
100.24	Sergius	ܕܝܠܝܬܐ		properties
100.29	Severus	ܕܝܠܝܬܐ		properties
101.22	Sergius	ܕܝܠܝܬܐ		propriety
101.24	Sergius	ܕܝܠܝܬܐ		properties
102.2	Sergius	ܪܫܡܐ		sign
102.8	Cyril	ܕܝܠܝܬܐ	ἀνθρωπίνοις τε αὖ καὶ τοῖς ὑπὲρ ἄνθρωπον ἰδιώμασιν	properties

102.11	Sergius	ܕܝ̈ܠܝܬܐ		proprieties
102.12	Sergius	ܕܝܠܝܬܐ		propriety
103.23	Severus	ܕܝܠܝܬܐ		particularity
103.23	Severus	ܐܝܟܢܝܘܬܐ		quality
105.19	Severus	ܕܝܠܝܬܐ		peculiarity
106.27	Severus	ܐܝܟܢܝܘܬܐ		quality
106.31	Severus	ܕܝܠܝܘܬܐ		particularity
107.1	Severus	ܐܝܟܢܝܘܬܐ		quality
109.1	Severus	ܐܝܟܢܝܘܬܐ	*Marginal note* states that where there is ܐܝܟܢܝܘܬܐ it is *ποιότης*	quality
121.2	Cyril	ܕܝ̈ܠܝܬܐ	*ἀνϑρωπίνοις τε αὖ καὶ τοῖς ὑπὲρ ἄνϑρωπον ἰδιώμασιν*	properties
121.6	Sergius	ܕܝ̈ܠܝܬܐ		properties
121.8	Sergius	ܕܝܠܝܬܐ		particularity
121.10	Cyril	ܕܝ̈ܠܝܬܐ	*ἀνϑρωπίνοις τε αὖ καὶ τοῖς ὑπὲρ ἄνϑρωπον ἰδιώμασιν*	properties
121.11	Severus	ܕܝܠܝܬܐ		particularity
121.13	Severus	ܐܝܟܢܝܘܬܐ		quality
121.13	Severus	ܕܝ̈ܠܝܬܐ		properties
121.15	Severus	ܕܝ̈ܠܝܬܐ		properties
121.16	Severus	ܕܝ̈ܠܝܬܐ		properties
121.17	Severus	ܐܝܟܢܝܘܬܐ		quality
121.23	Severus	ܐܝܟܢܝܘܬܐ		quality
121.25	Severus	ܕܝ̈ܠܝܬܐ		properties
121.25	Severus	ܕܝ̈ܠܝܬܐ		properties
121.27	Severus	ܕܝ̈ܠܝܬܐ		properties

(*continued overleaf*)

Appendix A (*cont.*)

Page	Writer	Word	Greek or Latin	Translation
121.27	Severus	ܕ̈ܝܠܝܬܐ		properties
122.6	Sergius	ܡܫܘܕܥܢܘܬܐ		quality
122.7	Sergius	ܕܝܠܝܬܐ		particularity
122.8	Severus	ܡܫܘܕܥܢܘܬܐ		quality
122.9	Severus	ܕܝܠܝܘܬܐ		particularity
122.12	Sergius	ܕܝܠܝܬܐ		particularity
122.14	Leo	ܕܝܠܝܘܬܗ	Tenet enim sine defectu *proprietatem suam* utraque natura	particularity
122.17	Severus	ܗܠܝܢ ܕܝܠܗ		in those things which are its own
122.24	Severus	ܕ̈ܝܠܝܬܐ		properties
123.10	Severus	ܕܝܠܝܬܐ		particularity
123.11	Sergius	ܡܫܘܕܥܢܘܬܐ		quality
124.11	Sergius	ܡܫܘܕܥܢܘܬܐ		quality
125.11	Severus	ܡܫܘܕܥܢܘܬܐ		quality
134.2	Cyril	ܫܘܕܥܐ	*ποιεῖσθαί φαμεν τὴν δήλωσιν*	sign, indication
134.12	Cyril	ܫܘܕܥܐ	*τὴν ἑνὸς ποιεῖται δήλωσιν*	sign
134.28	Severus	ܡܫܘܕܥܢܘܬܐ		quality
134.30	Severus	ܡܫܘܕܥܢܘܬܐ		quality
135.14	Severus	ܕ̈ܝܠܝܬܐ		properties
135.15	Severus	ܫܘܕ̈ܥܐ	in Harvard syr. 22, for ܡܫܘܕ̈ܥܢܘܬܐ	signs
135.16	Severus	ܕܝܠܝܬܐ		property
136.4	Severus	ܡܫܘܕܥܢܘܬܐ		quality
136.14	Severus	ܕܝܠܝܬܐ		propriety

136.15	Severus	ܕܝܠܝܬܐ	propriety
136.25	Severus	ܕܝܠܝܬܐ	propriety
136.27	Severus	ܕܝܠܝܬܐ	propriety
137.12	Severus	ܕܝܠܝܬܐ	propriety
137.19	Severus	ܕܝ̈ܠܝܬܐ	properties
137.22	Severus	ܕܝܠܝܬܐ	propriety
137.28	Evagrius	ܕܝܠܝܬܐ	property
138.24	Severus	ܕܝܠܝܬܐ	propriety
138.26	Severus	ܕܝܠܝܬܐ	propriety
138.29	Severus	ܕܝܠܝܬܐ	propriety
139.2	Severus	ܕܝ̈ܠܝܬܐ	properties
139.5	Severus	ܕܝ̈ܠܝܬܐ	properties
139.7	Severus	ܕܝ̈ܠܝܬܐ	properties
144.8	Severus	ܕܝܠܝܬܐ	particularity
144.9	Severus	ܡܫܘܕܥܘܬܐ	quality
144.12	Severus	ܡܫܘܕܥܘܬܐ	quality
144.12	Severus	ܕܝܠܝܘܬܐ	particularity
150.24	Sergius	ܡܫܘܕܥܘܬܐ	quality
150.26	Sergius	ܫ̈ܘܕܥܐ	signs
152.1	Sergius	ܡܫܘܕܥܘܬܐ	quality
152.2	Sergius	ܡܫܘܕܥܘܬܐ	quality
152.3	Sergius	ܡܫܘܕܥܢܘܬܐ	signification
152.13	Sergius	ܕܝܠܝܬܐ	propriety
153.3	Sergius	ܕܝ̈ܠܝܬܐ	properties
153.11	Sergius	ܕܝ̈ܠܝܬܐ	properties
154.11	Sergius	ܡܫܘܕܥܘܬܐ	quality
154.16	Sergius	ܗܠܝܢ [ܕܝ̈ܠܝܬܐ]	properties

(*continued overleaf*)

Appendix A (*cont.*)

Page	Writer	Word	Greek or Latin	Translation
155.4	Sergius	ܪܘܫܡ̈ܐ		signs
155.6	Sergius	ܐܝܟܢܝܘܬܐ		quality
155.7	Sergius	ܪܘܫܡ̈ܐ		signs
155.9	Sergius	ܪܘܫܡ̈ܐ		signs
155.16	Sergius	ܕܝܠܝܬܐ		propriety
155.19	Sergius	ܕܝܠܝܬܐ		propriety
155.21	Sergius	ܕܝܠܝܬܐ		propriety
155.24	Sergius	ܕܝܠܝܬܐ		propriety
158.20	Severus	ܕܝܠܝܬܐ		particularity
158.25	Severus	ܕܝܠܝ̈ܬܐ		particularities
159.1	Severus	ܐܝܟܢܝܘܬܐ		quality
159.6	Severus	ܕܝܠܝܘܬܐ		particularity
159.26	Severus	ܕܝܠܝܘܬܐ		particularity
160.14	Severus	ܐܝܟܢܝܘܬܐ		quality
161.4	Severus	ܐܝܟܢܝܘܬܐ		quality
161.6	Sergius	ܕܝܠܝ̈ܬܐ		properties
161.8	Sergius	ܕܝܠܝܬܐ		particularity
161.13	Severus	ܐܝܟܢܝܘܬܐ		quality
161.13	Severus	ܕܝܠܝܬܐ		particularity
161.21	Severus	ܐܝܟܢܝܘܬܐ		quality
161.25	Severus	ܐܝܟܢܝܘܬܐ		quality
161.27	Severus	ܪܘܫܡܐ		meaning
162.15	Severus	ܐܝܟܢܝܘܬܐ		quality
162.25	Sergius	ܐܝܟܢܝܘܬܐ		quality

162.25	[of] Sergius	ܡܫܘܕܥܘܬܐ	quality
163.18	Severus	ܡܫܘܕܥܘܬܐ	quality
164.11	Severus	ܫܘܕܥܐ	sign
165.20	Severus	ܫܘܕܥܐ	meaning
166.30	Severus	ܫܘܕܥܐ	signification
168.7	Severus	ܡܫܘܕܥܘܬܐ	quality
168.12	Severus	ܡܫܘܕܥܘܬܐ	quality
168.14	Severus	ܡܫܘ̈ܕܥܘܬܐ	qualities
168.14	Sergius	ܡܫܘܕܥܘܬܐ	quality
168.15	Sergius	ܡܫܘܕܥܘܬܐ	quality
168.19	Severus	ܫܘ̈ܕܥܐ	signs
168.22	Sergius	ܕܝ̈ܠܝܘܬܐ	proprieties
168.27	Sergius	ܫܘ̈ܕܥܐ	signs, marks
172.22	Severus	ܫܘܕܥܐ	signification
172.23	Severus	ܕܝܠܝܘܬܐ	particularity
173.16	Severus	ܕܝܠܝܘܬܐ	propriety
173.20	Evagrius	ܕܝܠܝܘܬܐ	property
173.24	Sergius	ܕܝܠܝܘܬܐ	propriety
173.26	Severus	ܕܝܠܝܘܬܐ	propriety
174.1	Severus	ܕܝܠܝܘܬܐ	propriety
174.3	Severus	ܕܝܠܝܘܬܐ	propriety
174.6	Severus	ܕܝܠܝܘܬܐ	propriety
174.8	Severus	ܕܝܠܝܘܬܐ	propriety
174.8	Severus	ܕܝܠܝܘܬܐ	propriety
174.16	Severus	ܕܝܠܝܘܬܐ	propriety
174.18	Severus	ܕܝܠܝܘܬܐ	propriety
174.19	Severus	ܕܝ̈ܠܝܘܬܐ	proprieties
174.25	Sergius	ܕܝܠܝܘܬܐ	propriety

(*continued overleaf*)

Appendix A (*cont.*)

Page	Writer	Word	Greek or Latin	Translation
174.27	Severus	ܕܝܠܝܬܐ		property
177.4	Severus	ܫܘܕܥܐ	[LXX] ἐπίγνωσις	knowledge
178.29	Sergius	ܕܝܠܝܘܬܐ		propriety
180.3	Sergius	ܕܝܠܝ̈ܬܐ		properties
180.9	Nestorius	ܕܝܠܝ̈ܬܐ		properties
180.12	Theodoret	ܕܝܠܝ̈ܬܐ	τὰ ἴδια τῶν φύσεων	properties
180.14	Theodoret	ܕܝܠܝ̈ܬܐ	ἑκατέρας φύσεως τὰ ἴδια λέγοντες	properties
180.22	Leo	ܕܝܠܝܬܐ	Salva igitur *proprietate* utriusque naturae . . . . Tenet enim sine defectu *proprietatem*	particularity
180.23	Leo	ܕܝܠܝܬܗ	suam utraque natura	particularity
180.24	Leo	ܕܝܠܝܬܐ	Agit enim utraque forma cum alterius communione, *quod proprium est*	particularity
181.3	Chalcedon	ܕܝܠܝܬܐ	σωζομένης δὲ μᾶλλον τῆς ἰδιότητος	particularity
181.8	Sergius	ܕܝܠܝܬܐ		(an individuating) particularity
181.20	Sergius	ܕܝܠܝܬܐ		particularity
181.24	Sergius	ܕܝܠܝ̈ܬܐ		properties
182.6	Sergius	ܕܝܠܝܬܐ		particularity
182.8	Sergius	ܕܝܠܝ̈ܬܐ		properties
182.11	Sergius	ܕܝܠܝܘܬܐ		particularity
182.14	Sergius	ܕܝܠܝܬܐ		particularity

182.17	Sergius	ܕܝܠܝܬܐ			property
183.6	Sergius	ܕܝܠܝܬܐ			
		read:			
		ܕܝ̈ܠܝܬܐ			properties
183.18	Sergius	ܕܝ̈ܠܝܬܐ			properties
184.8	Sg (of Sev)	ܕܝ̈ܠܝܬܐ	(cf. 78.3)		properties
184.11	Sg (of Sev)	ܕܝ̈ܠܝܬܐ	(cf. 79.4)		properties
184.12	Sg (of Sev)	ܕܝ̈ܠܝܬܐ	(cf. 79.10)		properties
184.12	Sg (of Sev)	ܕܝ̈ܠܝܬܐ	(cf. 79.10)		properties
184.13	Sg (of Sev)	ܕܝ̈ܠܝܬܐ	(cf. 79.11)		properties
184.14	Sg (of Sev)	ܕܝ̈ܠܝܬܐ	(cf. 79.11)		properties
184.15	Sg (of Cyril)	ܕܝ̈ܠܝܬܐ	(cf. 80.6)	. . . . ἴδια μὲν	properties
184.15	Sg (of Cyril)	ܕܝ̈ܠܝܬܐ	(cf. 80.7)	. . . . ἴδια δὲ	properties
184.18	Sg (of Sev)	ܕܝ̈ܠܝܬܗܘܢ	(cf. 80.15)		properties
184.26	Sg (of Sev)	ܕܝ̈ܠܝܬܐ	(cf. 86.2)		properties
185.1	Sg (of Sev)	ܕܝ̈ܠܝܬܐ	(cf. 87.8)		properties
185.6	Sg (of Sev)	ܕܝ̈ܠܝܬܐ	(cf. 88.3)		properties
185.13	Sg (of Sev)	ܕܝ̈ܠܝܬܐ	(cf. 94.2)		properties
185.16	Sg (of Sev)	ܕܝ̈ܠܝܬܐ	(cf. 94.5)		properties
185.17	Sg (of Sev)	ܕܝ̈ܠܝܬܐ	(cf. 121.25)		properties
185.18	Sg (of Sev)	ܕܝ̈ܠܝܬܐ	(cf. 121.25)		properties
185.19	Sg (of Sev)	ܕܝ̈ܠܝܬܐ	(cf. 121.27)		properties
185.20	Sg (of Sev)	ܕܝ̈ܠܝܬܐ	(cf. 121.27)		properties
185.21	Sg (of Sev)	ܕܝ̈ܠܝܬܐ	(cf. 139.5)		properties
185.22	Sg (of Sev)	ܕܝ̈ܠܝܬܐ	(cf. 139.7)		properties
185.27	Sergius	ܕܝ̈ܠܝܬܐ			properties
185.28	Sergius	ܕܝ̈ܠܝܬܐ			properties
186.1	Sergius	ܟܠܗܝܢ ܗܠܝܢ ܕܒܣܪܐ			to express "all the properties of the flesh"
186.5	Sergius	ܕܝ̈ܠܝܬܐ			properties

Appendix B

Occurrences of ܫܘܕܥܐ, ܡܫܘܕܥܢܘܬܐ and ܡܫܘܕܥܘܬܐ

Page	Writer	Word	Greek or Latin	Tranlsation
94.22	Severus	ܫܘܕܥܐ		signification
99.31	Sergius	ܫܘܕܥܐ		a mark
100.4	Sergius	ܡܫܘܕܥܢܘܬܐ		a mark, token
102.2	Sergius	ܫܕܥܐ		a sign
134.2	Severus quoting Cyril	ܫܘܕܥܐ	δήλωσις	a sign
134.12	Severus quoting Cyril	ܫܘܕܥܐ	δήλωσις	a sign
[135.15	Severus	ܫܘܕ̈ܥܐ	= rdg of Harvard Syriac 22]	signs
150.26	Sergius	ܫܘܕ̈ܥܐ		signs
152.3	Sergius	ܡܫܘܕܥܘܬܐ		signification
155.4	Sergius	ܫܘܕ̈ܥܐ	(cf. rdg of Harvard Syriac 22, at 135.15)	signs
155.7	Sergius	ܫܘܕ̈ܥܐ		signs
155.9	Sergius	ܫܘܕ̈ܥܐ		signs
161.27	Severus	ܫܘܕܥܐ		meaning
164.11	Severus	ܫܘܕܥܐ		sign, designation
165.20	Severus	ܫܘܕܥܐ		meaning
166.30	Severus	ܫܘܕܥܐ		signification
168.19	Severus	ܫܘܕ̈ܥܐ	(a semi-quotation of Sergius' use)	signs
168.27	Severus	ܫܘܕ̈ܥܐ	(a quotation of Sergius: cf. 155.4 and 135.15 H)	signs
172.22	Severus	ܫܘܕܥܐ		signification
177.4	Severus	ܫܘܕܥܐ	LXX = ἐπίγνωσις	knowledge

Appendix C

Mixture words

Below is listed every occurrence of these words, in verbal or noun form, in this text, giving the cross-reference to the Greek in Migne where it is available. The first numeral refers to the page in Lebon's Syriac text, and the second numeral refers to the line: thus under ܒܠܒܠ, "113.28 (ἀνάχυσις)" means that on page 113, line 28, the word ܒܘܠܒܠܐ occurs, and the corresponding Greek is ἀνάχυσις.

ܚܒܟ: 71.11; 74.16 (οὐ πέφυρται); 77.26 (οὐ συγχέων); 79.7; 106.28; 113.4; 122.2 (in pair with ܒܠܒܠ); 134.22 and 23; 144.13; 149.20; 158.29; 160.17; 162.8; 162.12; 163.21.

ܒܠܒܠ: 75.26; 77.7; 80.21; 86.5; 99.12 (συγχέων); 99.15; 100.17; 104.21 (συγχέων); 105.3; 107.6; 107.11; 107.27 (φυρμόν); 108.27; 113.13 (ἀνάχυσις); 113.28 (ἀνάχυσις); 115.6; 122.2 (in pair with ܚܘܒܟܐ); 125.3; 125.12; 126.23 (συγχέωμεν); 129.25; 144.4 (adv.); 148.8; 149.17; 159.17; 159.22; 159.28; 160.3; 160.27; 161.3; 162.10; 180.9.

ܡܙܓ: 77.26 (ἀνακιρνῶν); 88.13 (σύγκρασιν); 99.13 (ἀνακιρνῶν); 99.15; 99.21; 100.17; 100.18; 100.21; 104.21 (ἀνακιρνῶν); 104.23; 105.3; 105.15; 105.20; 106.3 (κρᾶσις); 107.7; 107.8; 107.10; 107.11; 107.14; 107.28 (σύγκρασιν); 108.27; 108.30; 113.1; 113.11 (κράσεως); 113.14 (συγκεκραμένων); 113.25 (συγκεκραμένους); 113.27 (συνανακιρνᾶσθαι); 114.12 (κρᾶσις); 114.17; 115.6; 115.7; 119.10; 127.21; 127.23 (κρᾶμα); 127.31; 129.16; 129.22; 131.4 (ἀνακιρνάντων); 131.11; 132.2; 132.6 (κεκερασμένος); 144.20; 144.22; 149.12; 154.9; 154.14; 160.13; 160.18; 160.19; 160.21; 160.27; 161.2; 161.3; 161.18; 161.23.

ܚܠܛ: 84.10; 84.15; 99.15; 99.23; 102.11; 104.23; 106.3 (μίξις); 109.18 (συνάπτουσιν); 113.4; 114.11 (μίξις); 121.11; 122.1; 144.19; 147.14; 149.13; 149.26; 160.27; 177.18.

Bibliography

Abramowski, L., and Goodman, A., *A Nestorian Collection of Christological Texts*, Vol. 1 Syriac Text, Vol. 2 Introduction, translation and indexes (Cambridge, 1972).

Alexander of Aphrodisias on Stoic Physics. A study of the *De Mixtione* with preliminary essays, text, translation and commentary by Robert B. Todd (Leiden, 1976).

Aristotle, *Categories and De Interpretatione*, transl. with notes by J. L. Ackrill (Oxford, 1963).

——*On Coming-to-be and Passing-away*, transl. by E. S. Forster (Loeb Classical Library, London, 1955).

——*On Coming-to-be and Passing-away*, a revised text with introduction and commentary by H. H. Joachim (Oxford, 1922).

Athanasius (of Antioch), *The Conflict of Severus*, ed. and transl. from the Ethiopic by E. J. Goodspeed, *Patrologia Orientalis*, 4 (Turnhout, 1971), 575–717.

Austin, J. L., *Sense and Sensibilia* (Oxford, 1962).

Basil of Caesarea, *The Letters*, transl. by R. J. Deferrari (Loeb Classical Library, London, 1926–34).

——*The Letters*, transl. by Blomfield Jackson (*The Nicene and Post-Nicene Fathers*, Vol. 8, London 1894).

Bethune Baker, J. F., *Early History of Christian Doctrine* (London, 1962).

Bindley, T. H., and Green, F. W., *The Oecumenical Documents of the Faith* (London, 1950).

Brière, M., 'Introduction générale aux homélies de Sévère d'Antioche', *Patrologia Orientalis* 29 (Paris, 1960), 7–72.

Brock, Sebastian P., *The Syriac Version of the Pseudo-Nonnos Mythological Scholia* (Cambridge, 1971).

——"Some New Letters of the Patriarch Severos", *Studia Patristica* 12 (*Texte und Untersuchungen zur Geschichte der altchristlichen Literatur*, Band 115), (Berlin, 1975), 17–24.

Bury, J. B., *History of the Later Roman Empire*, 2 Vols. (London, 1923).

Casey, R. P., "Julian of Halicarnassus", *Harvard Theological Review*, 19 (1926), 206–213.

Chadwick, Henry, *The Early Church* (Harmondsworth, 1967).

——"Eucharist and Christology in the Nestorian Controversy", *Journal of Theological Studies*, N.S. 2 (1951), 145–164.

Chesnut, Roberta C., *Three Monophysite Christologies: Severus of Antioch, Philoxenus of Mabbug and Jacob of Sarug* (Oxford, 1976).

Chronicon anonymum ad AD 846 pertinens, ed. E. W. Brooks, *Corpus Scriptorum Christianorum Orientalium* 3 (Syr. 3, 1904), transl. I. B. Chabot, *Corpus Scriptorum Christianorum Orientalium* 4 (Syr. 4, 1904).

Crum, W. E., "Sévère d'Antioche en Egypte", *Revue de l'orient chrétien*, 3 ser., 3 (1922–3), 92–104.

Curteis, A. M., *History of the Roman Empire, AD 395–800* (London, 1875).

Cyril of Alexandria, *Opera*, text ed. P. E. Pusey, 7 vols. (Oxford, 1868–77), repr. 1965.

——*Deux Dialogues Christologiques*, introd., text, transl. and notes by G. M. de Durand (Paris, 1964).

——*Five Tomes against Nestorius; Scholia on the Incarnation; Christ is One; Fragments against Diodore of Tarsus, Theodore of Mopsuestia, The Synousiasts*, transl. E. B. Pusey (Oxford, 1881).

De Halleux, A., "La Philoxénienne du symbole", Symposium Syriacum 1976 (*Orientalia Christiana Analecta* 205, Rome, 1978), 295–315.

Diekamp, F., *Doctrina Patrum de Incarnatione Verbi* (Münster in Westf., 1907).

Dionysius the Areopagite, *On the Divine Names and The Mystical Theology*, transl. C. E. Rolt (London, 1920).

Dragas, G. D., "St Athanasius' Two Treatises *Contra Apollinarem*", Abba Salama, 6 (1974), 84–96.

——"A note concerning Athanasius' soteriology", *Ekklesiastikos Pharos*, 61 (1979), 210–220.

Draguet, R., "La Christologie d'Eutychès d'après les Actes du Synode de Flavien, 448". *Byzantion*, 6 (1931), 441–457.

——*Julien d'Halicarnasse et sa controverse avec Sévère d'Antioche sur l'incorruptibilité du corps du Christ* (Louvain, 1924).

Dratsellas, C., "Questions on Christology of St Cyril of Alexandria", *Abba Salama*, 6 (1974), 203–232.

——*Questions of the Soteriological Teaching of the Greek Fathers* (Athens, 1969).

Evagrius, *The Ecclesiastical History*, ed. with introd. and notes by J. Bidez and L. Parmentier (London, 1898).

——*A History of the Church in Six Books* (A new translation from the Greek) (London, 1846).

Fouyas, M., *The Person of Jesus Christ in the Decisions of the Ecumenical Councils* (Addis Ababa, 1976).

Franks, R. S., *The Doctrine of the Trinity* (London, 1953).

Frend, W. H. C., *The Rise of the Monophysite Movement* (Cambridge, 1972).

Garitte, G., "Textes hagiographiques orientaux relatifs à saint Léonce de Tripoli. II L'homélie copte de Sévère d'Antioche", *Le Muséon*, 79 (1966), 335–386.

Graffin, F., "La catéchèse de Sévère d'Antioche", *L'Orient syrien*, 5 (1960), 47–54.

Greer, R. A., "The Antiochene Christology of Diodore of Tarsus", *Journal of Theological Studies*, N.S. 17 (1966), 327–341.

Gregory of Nazianzus, *Orations and Letters*, transl. by C. G. Browne and J. E. Swallow (*The Nicene and Post Nicene Fathers*, Vol. 7, Michigan, 1974).

Grillmeier, A., *Christ in Christian Tradition*, Vol. 1 (London, 1975).

Hardy, E. R., (ed.), *Christology of the Later Fathers* (*Library of Christian Classics*, Philadelphia, 1954).

Hathaway, R. F., *Hierarchy and the Definition of Order in the Letters of Pseudo-Dionysius* (The Hague, 1969).

Hefele, C. J., *A History of the Councils of the Church*, 5 Vols. (Edinburgh, 1895).

Hespel, R., "Le Florilège Cyrillien réfuté par Sévère d'Antioche: Étude et édition critique", *Bibliothèque du Muséon*, 37 (1955), 1–255.

Hongimann, E., *Évêques et évêchés monophysites d'Asie antérieure au VIe siècle, Corpus Scriptorum Christianorum Orientalium* 127, Subsidia 2 (Louvain, 1951).

John of Beth Aphthonia, *Vie de Sévère*, ed. and transl. by M.-A. Kugener, *Patrologia Orientalis*, 2 (Paris, 1907), 207–264.

Kelly, J. N. D., *Early Christian Creeds* (London, 1968).

Lang, D. M., "Peter the Iberian and his Biographers", *Journal of Ecclesiastical History*, 2 (1951), 158–168.

Lash, C. J. A., "The Scriptural Citations in the *Homiliae Cathedrales* of Severus of Antioch and the Textual Criticism of the Greek Old Testament", *Studia Patristica*, 12 (*Texte und Untersuchungen zur Geschichte der altchristlichen Literatur*, Band 115), (Berlin, 1975), 321–327.

Lebon, J., "La Christologie de Timothée Aelure", *Revue d'histoire ecclésiastique*, 9 (1908), 677–702.

——*Le Monophysisme sévérien. Étude historique littéraire et théologique sur la résistance monophysite au concile de Chalcédoine jusqu'à la constitution de l'Église jacobite* (Louvain, 1909).

——"Le pseudo-Denys l'Aréopagite et Sévère d'Antioche", *Revue d'histoire ecclésiastique*, 26 (1930), 880–915.

——"Encore, le pseudo-Denys l'Aréopagite et Sévère d'Antioche", *Revue d'histoire ecclésiastique*, 28 (1932), 296–313.

——"La Christologie du monophysisme syrien", in *Das Konzil von Chalkedon: Geschichte und Gegenwart*, ed. by A. Grillmeier and H. Bacht (Würzburg, 1951), I, 425–580.

Lietzmann, H., *Apollinaris von Laodicea und Seine Schule* (Tübingen, 1904).

Loofs, F., *Nestoriana* (Halle, 1905).

——*Nestorius and His Place in the History of Christian Doctrine* (Cambridge, 1914).

Lossky, V., *The Mystical Theology of the Eastern Church* (London, 1957).

——*The Vision of God* (London, 1963).

Meijering, E. P., *God being History* (Amsterdam, 1975).

——*Orthodoxy and Platonism in Athanasius, Synthesis or Antithesis?* (Leiden, 1968).

Meyendorff, J., *Christ in Eastern Christian Thought* (Washington and Cleveland, 1969).

——"Chalcedonians and Monophysites After Chalcedon", *Greek Orthodox Theological Review*, 10 No. 2 (1964–5), 16–30.

Moeller, C., "Nephalius d'Alexandrie: un représentant de la Christologie néochalcédonienne au début du sixième siècle en orient", *Revue d'histoire ecclésiastique*, 40 (1944), 73–140.

Nestorius, *The Bazaar of Heracleides*, transl. by G. R. Driver and L. Hodgson (Oxford, 1925).

——*Le Livre d'Héraclide de Damas*, ed. by P. Bedjan (Paris, 1910).

——*Le Livre d'Héraclide de Damas*, transl. by F. Nau (Paris, 1910).

Norris, R. A., *God and the World in Early Christian Theology* (London, 1966).

——*Manhood and Christ: A Study in the Christology of Theodore of Mopsuestia* (Oxford, 1963).

Philoxenus of Mabbug, *The Discourses of Philoxenus, Bishop of Mabbogh*, ed. and transl. by E. A. W. Budge, 2 Vols. (London, 1894).

Polanyi, M., *The Tacit Dimension* (London, 1966).

Porphyry the Phoenician, *Isagoge*, transl. introd. and notes by E. W. Warren (Toronto, 1975).

Prestige, G. L., *God in Patristic Thought* (London, 1936).

——*Fathers and Heretics* (London, 1940).

Proclus, *The Elements of Theology*, transl., introd. and commentary by E. R. Dodds (Oxford, 1963).

Raven, C. E., *Apollinarianism: An Essay on the Christology of the Early Church* (Cambridge, 1923).

Roques, R., *L'Univers Dionysien: Structure hiérarchique du monde selon le pseudo-Denys* (Lyon, 1954).

Samuel, V. C., "The Christology of Severus of Antioch", *Abba Salama*, 4 (1973), 126–190.

——"One Nature of God the Word", *Greek Orthodox Theological Review*, 10 (No. 2) (1964–5), 37–51.

——"Further Studies in the Christology of Severus of Antioch", *Ekklesiastikos Pharos*, 58 (Pts. 3–4) (1976), 270–301.

Schwartz, E., (ed.) *Acta Conciliorum Oecumenicorum* (Berlin and Leipzig, 1914–40).

Sellers, R. V., *Two Ancient Christologies* (London, 1940).

——*The Council of Chalcedon* (London, 1961).

Severus of Antioch, *Orationes ad Nephalium*, ed. and transl. by J. Lebon, *Corpus Scriptorum Christianorum Orientalium*, 119, 120 (Syr. 64, 65) (Louvain, 1949).

——*Le Philalèthe*, ed. and transl. by R. Hespel, *Corpus Scriptorum Christianorum Orientalium*, 133, 134 (Syr. 68, 69) (Louvain, 1952).

——*Eiusdem ac Sergii Grammatici: Epistulae Mutuae*, ed. and transl. by J. Lebon, *Corpus Scriptorum Christianorum Orientalium*, 119, 120 (Syr. 64, 65) (Louvain, 1949).

——"A Collection of Letters from Numerous Syriac Manuscripts", ed. and transl. by E. W. Brooks, *Patrologia Orientalis*, 12, 14 (Paris, 1919–20), 163–342; 1–310.

——*The Sixth Book of the Select Letters of Severus, Patriarch of Antioch, in the Syriac Version of Athanasius of Nisibis*, ed. and transl. by E. W. Brooks, 4 Vols. (London, 1902–4).

——"Severos' letter to John the soldier", ed. with introd. and translation by Sebastian Brock, *Göttinger Orientforschungen* (Veröffentlichungen des Sonderforschungsbereiches Orientalistik an der Georg-August-Universität Göttingen) I. Reihe: Syriaca, Band 17, (Wiesbaden), 53–75.

——*Les HOMILIAE CATHEDRALES de Sévère d'Antioche* in the Syriac translation of Jacob of Edessa, ed. and transl. in *Patrologia Orientalis* (Turnhout, Belgium, and Paris, 1922–72).

Homilies 32–39, ed. and transl. by M. Brière, F. Graffin and C. J. A.

Lash, *Patrologia Orientalis*, 36 (Turnhout, Belgium, 1972), 396–528.
Homilies 40–45, ed. and transl. by M. Brière and F. Graffin, *Patrologia Orientalis*, 36 (Turnhout, Belgium, 1971), 8–137.
Homilies 46–51, ed. and transl. by M. Brière and F. Graffin, *Patrologia Orientalis*, 35 (Turnhout, Belgium, 1969), 288–379.
Homilies 52–57, ed. and transl. by R. Duval, *Patrologia Orientalis*, 4 (Paris, n.d.), 1–94).
Homilies 58–69, ed. and transl. by M. Brière, *Patrologia Orientalis*, 8 (Paris, n.d.), 209–396.
Homilies 70–76, ed. and transl. by M. Brière, *Patrologia Orientalis*, 12 (Paris, n.d.), 1–163.
Homily 77, Greek and Syriac texts ed. and transl. by M.-A. Kugener and E. Triffaux, *Patrologia Orientalis*, 16 (Paris, 1922), 761–863.
Homilies 78–83, ed. and transl. by M. Brière, *Patrologia Orientalis*, 20 (Paris, 1928), 273–434.
Homilies 84–90, ed. and transl. by M. Brière, *Patrologia Orientalis*, 23 (Paris, 1932), 1–176.
Homilies 91–98, ed. and transl. by M. Brière, *Patrologia Orientalis*, 25 (Paris, 1935), 1–174.
Homilies 99–103, ed. and transl. by I. Guidi, *Patrologia Orientalis*, 22 (Paris, 1929), 207–312.
Homilies 104–112, ed. and transl. by M. Brière, *Patrologia Orientalis*, 25 (Paris, 1943), 625–815.
Homilies 113–119, ed. and transl. by M. Brière, *Patrologia Orientalis*, 26 (Paris, 1947), 265–450.
Homilies 120–125, ed. and transl. by M. Brière, *Patrologia Orientalis*, 29 (Paris, 1960), 74–262.
——"La Première Homélie cathedrale de Sévère d'Antioche", transl. by E. Porcher, *Revue de l'orient chrétien*, 19 (1914), 69–78; 135–142.
——"The Hymns of Severus and Others in the Syriac Version of Paul of Edessa, as revised by James of Edessa", ed. and transl. by E. W. Brooks, *Patrologia Orientalis*, 6, 7 (Paris, 1911), 1–179; 593–802.
——*Liber contra impium Grammaticum*, ed. and transl. by J. Lebon, *Corpus Scriptorum Christianorum Orientalium*, 93, 94; 101, 102; 111, 112 (Syr. 45, 46; 50, 51; 58, 59) (Paris and Louvain, 1929–1938).
——*La Polémique antijulianiste*, ed. and transl. by R. Hespel, *Corpus Scriptorum Christianorum Orientalium*, 244, 245 (Syr. 104, 105) (Louvain, 1964).
Stead, G. C., "The Concept of Divine Substance", *Vigiliae Christianae*, 29 (1975), 1–14.
——*Divine Substance* (Oxford, 1977).
Thunberg, L., *Microcosm and Mediator: The Theological Anthropology of Maximus the Confessor* (Lund, 1965).
Timothy Aelurus of Alexandria, *Fragments*: "Textes monophysites: B. Extraits de Timothée Aelure", ed. and transl. by F. Nau, *Patrologia Orientalis*, 13 (Paris, 1919), 202–236.
——"A Collection of Unpublished Syriac Letters of Timothy Aelurus", introduction, text, translation and notes by R. Y. Ebied and L. R. Wickham, *Journal of Theological Studies*, N.S. 21 (1970), 321–369.

Torrance, T. F., *Theology in Reconstruction* (London, 1965).
—— *Theology in Reconciliation* (London, 1975).
Urmson, J. O., *Philosophical Analysis* (Oxford, 1966).
van der Meer, F., and Mohrmann, C., *Atlas of the Early Christian World* (London, 1958)..
Vööbus, A., "Découverte d'un memra de Giwargi évêque des arabes, sur Sévère d'Antioche", *Le Muséon*, 84 (1971), 433–436.
——"Discovery of New Important *memre* of Giwargi, the Bishop of the Arabs", *Journal of Semitic Studies*, 18 (1973), 235–237.
Wigram, W. A., *The Separation of the Monophysites* (London, 1923).
Wolfson, H. A., *The Philosophy of the Church Fathers* (Cambridge, Mass., 1964).
Zacharias the Scholastic, *The Syriac Chronicle Known as that of Zachariah of Mitylene*, transl. by F. J. Hamilton and E. W. Brooks (London, 1899).
——"Vie de Sévère", ed. and transl. by M.-A. Kugener, *Patrologia Orientalis*, 2 (Turnhout, 1971), 1–115.
Zambolotsky, N., "The Christology of Severus of Antioch", *Ekklesiastikos Pharos*, 58 (Pts. 3–4) (1976), 357–386.